Maryland

Lost and Found...Again

Maryland
Lost and Found....Again

Eugene L. Meyer

WOODHOLME
HOUSE
PUBLISHERS

Baltimore, Maryland

Printed and bound in the United States of America.

1 2 3 4 5   09 08 07 06 05 04 03 02 01 00

Library of Congress Cataloging-in-Publication Data

Meyer, Eugene L.
    Maryland lost and found...again / Eugene L. Meyer.
        p.   cm.
    Updated and expanded ed. of: Maryland lost and found. c1986.
    Includes index.
    ISBN 1-891521-08-X (alk. paper)
        1. Maryland—Social life and customs. 2. Maryland—Description and travel.
    3. Maryland—History. I. Meyer, Eugene L. Maryland lost and found. II. Title.

    F181.M47 2000
    975.2—dc21   99-089771

Woodholme House Publishers
131 Village Square I
Village of Cross Keys
Baltimore, Maryland 21210
Fax: (410) 532-9741
Orders: 1-800-488-0051   *Book and cover design:* Jason Lawrence
email: info@woodholmehouse.com   *Backcover photograph:* James Thresher

Cover art: Detail of Esso Marketers' "Pictorial Guide to Happy Motoring in Maryland, Delaware, Virginia, and West Virginia," 1939

Inset images: Baltimore harbor (early twentieth century); Route 40 (National Highway) narrows near Cumberland; Chesapeake Bay patent tonger; Patapsco River and Baltimore's Inner Harbor (photographs: Eugene L. Meyer)

Unless otherwise noted, postcards, photographs, and artifacts are from the author's collection.

To Emma and Gerry Meyer,
of blessed memory,
who first took me to Maryland, and

for my wife Sandra and sons Eric, David, and Aaron—
fellow travelers in the Free State

Acknowledgments

Over the years, a succession of editors at the *Washington Post* has indulged my Maryland wanderlust. Among them, David Maraniss dispatched me to the western slope of Backbone Mountain, about as far as you can go in that end of the state without leaving it, and Bob Woodward blessed my voyage of discovery up and down the Chesapeake Bay.

Other *Post* editors who have traveled Maryland with me through reams of copy have included Fred Barbash, Don Baker, Laura Stepp, Leslie Walker, Judy Havemann, Bill Hamilton, Steve Reiss, Bob Thomson, Bob McCartney, Miranda Spivack, and Ashley Halsey. Ben Bradlee, who shares my love of Chesapeake Country, graciously granted me a leave of absence to write the original hardcover book.

Gregg Wilhelm, at Woodholme House, was as enthusiastic and creative as any author could hope a publisher to be.

Finally, I would like to thank my wife and partner, Sandra Pearlman, for her support and encouragement during my revisionary efforts.

Contents

*G*rowing up on Long Island in the 1950s, I wanted most of all to travel. Years later, I would tour the country, crisscrossing it a dozen times by car, drive the Alcan Highway to Alaska, and venture overseas. But the farthest we ventured back then was to Washington, D.C. What I remember most about that long-ago trip are images of the passing scene: the Baltimore bottleneck; endless rows of attached houses, each with identical white marble steps; and the signs that warned of "Soft Shoulders" along old Route 1, the Main Street of East Coast America before the interstates.

This was, in fact, my first fleeting glimpse of Maryland.

My wanderlust might have been cured at an early age had we used U.S. 1 as a springboard to explore the rest of the state. Fortunately, we did not. There remained much to discover and to savor after I returned to the area many years later to live and work.

I moved, it so happened, to Washington, D.C., which was once a part of Maryland. For twelve years, I lived, in fact, two blocks from the state. But I felt even closer to it than that. At the *Washington Post*, Maryland became my beat. The assignment allowed me to rediscover a state I had long ago only glimpsed, then lost and found again. The *Post* gave me wide latitude to roam the state and write about its places and people. I drove its highways and back roads, sailed its waters, hiked its hills. Its variety always astonished, its people often delighted me. My wanderings were full of wondrous discovery of both a past and a present too little known or recognized. Thus, in many cases, I learned in the course of a reporting excursion that I was breaking new ground. The literature I wanted to read in preparation for each trip just didn't exist. What was missing most, it seemed, was a book about the entire state, end to end, one combining currency and history, using ordinary people and places to link the present and the past. That is why I wrote *Maryland Lost and Found*.

And that is why, fifteen years later, there is *Maryland Lost and Found...Again*. As I reread the chapters and revisited many of the locales, I was struck by how little has changed. Sure, some roads have been widened, suburban frontiers have expanded, new politicians have come on the scene. But the scenery is strikingly the same, and so are the abiding themes, region by region and across the state: the Eastern Shore and secession; the ghosts of the slot machines; tobacco, hanging on, if only by a leaf; the Baltimore-Washington region, now combined statistically if not culturally; the inexorable march of former city dwellers into the suburbs and now the exurbs, gobbling up rural land, and challenging country ways. To be sure, time has not completely stood still, and, where appropriate, I have updated statistics and other information, added and subtracted here and there. In some chapters, the changes have been woven into the text; to other chapters, I have added short epilogues. In addition, *Maryland Lost and Found...Again* has many more illustrations to accompany the printed word.

With the passage of time, of course, some of the characters in this book are gone: Bill Newnam, whose Maryland Airlines ferried the rich and reclusive to their Eastern Shore retreats and who became an invaluable source on many matters, and a good friend; the elderly ladies driven by the erosive forces of nature to move from Poplar to Tilghman Island; Charlie Elgin, longtime mayor of Poolesville, who with quiet dignity clung to the memory of his Confederate ancestors. These and many others who have passed on are memorialized within the stories found in these pages.

Not for nothing has Maryland been called "America in Miniature." For to write about Maryland is, in a sense, to write about America. Indeed, within its borders is a generous slice of American pie: megalopolis, Appalachia, the Chesapeake Bay, the Deep South, the industrial North, rich farmland, a major port, the nation's capital, the primary car and rail routes carrying East Coast interstate traffic.

By any measure, Maryland spells diversity, if not unity. Politically, the state nearly split apart during the Civil War. That Maryland is a state of the Union, once in question, is now settled. But what else is it? "Maryland—more than you can imagine" was another slogan that sought to capture its majestic scope. Whether that's true or not, the nice thing about Maryland is that it's not "more than you can visit." It's big enough to entice and intrigue, but not so huge as to overwhelm.

State lines may be largely arbitrary, but these political boundaries impose their own reality, their own order. Thus did the German settlers in the Shenandoah Valley of Virginia secede with their state, while their ethnic and religious brethren in the same valley in Maryland did not. So here we focus not on the Great Valley, but on the State of Maryland.

What is beyond debate is a simple fact: the state owes its existence to the overriding forces of history and geography. Its boundaries are both natural and political, the Potomac River on the south, the Mason-Dixon line on the north. Although the southern boundary, dating back to the 1632 royal charter, has repeatedly been a matter of dispute between Maryland and Virginia, it is the northern border, determined by two colonial surveyors, that has had a more profound impact on the state's place among the states. That line located Maryland in the South—barely. Slavery and segregation flourished, but, being a border state, Maryland experienced cultural cross-currents from the North as well.

Historically and culturally, the city of Baltimore has walked both sides of the line: It has been an industrial hub with large immigrant communities typical of the North, and it has been a social and economic center for the Upper South, especially when steamships provided the main mode of transport and commerce well into the 1930s. Its ties to the Bay, the Eastern Shore, and shipping have made it look eastward, even as rail and highway connections have directed it westward for markets.

There are also two major military bases, in Maryland but not really of it. One is an international dateline, the other merely an exit on the Baltimore-Washington Parkway: Andrews Air Force Base and Fort Meade are only twenty miles apart, yet their worlds spin in different orbits. The former is brassy and bustling; the latter, sleepy and secure...for now at least. Military Maryland is part of the American drama and only incidentally part of the state scene.

If the state lacks coherence—as I contend that it does—it is this fact that makes it so endlessly fascinating. Boosters prefer to call its incoherence "diversity." So be it. Its diversity made my task both challenging and rewarding. And it may account for the lack of literature that treats the state as a whole. As I took up the challenge, I came to recognize that even this book could not be comprehensive. There are, of necessity, omissions. You won't find much about Ocean City and the collegiate rites of passage or about horses and racetracks, two staples of what is widely perceived to be "Maryland life." Yet, it was my intention to achieve, and it is my hope that I have achieved, the larger view, including representative sections without dwelling on the obvious.

The fact is that many Marylanders have little sense of place about their state outside of their own geographical locales. Most out-of-staters who casually pass through see even less, so narrow is their peripheral vision as they drive along the interstate or travel by train. It has, therefore, been my mission to give readers a sense of place—and a connection to the past. This is the link so often missing from our individual and collective awareness, and it tells us who and what we are, and why.

It is my hope that readers, Marylanders and otherwise, will find in these pages a guidebook not to the roads and resting places but to the ways and means of Maryland. This is not a travel book in the traditional sense but, hopefully, it is a book for travelers, armchair and otherwise

This is decidedly not an "issues" book in the sense that it takes sides. Although I confess to a passionate feeling for humanity in general and a special warmth toward persons I would describe as individualists, I happily leave the polemics and the partisanship to others. Readers looking for an environmentalist tract or a pro-industry slant will be disappointed. My focus is on the environment only to the extent that it shapes the lives of the people. But this is not a book about famous—or infamous—people, or about politicians, either. My interest lies less with those who are household names and more with the households and their occupants, whose life and times tell the story of the state.

Nor is this a book about me. While my Maryland experience has undoubtedly affected my world view, I am by training and temperament a reporter. I strive to be an unobtrusive guide, whose purpose is to introduce the places and people of Maryland but not to overshadow them.

It might be said, too, that the nature of the news business is such that I have been drawn inevitably into areas of controversy. Conflict can define more sharply the central questions of human existence. If tales based on contention tend to sound downbeat at first, it should be said that, in most cases, good sense, good humor, and good will manage somehow to prevail.

The Marylanders I've gotten to know well almost invariably exhibited these character traits. Unlike some of their more mobile cosmopolitan counterparts, they didn't seem rootless; they knew their place. Of course one Marylander's place can be so different from another's. Maryland is no artful mosaic, no tapestry of fabrics carefully woven into a whole cloth. It is more a colorful kaleidoscope, bits and pieces thrown together. Maryland is the damnedest place. Or places.

One evening on Tilghman Island, I listened while a roomful of restaurant patrons sang, with great gusto: "We don't give a damn for the whole state of Maryland, we're from the Eastern Shore." This was three decades after the Chesapeake Bay Bridge connected its shores. Yet, the separation has persisted. Farther south, in the middle of the Bay, I have heard Smith Islanders talk of the state line with Virginia as little more than an economic encumbrance. They live, in fact, in what amounts to another country, with its own accent and customs. You almost need a passport to go there.

In Cecil County, straddling the Eastern and Western shores at the upper end of the Bay, the folks root for the Phillies and commute to jobs in Wilmington. Predictably, one evening while I was covering the Maryland General Assembly, in 1981, a state senator from there lamented, "The Eastern Shore don't want us, the Western Shore won't have us. Cecil County may as well be made a part of

Delaware." That sentiment led to the introduction of legislation in 1998 (ultimately unsuccessful) to provide for a referendum that could have led to the nine Eastern Shore counties seceding.

The lament was echoed by a car dealer in Garrett County, on the Allegheny plateau: "Maryland don't want us, West Virginia won't have us, and we don't want Pennsylvania. We want a state of our own." In the three Appalachian counties of Maryland, I have been told time and again, "The rest of the state thinks Maryland ends somewhere down around Frederick."

Today's Western Marylanders root for the Pittsburgh Pirates and Steelers, and watch Pennsylvania, West Virginia, and Ohio television. They care little for the Baltimore Orioles, less about the Washington Redskins. Years before, the German Protestants who migrated from Pennsylvania into Western Maryland had little in common with the English Catholics who settled Southern Maryland. The rhythms of life in that peninsula between Chesapeake and Potomac more resembled those of Tidewater Virginia, with which it enjoyed familial and commercial ties (except for occasional, bitter battles between watermen over oyster beds) into the twentieth century. Descendants of the settlers in Western and Southern Maryland share a rural conservatism but little else.

Most suburbanites who live near the nation's capital, meanwhile, consider themselves "Washingtonians," even though they live, vote, and pay taxes in Maryland. Many are transplants who tend to think they live in the North, which shows how much they know about their adopted state. That leaves Baltimore, Annapolis, and some surrounding territory for those who feel they are full-fledged citizens only of the state of Maryland. Call it Central, Heartland, or simply Middle Maryland, if you like.

The shape of Maryland is oddly configured, resembling a pistol with the barrel pointed to the west. Maryland spans three hundred and fifty miles from the Atlantic to its westernmost mountains. At its narrowest, where the Potomac snuggles up to the Mason-Dixon line, it is a mere two miles wide.

Seen from the air, Maryland is a patchwork of shapes and colors. It extends from the winding rivers and creeks of Tidewater to the plowed fields of Piedmont to forested mountain upon mountain to the very tabletop plateau of the Alleghenies. The climate at ground level ranges from the horrible heat and humidity of an August day on the mosquito-infested lower Eastern Shore to the bone-chilling temperatures and snow squalls of Garrett County in January. I've experienced both: a crowded crabfest in Crisfield, in Somerset County, everyone and everything steaming and sizzling in the stultifying summer heat, and a twenty-two-mile round trip in a blinding blizzard, all for the sake of breakfast in the Garrett County seat of Oakland. They are endearing, and enduring, memories.

Other memories of Maryland—my Maryland—linger. They include an early-morning drive east from Chestertown on the Eastern Shore, the mist hovering gently over the fields; the drive down U.S. 1, yesterday's interstate, offering a fading view of our recent past; a detour to a place called Detour, on the Frederick-Carroll County line; the back way to Kempton, a ghost town at the far southwestern corner of the state; the road and bridge to the lower end of Hooper's Island, a sliver of land that seems much farther than it really is from the traffic and congestion of megalopolis; a Southern Maryland tobacco auction in progress, the air thick with dust as auctioneers move up and down the rows; a tugboat ride from St. Mary's up the Potomac River, passing under the Route 301 Bridge at sunset; countless boat rides to Smith Island, a passage in time and space across twelve miles of open bay.

And, of course, the people: families of tenant tobacco farmers sharing a single outdoor water pump, watermen whose working days start before dawn and end by lunchtime, ageless men and women whose homespun wisdom is written not in formal degrees but in weathered faces and warm hearts.

I have found, just beyond Maryland's major thoroughfares, its Washington and Baltimore beltway bustle, a collection of scenes exotic to most urbanites. These include annual coronations of homegrown royalty, including a Little Miss Crustacean and queens of the pork, poultry, wool, and dairy persuasions. The pageants may seem like bits of nostalgia at best, or reminders of roles better relegated to history, but they are serious affairs for many Marylanders. Underpinning such events are the traditional values that prevail from the lowlands of the Eastern Shore to the highlands of Garrett County. This is the philosophical thread that joins the people in the far-flung corners of the state. Theirs is a world suspicious of government, disdainful of metropolitan life, and protective of the individual, especially in matters of property. This world may seem to some to represent the past, but it is a past that is also present—if threatened, increasingly, by change.

If some parts of the state seem to be standing still, or at least hoping to hold their ground, others are a virtual blur of movement and change. I-95 and the northeast corridor of the high-speed trains course through the state's veins. Megalopolis, the ever-expanding concentration of humanity, spreads amoeba-like from its heart. I have heard supposedly worldly city folk decry the sameness they see around them, unaware of how different life is just miles from home.

They are creatures of the Beltways, spinning in their own orbits. They are always amazed to learn their state contains sections so remote (except to those who live there) that television is still somewhat novel and drinking water comes not from the tap or the store but in jugs from a nearby stream or spring.

Marylanders of my acquaintance have been blue-collar ethnics, white-collar bureaucrats, Amish farmers, Chesapeake Bay watermen, country gentry, city slickers, politicians from ward heelers to suburban smoothies to "good old boys." They are harried commuters, glued to cell phones, and welfare recipients just trying to survive. They are black, white, Hispanic, and Asian. They are America.

Dixie, let it be said, also lives on in Maryland: The official state song remains a fiercely secessionist hymn protesting the federal "despot's heel" on Maryland soil. Those who try to update the lyrics quickly discover the state hymn is not to be trifled with, lest we forget. My travels helped me remember, for the hidden legacy of the Civil War in Maryland is closer to the surface than you might think.

I have learned this many times and many ways. There's the obscure cemetery in Montgomery County, a scant twenty-five miles from downtown Washington, with its monument to Confederate dead. There's the annual John Wilkes Booth escape route tour through Southern Maryland, where I was informed that Abe Lincoln received only one vote in Prince George's County in 1860. Nor will I ever forget the palpable outrage with which a granddaughter of the infamous Dr. Samuel Mudd, who tended to Booth's broken leg, described the depredations of Union troops around the family homestead in Charles County during the search for the assassin. She was born after Dr. Sam's death, but she spoke as if the events had taken place the day before.

Strangest of all, perhaps, was a letter I received from a reader reacting to a newspaper story on another subject. My correspondent wrote of "the general decline in the quality of life which has been the hallmark of Southern Maryland ever since the tragic victory of A. Lincoln's carrion birds who invaded and occupied the region in order to terrorize and otherwise punish our people for our strong Confederate sympathies, and to force an unwanted 'union' on us—just as powerful outside agencies continue to this day to trample upon the wishes of what is left of Southern Marylanders."

For generations, Maryland has shared the classic American conflicts over region and race. The state was held in the Union forcibly, by martial law. Many of its legislators and other leading citizens were thrown in prison. Reconstruction followed war north of the Potomac as well as south of it. Jim Crow prevailed in fact and in law for almost a century. And it long lingered in places.

How well I remember the "Colored Only" signs on U.S. 1 motels I saw while driving north from Washington as late as 1965. As a northerner newly returned to Washington half a decade later, I attended a Christmas service in a country church in Southern Maryland. Its congregation was all white. Next-door was a church whose parishioners were all black. Descendants of slaveowners worshipped next to, but not with, descendants of slaves. "Everything down here is black and white," a white churchgoer told me. If the feeling may have been mutual, then so was the place: Mutual, Maryland.

My northern naiveté has been further diminished as, in years since, I have talked to tobacco sharecroppers and listened to Deep South transplants wax eloquent over the familiar surroundings they found here just north of the Potomac, where tract homes and supermarkets share the countryside with rural shacks and Southern States stores. In all my travels throughout the country, I saw no place as completely and self-consciously segregated as Cambridge, on Maryland's Eastern Shore.

There's at least one relatively benign aspect to the regional identity crisis afflicting many Marylanders. "Down South, I'm a 'Damn Yankee,' while up North, they say I have a southern accent," said a friend with Eastern Shore roots and Baltimore blueblood.

If regional schizophrenia divides the state, the Chesapeake Bay, as much as anything, binds it. I've seen crabcakes on the menu well into Western Maryland, although, if the truth be known, I probably wouldn't order one much west of Baltimore. Nonetheless, even though half of it is in Virginia, the Bay is about as "Maryland" as you can get. The 4,400-square-mile Chesapeake with its 7,325-mile coastline is the nation's largest estuary. Exploring it in 1608, Captain John Smith found a bounteous bay full of fish such as "brettes, mullets, white Salmonds, Trowts, Soles, Plaice, Herrings, Rockfish, Eeles, Shades, Crabs, Shrimps, Oysters, Cocles and Muscles.... In somer," he wrote, "no place affordeth more plentie of Sturgeon, nor in winter more abundance of fowle.... In the small rivers all the years there is good plentie of small fish, so that with hookes those that would take paines had sufficient."

Indeed, the Bay has long been viewed as an almost endless resource. But, inexorably, change has come to the Chesapeake. Its harvests of oysters and crabs have declined, along with the underwater grasses that nurture aquatic life. There's an emerging consensus that blames the change on human gluttony: too many bivalves scooped from its waters; too many chemicals dumped into them; too much land developed, with too little thought given to sediment spilling into the Bay.

Over the years, the Bay has been plied by workboats, warships, ferries, freighters, and pleasure craft. Its bounty has supported a work force on land and water. It has even provided a living of sorts for journalists like myself, who seize every opportunity to be on the Bay and write about it. What we all extol and fret over is an estuary that has shaped the lives of generations of Americans who carved out a regional culture as unique in its own way as those identified with the frontier West, plantation South, or urban North.

Despite growing concern over crowded waters—and they are crowded around Annapolis and the Bay Bridge on nice weekends—much of the Bay remains empty most of the time. Watermen confront a lonely vista when they invade the Bay's predawn darkness and even when, by midday, their work is done. The large freighters keep to the middle of the estuary, where the channel is deepest. Almost anywhere on its surface, the forces of the Bay can be relentless. I've never seen a waterspout, the Bay equivalent of a twister, but I've bounced on the bowsprit as our craft lurched through the water one knot or so ahead of an afternoon squall. The wind-whipped waves, welling up so suddenly in summer storms, have eroded the Bay's shores and erased its islands, submerging buildings and bulkheads and all other man-made intrusions on its surface. Whole island communities have washed away over the years, their homes, their cemeteries, their land, forever gone. My search for the vanished islands was perhaps the ultimate quest for Lost Maryland—and among the most rewarding.

Other than natural forces shrink the land. In my few short years roaming the state, I have seen what I regarded as eternal countryside yield to what some view as progress in the form of highways and homes. "How can we stop the growth?" I was once asked by a fretting homeowner on South Mountain just inside Frederick County. He was fearful of the subdivisions marching like battalions of conquering troops inexorably across the Middletown Valley. My answer: "Pray for a Depression."

Still, as the century drew to a close, the state boasted 2.2 million acres in agriculture and $1.47 billion in gross farm income. Maryland is yet a place where the land provides, where, as on the Bay, days are measured by the sun, not by the clock, and traditional roles and ideas prevail. From the Eastern Shore flatlands to the hills and mountains of Western Maryland, the land provides. Chicken farms along with farms growing corn for chicken feed and soybeans thrive east of the Chesapeake. In Southern Maryland, tobacco remains the largest cash crop, despite litigation against cigarette companies and other external forces. Dairy predominates in Frederick and Carroll, wheat in Montgomery County. Washington County apple orchards are part of the passing scene for drivers heading west on the interstate or along old Route 40. Even in the cool, short summers of Garrett, farmers tend their crops.

Mindful of the economic and aesthetic worth of such things, Maryland's urban-dominated legislature has passed programs aimed at preserving the tillable soil. Voluntary programs that involve paying farmers not to develop are most palatable. But forms of forced conservation are regarded skeptically by the farmers themselves, an independent breed of American wary of government controls. In Anne Arundel and Howard, two rapidly suburbanizing counties, farmers mounted tractorcade protests against agricultural preservation laws that would restrict their rights. Some farmers I've met stubbornly resist the change. But most seem resigned or welcome it—indeed, look forward to cashing in on their inheritance, slow "smart" growthers be damned. Megalopolis, to them, means megabucks.

The superhighways I travel have expanded Maryland megalopolis. I-70, I-270, I-95, I-97, U.S. 50, and both beltways have turned what was once barely a corridor into a diamond-shaped metropolis that is now anchored by Annapolis on the east and Frederick on the west. Growth has pushed the frontiers outward, mostly from Washington, well into the Appalachian foothills.

But the influx of urbanites into the Maryland countryside has brought more than condos, shopping malls, and rush hours. It has also brought big city values to challenge the old ways. In Buckeystown, near Frederick, I met newcomers who were trying to start a sexually and racially integrated fire company. They had run afoul of all-white and all-male companies aided and abetted by women's auxiliaries. The upstarts would lose their battle but win the war. I also watched conflict in Howard County, between Baltimore and Washington, intensify as the "new town" of Columbia grew in population and political influence, pitting "countians" against Columbians in a war of tradition against trend.

In the middle of the diamond is Maryland's urban center. Baltimore is—let's face it—an old city with a fresh coat of charisma. "Charm City" is what its boosters called it after the sparkling redevelopment of its Inner Harbor. Behind the image, however, is the reality: Baltimore is also the financial capital of Maryland, but its factories have fallen on hard times, a microcosm of the American "Rust Belt" that has infected the nation's industrial core. It's a city of 277 neighborhoods, historically home to the range of immigrants and their families living in block upon block of lookalike rowhouses. But the newer generations have moved to the suburbs, leaving an increasing, and poor, black majority. Meanwhile, industrial pollution—without the jobs—has forced the complete abandonment of some neighborhoods, while others have for different reasons become ghost towns of boarded up homes.

A short, slim artery away from Baltimore is Maryland's self-possessed and scornful Second City: my erstwhile home, Washington, D.C. This may be an unconventional view of the nation's capital, but it is bolstered by several often-overlooked facts. To start with, what's left of the original diamond after Virginia reclaimed its share in 1846 came from Maryland. Georgetown, it will be recalled, was a Tidewater tobacco port of Southern Maryland long before its emergence on the cocktail and caviar circuit. Renegade Georgetowners and others still occasionally talk of rejoining Maryland.

The District of Columbia is, in fact, bordered on three sides by Maryland. The Potomac River, meanwhile, is more barrier than border between the District and Virginia. And, while Marylanders have scoffed at suggestions that the state take the District back, it is the combined might of the two metropolitan areas of Baltimore and Washington that dominates politics and priorities in Annapolis.

Blood, the saying goes, is thicker than water. And it has flowed freely between these two large cities, which are sometimes slurred together, as in the "Baltimore-Washington Parkway" or simply "B/W Parkway." Clans of Marylanders have migrated to the Second City, even as Washingtonians have moved into Maryland, pushing farther and farther into the once-sovereign region. Where once only the *Baltimore Sun* shone, the *Washington Post* now competes or dominates. (And nowadays, I can easily buy a *Sun* in any number of Washington suburbs.) In Baltimore City itself, Washington commuters increasingly occupy the restored townhouses of Federal Hill, and Washington real estate speculators and redevelopers have sought richer rewards on Baltimore's urban frontiers.

Maryland megalopolis sits astride the major road and rail rights-of-way of the East Coast. Maryland also has its westward routes, traditionally taking travelers beyond the borders of the state into such seemingly more exotic locales as Pennsylvania, Ohio, and the West. The sad fact is that for many years, Maryland has been a place to pass through, rather than a destination in and of itself. This rather unrewarding role began back in colonial times, when the King's Highway reached from New England to the South. Then came the railroads, beginning in and then passing through Baltimore, and, in this century, U.S. 1 and I-70 and I-95. The glimpses afforded passersby—including my parents and their two children nearly fifty years ago—are limited, and while the throughways have brought some people to Maryland, they have kept others from truly knowing it.

Before I "rediscovered" the state, I had regarded the crossing of the Susquehanna River, by train or by car on the interstate, as merely a milestone in the long journey between Washington and Civilization ("up north"). Although the river's scenic beauty was a welcome diversion, I never knew how limited was my view until I saw the crossing from the water itself. I now have a sense of place—the place where the Chesapeake Bay begins, just beyond the trees obscuring for all but the knowing the world beyond. It is this hidden view of Maryland I have sought to capture in these pages...again.

1

The Land of the Gentry

$\mathcal{T}$he seven-seat aircraft lined up behind the behemoth Boeing 727 and waited its turn to leave Washington National Airport. Finally, clearance to proceed crackled over the cockpit radio from the air traffic controllers, who must weave in the single-engine props with the jumbo jets.

Cleared for departure, the small plane turned onto the runway, taxied its length, and ascended into the humid haze. The four passengers sat at ease as pilot William S.D. Newnam, Jr., sunglasses in place, steered the plane toward the Chesapeake Bay and its Eastern Shore.

Maryland Airlines was heading home.

Newnam, the man at the controls, had never aspired to run a large airline providing steerage service to the airborne masses. A product of the barnstorming era, he was perfectly content to preside over a small airline, carrying the select few on short trips that mattered. In carrying out his mission, he had arrived at National's commuter terminal half an hour early and was prepared to delay his departure until all his important passengers were present and accounted for.

This afternoon, Alex Ray was late. The political consultant for the Republican National Committee was due in from Pittsburgh on a Northeastern flight that was behind schedule. When at last Ray came bounding into the terminal, Newnam was ready to go. "No dogfights on the way over," Ray admonished Newnam as he climbed aboard. The other Eastern Shore-bound passengers were Lyle Graham, a former vice-president of Philip Morris, Charles E. (Ted) Taylor, a heavyset, nattily dressed lawyer specializing in real estate and banking, and me.

Graham, formerly of New York and Hilton Head, South Carolina, was now residing on the Tred Avon River, one of many tidal fingers that jut inland from the Chesapeake Bay. He remained at Philip Morris as a company consultant and flew Maryland Airlines weekly to Washington. In addition, he and his wife often hired Newnam to fly them to Dulles or Baltimore-Washington International Airport.

Taylor had moved two years ago from Northern Virginia, where he continued to practice law, to a spot on the Wye River where his wife "raises a few horses," he said. He was now a regular commuter between his private peninsula and his Alexandria office.

"I leave the house at ten to eight. I'm in the office by a quarter to nine," he told me, a newcomer unaccustomed to such comings and goings but learning fast. "That's not bad, is it? Everybody asks me why I don't fly on my own plane to Washington. Well, it's a real job coming in and out of National; it's real hectic."

These were the country squires of Talbot (pronounced Tawlbit) County whose high-powered jobs in the corporate and political realms required frequent trips to the nation's capital and beyond. Newnam's small airline was their lifeline, providing what had evolved into a more or less regular if unscheduled service between their two very different worlds. While city commuters cursed the traffic and the crowds, the Eastern Shore puddle-jumper and jet set could rest secure. Thanks to Maryland Airlines, Washington was just a twenty-minute flight away.

My reasons for flying Maryland Airlines were also professional. I was writing about this unique shuttle service for the rich. Yet, after this first flight, I was to become a regular customer as well, using Maryland Airlines as a quick and convenient way to travel the distance while shifting mental gears from the whirl of Washington to the slower pace of the Eastern Shore. Through it all, Newnam was more than my pilot. He became a helpful guide to people and places in the land of the gentry, and a friend.

This afternoon, the small Aero Commander seemed like a midget in a land of giants dominating the Washington airport and the surrounding skies. The commuter craft rose above the Potomac River and the nation's capital, ascending to fourteen hundred feet, far below the jet stream of traffic, its speed climbing to 180 miles an hour. There it stayed, just low enough and slow enough to afford a bird's-eye view of Maryland below.

The plane passed over the Capital Beltway, a ribbon of traffic encircling Washington. Just beyond lay Andrews Air Force Base. Carved from the Maryland countryside during World War II to protect the Washington-Baltimore area with P-47s, it was now the home of the presidential aircraft in the midst of suburbia. Upper Marlboro, the Prince George's County seat, came next into view. It was still largely a sleepy southern tobacco town despite its prominent position as the capital of the state's second most populated county. The county office building—a clone of the modernistic and monumental Kennedy Center for the Performing Arts in Washington—loomed below, incongruously adjoining the town's traditional main street.

The Patuxent River, snaking its way for 110 miles from Piedmont to Tidewater to Chesapeake Bay, was next. Where once tobacco boats had navigated, the river had silted in. But development had not yet despoiled its banks, and it looked from the air like an oxbow twisting and turning through seemingly untouched wilderness.

The airplane proceeded on an easterly course over the lush farms and forests of Anne Arundel County, which is bisected by U.S. Route 50, a straight line from Washington to Annapolis and beyond. The flight path took us south of Annapolis, over Galesville, formerly a working watermen's town on the West River and now best known for its fancy marinas. From overhead, its harbor was a blue surface. On weekends it would be dotted with sails, but for now most of its craft remained docked or moored. Off to one side, unseen by most, even at ground level, was Woodfield Fish & Oyster Co. and its company houses occupied by black oyster-shuckers, the few left.

Newnam, my aerial tour guide to this land of the reclusive rich, pointed out the spectacular sights below. First came the Bay itself. Crossing it by air takes only a few minutes. On a clear day, the trip across seems even shorter. In foggy weather, it is difficult to see, or even imagine, an Eastern Shore.

To the north, above Annapolis, lay the William Preston Lane, Jr., Memorial Bridge, hidden on sultry summer days by haze, as if the span were an easily erased mistake. Better known as the Chesapeake Bay Bridge, it has connected the Eastern Shore with the rest of Maryland since 1952, when it was ceremoniously dedicated by Governor Theodore R. McKeldin and his otherwise obscure predecessor, after whom it is named.

According to conventional wisdom, the four-and-a-half-mile span forever ended the isolation of Maryland's otherworldly Eastern Shore, bringing to its somewhat backward inhabitants modern ideas and progressive values they had long been denied and an invasion of city dwellers to dominate the once-serene countryside. The conventional wisdom is mostly myth.

To be sure, completion of the bridge led to a rash of subdividing on Kent Island, its eastern terminus. But most lots long went undeveloped. And although a smattering of ex-urbanites who commute by car to jobs in Annapolis, Baltimore, and Washington now inhabit the newer bayside homes, no population explosion has greatly disrupted the demographics of the Eastern Shore.

What the bridge did, more than anything, was allow auto access to the oceanside beaches. (A ferry-and-rail link to Ocean City inaugurated in 1890 was short lived and had little lasting impact on Maryland's Atlantic resort.) The coming of the Bay Bridge left Western Shore resorts to wither or become year-round residences for Washington and Baltimore commuters. But it barely touched the vast flatlands of the Eastern Shore on either side of the beach-bound highway. Cars could be backed up for miles on steamy summer weekends—even after completion of a second, parallel, span in 1973—but weekday traffic was, and is, usually light. It was almost as if the bridge extended all the way to Ocean City without turn-offs, culturally leapfrogging the land between Chesapeake and Atlantic.

MARYLAND'S FAMOUS CHESAPEAKE BAY AND BAY BRIDGE

Postcard showing the original span of the William Preston Lane, Jr., Memorial Bridge completed in 1952.

New people had come to parts of the Eastern Shore before the bridge, although never in great numbers. Beginning around the turn of the century, Old Money from Pittsburgh, Philadelphia, and New York, as well as from Washington and Baltimore, began buying waterfront estates. Newer arrivals of the same ilk had quickly joined the rear guard against further incursions. And to them, Bill Newnam's steadiest customers, the Bay Bridge was an unnecessary and unwanted structure that potentially threatened their secluded way of life.

Yet, the fears were exaggerated. Motorists speeding along Route 50 ("the Ocean Gateway") saw nothing of their world of water, of private docks, tennis courts, and swimming pools, of big old plantation houses on secluded peninsulas jutting into tidal tributaries of the Chesapeake Bay. To these travelers, the whole Eastern Shore was little more than flat farmland, a place to pass through without stopping, except, perhaps, at the outlet stores. The other world, of large estates that have names but not street addresses, is visible only from the air.

This afternoon, visibility was good. The Eastern Shore appeared as a patchwork of land and water. The ground had been cultivated and was criss-crossed by straight, narrow roads. The water reached inland like outstretched hands with fingers extended, defining the shoreline.

Before the Eastern Shore itself, Newnam pointed to Poplar Island, once one thousand solid acres, now several islets almost washed away by the tides. "President Roosevelt had a lodge there during the war," Newnam said. "Dr. Elkins from Philadelphia gave part to the Smithsonian, still owns part." Newnam had flown Dr. Elkins back and forth on many occasions.

Poplar lay a mile or two offshore from the old Bay Hundred District, whose name originated in the English subdivisions of colonial times. The Bay Hundred looked from the air like an arm bent downward at the elbow. At its northern tip was Rich Neck, owned in its entirety by the former wife of a wealthy Washington lawyer, and the sleepy village of Claiborne, once a bustling ferry terminus. South of Poplar, the workboats of Knapp's Narrows and Tilghman Island—the last stronghold of the watermen in the land of the gentry—contrasted with the sailboats we had seen only minutes before. At Tilghman's southern end, two claw-like protrusions appeared. The longer one, known as Blackwalnut Point, formed a safe harbor in storms for oyster-dredging sailboats known as skipjacks.

Below Tilghman, the Bay's surface bore a slightly different hue, a telltale sign of a vanished isle. Once close enough to the point to be connected to it by a footbridge, Sharp's Island was several hundred acres of marsh and farmland owned by Newnam's paternal ancestors. His Aunt Maggie Parsons lived there when she was not teaching school in Oxford, a sailboat ride away. The steamboat from Baltimore stopped there, too, for the families who stayed at the island hotel. But over the years, the wind-whipped waters of the Chesapeake had erased the island from sight. All that was left was an underwater shoal on which sailors could run aground.

He flew over Oxford, where he had grown up, a collection of houses wedged on a peninsula between the Tred Avon and Town Creek. It was once a boisterous and bustling place of white-washed buildings and weathered faces, a watermen's town and, at one time, a port to rival Annapolis across the Bay. Oxford looked unchanged, but it had been gradually transformed from a working community to a retirement haven for the rich and retired who restored the homes inside and out, creating a "quaint" look the town had never had.

As Newnam piloted the plane up the Tred Avon River, he pointed out the private peninsulas of the people he had transported. "That's Ambassador Gerard Smith's house, with the long driveway," he said. "He was assistant secretary of state under Dulles. I've been flying him and his family for over thirty years." The estate, Ratcliffe Manor, covered an entire neck.

Upriver, Newnam noted the habitat of the man who owned the Chicago White Sox, and the former "plantation home" of television's one-time "Galloping Gourmet" on Peachblossom Creek. Next came Plaindealing Creek, whose residents included Harry W. Rodgers III, convicted along with former Maryland Governor Marvin Mandel of political corruption. Then came Cedar Point, where former Iowa Senator Harold Hughes had established a religious retreat and W. Alton Jones, the late board chairman of Citgo, had lived. And, finally, there was Broad Creek, on which Donald Hiss, brother of Alger Hiss, owned Sherwood Forest, which would later be sold to Europeans for a reported $1 million. "People are suffering around here," Newnam chuckled.

We landed easily at Easton Airport, descending over open fields and crossing Route 50 on the final approach. The plane bumped along the 2,500-foot runway, made a U-turn, and headed for a small parking area, where it stopped. Its passengers stepped out, retrieved their briefcases from a small rear compartment, and hurried off to their homes.

"Maryland Airlines makes my life possible," explained Stephen N. Connor the following day. His wife, three children, and four horses "at the moment" lived on thirteen acres with 758 feet of Miles River shoreline, a new barn, a pool, a "big old house" built in 1720. Eighty-three acres planted in corn and soybeans were tended by a sharecropper. There were also plenty of birds to shoot for sport, and several Labrador retrievers to fetch them. For a living, Connor was a lobbyist, consultant, and foreign agent for Saudi Arabia. An alumnus of Wall Street, he enjoyed the good life of the Eastern Shore but had to spend "a great deal of time in Washington," especially, he said, on Capitol Hill. He was one of Newnam's steadiest customers.

Commuting on Maryland Airlines was costing Connor upward of $10,000 a year when I spoke with him. "I use them for everything," he said. "Seldom does a week go by...."

Cape Centaur, an estate on the Miles River in Talbot County.
James Thresher, *Washington Post*

In one week, Maryland Airlines flew Connor to New York's Kennedy Airport to catch a Concorde to London. Maryland Airlines met him three days later at Dulles to bring him home. Connor flew the airline the next day to Washington and back. The following day, a Thursday, the airline took him to Washington again, this time to meet his son who was returning from camp, then ferried both back. On Friday, Connor and his wife flew Maryland Airlines to Washington National Airport to meet a scheduled flight to Lexington, Kentucky, for the "Summer Select Sale of Yearling Thoroughbreds."

Newnam, whose airline was so central to Connor's life, was undoubtedly a servant of the gentry, but he was also the master of Easton Airport. Of old Eastern Shore lineage, he began flying in 1932, from the county's first airport over by the Tred Avon. Wartime service had interrupted his domestic flying career. He had enlisted in the marines and emerged as a first lieutenant. He had trained to fly fighter planes, but the fight ended just as he arrived in the Pacific. Easton Airport, whose Quonset huts and hangers showed its wartime vintage, had been his base since 1946.

A short, soft-spoken man in his sixties who sported a crew cut, Newnam had acquired the airline in 1949. Hazel Newnam, his wife, worked in the office and also served as vice-president and secretary of the corporation. There were also a secretary (sometimes Newnam's daughter), two maintenance men, four full-time and four part-time pilots. Newnam's air force consisted of nine planes, mostly two- and four-seaters.

Behind Newnam's desk in his Quonset hut office was a picture gallery of the high and the mighty he had flown. Each photograph was inscribed. There were presidents, senators, congressmen, ambassadors, admirals, judges, and just plain rich folks, like the late Colonel Edgar W. Garbisch in his West Point football uniform before he had the good fortune to marry a Chrysler heiress.

For years, when they weren't living in their New York apartment or Palm Beach house, traveling here and there, or making ritual appearances in corporate board rooms, the couple lived on the six-hundred-acre estate given them by her father. Pokety, as it was called, encompassed four miles of Choptank River shoreline, a dock, guesthouse, greenhouse, pool, bowling alley, stables, the manager's and farmer's houses, and a large henhouse. Along with the Francis du Ponts of Horn Point, the Garbisches were almost the only gentry to settle south of the Choptank, in Dorchester rather than Talbot County.

Newnam flew them and their children and their guests about. Ed Garbisch, in turn, financed the purchase of Newnam's Aero-Commander at low interest, then credited the times he chartered the plane against the principal. Ben, their black chauffeur, would meet them at the airport, along with Eddie, a beloved cocker spaniel the colonel accidentally killed one day when the dog ran under his car. "They never got over that," Bill Newnam said.

As Garbisch's health declined, Newnam also flew the colonel's doctor down from New York and back. Toward the end, Bernice Garbisch sobbed she could not live without Ed. Then he died in December 1979. Within twenty-four hours, she, too, was gone. Some say she died of a broken heart.

Soon after the couple's death, Newnam received a basket of fruit and cheese the couple had sent him in their final days. It was a Christmas present to a devoted servant and—as much as class would allow—a dear friend. Months later, Pokety and its prized art and antiques were for sale. Newnam was called on to fly the officials of Sotheby Parke Bernet, the Madison Avenue auction house, back and forth. The auction, held in May 1980, grossed $16 million. Pokety went on the market for $3 million and eventually was sold to a Saudi Arabian for $1.9 million.

Over the years, Newnam had been by himself to Pokety several times, "not for any formal social function" with others, "but just to visit them," he said. "They said so many times about [my family] going over, but we just never did it. They had so many international guests, we just really appreciated the friendship we had."

Unlike most of his passengers, Newnam lived in a modest brick house by a highway, without a swimming pool, tennis court, or boat dock. His occasional visits to Pokety notwithstanding, he seldom saw the homes of those he flew, except from the cockpit. "We don't go to their cocktail parties," he said, adding with a laugh, "Somebody's got to work, you know. I'm about the only one. I'm getting tired, too."

Bill Newnam died in 1991. Three years before, he sold his small airline to a man who continued to operate commuter flights to and from Washington National until 1996. Today, only chartered planes make the trip. Easton's airport is busier than ever, though, with an expanded 5,750-foot runway and fifteen private jets based there. Bill's Quonset hut office is long gone, replaced by a spiffy new terminal. The airport also has a new name. It is now Easton Airport-Newnam Field.

"Tell everybody Talbot is hot, mosquito ridden, unfriendly, and way overpriced," suggested another Maryland Airlines regular. Peter Black, a mineral mogul in his sixties from New England and New York, had moved in 1968 to an 1840 home on Plaindealing Creek. Black was the lord of a three-hundred-acre manor farmed by a St. Michaels man. He also owned half a vineyard on the Tred Avon.

An active conservationist, Black was a trim, white-haired Boston Brahmin who enjoyed the good life of a country squire with easy access to the water. "We wanted to find a farm on navigable waters," he explained. "Maine was too cold and you can't farm. Connecticut is built up along the waterfront. New Jersey has nothing, and pretty soon you're in Maryland, so we followed the shoreline."

Here, he had his own duck blind "right at the end of the point." There was also a private pier for the Caroline, a fifty-foot ketch named after his wife, and a New England lobster boat used for fishing. The sailboat, he said, had done "a lot of ocean cruising. She went to Central America last winter, by way of Haiti and Jamaica, and will cross the Atlantic next summer."

The Blacks' boats could be seen from a screened-in back porch furnished in white wicker and cooled by a ceiling fan. After a few minutes, Black took me to the pier. With us was his son, Bill, who had prepped at the Country School in Talbot County, where "all the doctors send their kids." Appropriately, the younger Black, who had also learned flying from Bill Newnam, was a medical student in the British West Indies, where he had acquired an English accent in the course of his education.

Also residing on the estate were three Scotch terriers, a black Labrador retriever named Moxie, a miniature horse from Charleston, South Carolina, and two donkeys. Southerly, as the place is called, featured a Japanese garden constructed by World War II internees and a smokehouse at the end of a long driveway lined with loblolly pine and fig trees.

Houses in the land of the gentry generally adhere to the rule of the road: The rich live far from it, close to the water. Others (and there are others) live near the pavement. Some are tenant farmers, working the land owned by the wealthy. Mostly, the working people live in the flatlands east of Route 50 or in Talbot's few towns. "It is always more expensive to live in the country," a local real estate agent informed me. But one must, after all, eat and shop. Older ladies of leisure dine at Tidewater Inn in the chic shopping district of Easton. Working people can often be found at the H & G Restaurant, unfashionably located on Route 50 between a budget motel and a gas station.

There are almost no subdivisions in the usual suburban sense in Talbot County. Instead, there are "areas," collections of expensive contemporary homes. Opposition to higher-density development combined with the expense of estate living have held Talbot's population growth to a trickle. There were 23,000 residents in 1970; 36,000 a decade later; and just 33,065 in 1998. Not soaring interest rates or double-digit inflation or economic recession could dim the bright real estate market in very expensive waterfront properties. Little wonder when many buyers can pay cold cash.

That one of every eight Talbot citizens still lived below the poverty line, often in crowded and dilapidated housing, did not directly concern the gentry. ("It may have been astounding news to some that five-hundred families in Easton are in need of low-to-moderate-income housing," began an editorial in the *Easton Star-Democrat.*) Which is not to say the rich don't have problems.

Consider, for example, the plight of the elderly woman of wealth recently widowed. She and her husband came here for the good life in retirement, but soon she was left to rattle around in a large mansion all by herself. "I want to stay on the Eastern Shore," sighed the woman, who still lived in the couple's rambling brick house on Trippe's Creek. "But as I get older," she said, "I can't maintain this. There is no place for me to go."

Even pricey townhouses are frowned on by the Talbot County gentry, which tends to view all development the way one widow transplanted from Washington regarded the starlings nesting in her purple martins' house. "Well," she said, recalling her reaction to the arrival of the dirty birds as we-sipped cocktails on her back porch, "there goes the neighborhood."

The land of gracious living is also hard on the affluent young, most of whom leave for the cities. The average age here, naturally, is higher than elsewhere. This fact attracts many doctors to Talbot—the phonebook listed nearly seventy—to heal the well-heeled of the county, a group they quickly join. "You have to call to make an appointment weeks in advance," complained Peter Black. "They're all off goose hunting, cruising, or something else."

But with the wealth had come a measure of noblesse oblige to Talbot County. Peter Black, the squire of Southerly, had paid his civic dues as founder of the Maryland chapter of the Nature Conservancy and as president of the Chesapeake Bay Maritime Museum in St. Michaels. He was also a member of the exclusive Chesapeake Bay Yacht Club. It is, they say, "the only inland yacht club on the Chesapeake Bay." Its stately old two-story brick building was in Easton, just a block from the county courthouse with the Confederate statue out front testifying to Talbot's southern sympathies during the Civil War.

The club, formed in 1887, hosted an annual regatta in August. It had 160 members. No more, no less. The likes of Bill Newnam do not belong. It is not a workingman's club. But belonging is more than a matter of money and class. Race and sex also counted. When Peter Black escorted me through its hallowed halls in 1980, there were no black members, and women were relegated (without any audible complaints) to a sort of ladies' auxiliary known as the Harbor Club. The wives met downstairs and were allowed upstairs but once a year, for the annual anniversary party in November.

The sacrosanct second floor consisted of a dining room, sitting room, and library. There was a small wooden ballot box for voting on prospective members (one blackball was one too many) and these posted instructions: "Ascertain in some way, without suggesting you will propose him, that the nominee wants to join.... The membership committee will, as discreetly as possible, attempt to ascertain the acceptability of the person to general membership.... Potential embarrassment can be avoided by strict adherence."

The century-old club oozed tradition, from the paneled poker rooms to the wooden bar, tended by a black bartender of long service. It seemed a fitting symbol for the ways of the gentry on the Eastern Shore of the Chesapeake Bay. Reflected Peter Black at the Yacht Club bar, "There is little enthusiasm for change, and it's a good thing."

When change does come to the self-styled "Land of Pleasant Living," it's glacial at most. In the larger scheme of things, even the gentry are, after all, newcomers. Still, the natives are often out of sight and out of mind of both gentry and tourist. The sailboats anchor in St. Michaels harbor, their occupants coming ashore to the Crab Claw Restaurant or the Maritime Museum. A few remaining watermen cling, meanwhile, to a dwindling number of public slips, their workboats outnumbered by pleasure craft. In Oxford, where Bill Newnam had lived, gone to school, and grown to manhood, there was hardly a waterman left in what was once a waterman's town. Yet, oddly, Oxford looks old, unchanged.

The signposts of history are everywhere, reminding the visitor that Oxford was platted in 1683, that the ferry across the Tred Avon to Bellevue had run ever since, that the restored Robert Morris Inn was built in 1710, that the cemetery dated to 1808. "Please bear with us while our eighteenth-century doors are being refinished," said a sign at the inn. "In the meantime, we have provided the very latest in twentieth-century doors for your convenience." What appears to be Old Oxford, a town that seemingly makes vintage a virtue, is really New Oxford in period dress.

"Hardly any of the people we knew are still here," said Hazel Newnam, who lived there with her husband just before World War II. They still attended the Oxford Methodist Church, of which Bill was a trustee, but knew few of the town's residents. It had been so different, once. Newnam drove me down Morris Street, the main road, one drizzly March day, pointing out the houses formerly inhabited by a slew of aunts. All the homes were painted white then, a familiar color in a familiar town. Now, they bore bright pastel shades chosen by strangers.

Newnam's father had owned a grocery store, and his mother took in summer boarders in their twelve-room house with its eighteenth-century grapevine on Morris Street. The grocery store burned down during the Depression, along with the drug store, the doctor's office, and the combination firehouse-police station. The police chief, Newnam recalled, was the town's principal bootlegger. He kept his hooch under the cot in the jail where, the story goes, the prisoners drank it. What was left went in the fire. Afterward, a new town hall and police headquarters were built on the site of the old grocery.

"To me, I hate to see Oxford the way it is," Newnam said. "It's almost like a small city, the way people treat each other. They don't make any effort to find out who lives next-door."

One of the few old-timers who remained was William Benson, Newnam's brother-in-law. Benson ran the ferry from 1938 until 1974. "I couldn't afford to buy a home in Oxford today," he said, emerging from retirement one fall day to pilot the ferry across the Tred Avon. "What few ordinary workingmen live in Oxford today couldn't buy a house here if they didn't already have one."

Even as the buildings were spruced up, the human heritage slipped away.

The number of watermen had declined from more than one hundred to fewer than a handful, and the black oyster-shuckers and crab-pickers were all but gone. I found one of the four or five semi-retired Oxford watermen repairing a crab net on his workboat, at his backyard dock. Epps Abbott, nearing seventy, had made a living for years trotlining for crabs in the nearby rivers and creeks.

"There were close to one-hundred-and-twenty-five crab and oyster boats, at least eight or ten dredge boats—skipjacks, bugeyes, even one schooner—and three buy boats," he recalled. "There were eight big oyster and crab houses. They had a couple of boatyards here but they didn't have any such thing as a marina. There were fifteen stores on Main Street—hardware, drug store, butcher shop, two barber shops. You didn't have to leave Oxford to buy nothing. Now, the town's got nothing to sell anymore but service—food and sailboats."

Downes Curtis's life also spanned both eras. A master sailmaker who plied his craft from a second-story loft, Curtis at sixty-eight remembered when Oxford had more blacks like himself, families with lots of offspring, and men who worked on the water or in the seafood and packing houses that thrived here.

"I'm not running the town down, but it ain't worth a damn now, so far as people," he said. "You'd like to live here if you didn't have anything to do and had a lot of money." His brother, Albert, agreed. "Now, it's mostly for retirement age," he said. "They want to keep the community quiet."

"The ones of us who really think about life in this town want it to stay as it is with a contented mixture of black, white, young, and old instead of as an enclave for wealthy widows and aging couples who can no longer get help for their big estates or for extremely well-to-do younger couples," a recent arrival had earnestly assured me.

Yet, despite such sentiments, two businesses owned by and catering to natives were replaced in a single year by restaurants only affluent tourists and newly resident rich could afford. First, the black-owned Aloha, a local hangout, became the Masthead, with a prix fixe menu. Then, Pope's Tavern, Oxford's last workingman's bar, was gone, transformed by a Johnson and Johnson Band-Aid heir into a "nice restaurant" without pool table, juke box, and men in gum boots who smell like oysters and crabs.

As expected, the "new" Pope's urged patrons to make reservations and advertised "sophisticated, innovative cuisine in a uniquely beautiful atmosphere." The new owner spent $85,000 renovating and hired a staff of thirteen. In less than two years, however, Pope's had closed. The former proprietors of Pope's, meanwhile, opened Duck's Tavern in the corner of a gas station on the outskirts of town, but everyone agreed it wasn't the same.

"We really need the waterman—that worries all of us—you want the local person," said Mary Hanks, a resident and a real estate agent who used terms of her art such as "a gem" and "real choice" to describe her adopted hometown, where tiny lots brought $80,000 and stately homes upward of $300,000. "Everything here is really a plus," she hastened to add. "The whole town is a family. You've never been in a big family that didn't have a controversy."

In this feuding family, children were an endangered species. A shrinking enrollment had forced the town's public school to shut down, and young people were left with simply nowhere to go except the sidewalk and street in front of a small cluster of chic shoppes and stores that passed for "uptown."

One year, in their zeal to preserve a "peace" of the past that never was, the Oxford commissioners even tried to outlaw kids. It began with an 11 p.m. curfew for anyone under eighteen. Then came the "No Swimming" signs by the ferry dock, where generations of youngsters swam before, and ten-dollar tickets for bicycles parked on sidewalks. Finally, an anti-loitering ordinance was proposed to further limit the youthful presence.

Through it all, there was little opposition to the so-called "children's ordinances" enacted by the town fathers. Then, one of the Oxford commissioners made a racial remark, singling out black teenagers for criticism.

At the sparsely attended but tape-recorded town meeting, Commissioner

Fletcher Hanks had wondered "how you're gonna get these blacks off the street." The chief commissioner quickly interjected, "That was not said." But it was. Then, when a citizen proposed free movies for the teenagers, Hanks said, "Those people are illiterates. We have a group, all you're doing is you're going to show films to these people that are supposed to be studying at nighttime, and they're illiterate and are gonna be a burden to us taxpayers for the rest of our lives."

The *Easton Star-Democrat* reported the remarks most of the townspeople had missed. The reaction was volcanic. Within weeks, 270 citizens had signed petitions against Hanks. The commissioner would not resign, and the petitioners learned Oxford's charter contained no provision for recall.

Hanks attributed the flap over his racial remarks to his outspoken opposition to marinas which had helped get him elected. "I don't mince words, so I've naturally made enemies," he said.

He had always been a contrary sort, according to Bill Newnam, who had lived two doors away when they were growing up together as second cousins in Oxford. Even when they were kids, playing a golf-like game called caddy, Newnam remembered, Fletcher Hanks would grab the "ball" and go home. "He was never much of a team player," Bill Newnam said.

Hanks's term in office had been stormy from the start. He was credited, rightly or wrongly, with having the "Welcome to Oxford" sign removed from the road leading into town. He was instrumental, too, in ordering trees cut down and shrubbery pruned in the town park. The trees, he observed at the time, blocked his front-window view of the Tred Avon. The shrubs, he said later, provided "a harbor for defecating and fornicating." With only a little more delicacy, another commissioner said the foliage had been used as "portable toilets and dressing rooms."

The summary execution of the trees had come without the permission of the town beautification committee, headed for sixteen years by Mary Hanks, who had once been married to Fletcher's brother. Her public protest brought the dissolution of her group. "It was so, well, unsophisticated," she said of the whole affair.

Fletcher Hanks was, in his own way, sophisticated enough. A shoreman on his mother's side, he had left Oxford to fly for foreign governments during World War II, then returned home to patent a clam dredge and operate a seafood business.

"I sold a lot of fish among the blacks," he recalled. "They used to kid me I was the first white person they'd ever seen who'd clean fish for black people. I believe I've hired more black people than anybody in Talbot County."

In semi-retirement, Hanks had become a self-styled ultraconservative, decrying what he regarded as permissiveness among today's youth, including his own five grown children. A lanky figure with close-cropped hair who now lived alone, Hanks spun a web of Social Darwinism to describe his hometown: "We took the wealth out of the water and educated our children. The bright ones left. The more ambitious left. The others stayed. It stratified society without improving it."

In his view, the influx of wealth, of educated, older people, had saved Oxford, and protecting the gentry had become his mission. "Older people like peace and quiet," he declared. "As the population changes, we have to change the way we run the town. There must be a more orderly form of government."

So the anti-loitering ordinance was proposed, along with the rest of the children's bills. Taking this flurry of legislative action into account, the Easton paper sarcastically suggested the town government might want to pass one all-encompassing law establishing residency requirements for Oxford.

It was all a bit much for the chief commissioner, himself a father of five. He decreed the loitering law "tabled indefinitely" and added, meekly, "I'd like to go on record as defending the young people " A year later he would be succeeded by Hanks, who did not repeat his indiscretion. A recall provision for "misconduct in office" had been added to the town's charter.

But in the immediate aftermath of the battle of the "children's ordinances," who could foretell the future? The present was quite enough. Over at the Masthead, they celebrated the town's first newborn in two years. "I think it's nice to be someplace where you can close up every bar in town and still be in bed by midnight," remarked a visitor from Connecticut.

"You can do almost anything in Oxford, only don't ride your bicycle on the sidewalk," observed Masthead owner Marie Hilliard, a bubbly Briton who was also tending bar. "As they say in the Bahamas, stay awhile and live longer."

2

A Bridge in Time

*E*asily overlooked at the north end of the Choptank River Bridge, it was a landmark nonetheless. Southbound, the sign announced "Last Chance Liquors." The reverse side said "First Chance Liquors." Hordes of motorists drove by the sign each summer on their way to and from Ocean City without giving it a passing thought.

The two-way sign harkened to a time, before 1949, when the river divided the Eastern Shore into wet and dry. While liquor had long been sold south of the bridge (though only from county-operated stores), the sign remained as sort of a quaint anachronism.

It was also an official boundary marker. Like the Rio Grande and the Rhine, the Choptank is a cultural divide. As significant in its own way as the Mason-Dixon Line, it separates the Upper and Lower shores. Heaven and earth may not be on opposite sides of the bridge, but there are distinct and deep differences.

Above lies the land of the gentry, conservative in many ways but occasionally open to new ideas. Below the Choptank, there are trees, chickens, marsh, mosquitoes, and migrant workers. Here, there is unalloyed conservatism in all things. Government is generally regarded with suspicion and mistrust. Dorchester County voters twice rejected a modest home rule charter similar to ones in effect in other Eastern Shore counties; too much government, they said. Yet, in the midst of it all is a government reservation of twenty-four thousand acres—fourteen thousand owned by Uncle Sam, ten thousand by the state—comprising one-quarter of the county. When the government sought to expand its Blackwater Wildlife Refuge, the citizens rebelled—and won. Wrote a sympathetic county planner: "The residents of this county have said and are continuing to say...keep the sometimes well-meaning, but invariably inconsistent, federal or state bureaucrat in Washington, D.C., or Annapolis, Maryland, and let the Delmarva Fox Squirrel, the egret, the Bald Eagle, and, last but not least, the people, live in harmony without undue environmental damage as we have done for over three hundred years. If we need help for the preservation of either species, the animals or the people, rest assured we will call for help."

Dorchester County comprises a broad and bulging peninsula of woods and wetlands bounded by the Choptank on the north and the Nanticoke on the south. If wetlands are included, the county is the state's largest—688 square miles—and it is virtually empty. Only about thirty thousand people live there, nearly half of them in and around the town of Cambridge, at the southern terminus of the Choptank Bridge. From the air, the view of forest, river, and marsh is broken only occasionally by a country crossroads, a small cluster of houses. It is rugged country. Along with the trees, rugged individualists grow here, their roots as firmly planted in Eastern Shore soil.

Below the Choptank, old habits die hard. Ageless women are addressed by their first names, always preceded by "Miss," as a sign of respect. They are Democrats here, but the white majority, at least, are southern Democrats, registering as they have for generations in the party of Jefferson and Jackson but usually gritting their teeth as they pull the primary levers for other than local office. (At the state's smallest precinct, Henry's Crossroads, which is located in the Dorchester hinterlands, the Democratic majority gave Republican Ronald Reagan an 87.5% victory in 1980's presidential sweepstakes.)

This is the land Harriet Tubman left, fleeing from slavery to organize the Underground Railroad. People still flee from here, in search of equal opportunity. And little wonder. The public outrage generated by Fletcher Hanks' racial remarks in Oxford was unthinkable below the Choptank.

The land below the Choptank was the bedrock of resistance to the state's own public accommodations act, from which the Eastern Shore was exempted. (Paradoxically, the law was enacted under the administration of Governor J. Millard Tawes, who came from Crisfield, farther down on the Lower Eastern Shore.) Cambridge, where resistance was greatest, was the scene of the nation's longest occupation by federal troops, as civil rights groups challenged segregationist barriers. It is a place where race remains an overriding fact of life.

Ocean-bound motorists passing through on the "Sunburst Highway" see and feel none of this. To them, the fast-food outlets on U.S. 50 are a sure sign of modern civilization. The bridges across the Chesapeake Bay and the Choptank River bring them through, not to, here, and neither they nor the natives, generally, are the wiser for it.

The Choptank is in no small measure the reason all below it is different. From its broad mouth, the tidal river runs a good fifteen miles before reaching Cambridge. It flows an equal distance before winding northeasterly another fifteen miles or so, past the Caroline County seat of Denton. Until modern times, no bridge spanned it for most of its length. At one time a ferry made the crossing near Cambridge, but the primitive road north from Ferry Neck, on the Talbot County side, discouraged travel and commerce.

A trip between Talbot and Dorchester counties more often followed a roundabout route over rough country roads and included an upriver crossing known as the Dover Bridge. "When we went to Cambridge to go shopping," recalled Bill Newnam, "we used to take our lunch because it was a whole day's outing." Cambridge residents rarely ventured north. If the Eastern Shore was isolated from the rest of Maryland, the Lower Shore was even more so.

Private plans to bridge the river crashed in 1929 with the stock market. But by 1934 work was underway—with government support. The project was part of Franklin D. Roosevelt's pump-priming New Deal to lift America from the Depression.

Among those who built the bridge was Bill Newnam. Fresh from Oxford High School, he painted concrete conduits that carried electricity to the bridge lights and draw span. Frederick C. Malkus, Jr., later a state senator from Cambridge, earned thirteen dollars a week wrapping wire around steel bars. Malkus described the project nearly half a century later as "a monument to putting people to work."

Republican Governor Harry W. Nice named the new bridge after Emerson Harrington, a Cambridge native who was narrowly elected governor in 1915 and served one term. He had capped his career in office by rejecting suffragette calls for a special session of the General Assembly to ratify the Nineteenth Amendment. Women's suffrage became the law of the land without Maryland, and the governor responsible for this omission was immortalized by a span nobody ever called by its right name: the Emerson G. Harrington Bridge.

Its entrances heralded on both sides by two triumphal pylons, the bridge was 1.75 miles long, a marvel of modern engineering and at that time the longest span in the state. The $1.4 million structure was ceremoniously dedicated on October 26, 1935. President Roosevelt sailed over from Annapolis for the occasion, and the presidential yacht Sequoia was the first through the draw of "that splendid bridge," as FDR called it.

The bridge did not bring the multitudes to Dorchester County, even though a new, improved road joined the area to Easton, sixteen miles north of the Choptank. At first boats going through the draw nearly outnumbered cars passing over it. By and large, the urbanites of the Western Shore still flocked to the Chesapeake resorts, and Ocean City lured only the most venturesome vacationers with its few frame hotels.

Then, in the 1950s, as soon as the Bay Bridge was built, the two-lane Choptank Bridge became overcrowded. By the 1980s it was also crumbling and dangerous. So few boats passed through, its drawbridge tenders were reduced to watching television, reading books, and practicing the trumpet, while on peak

A 1940s postcard offers a road-view perspective
of the Choptank River Bridge.

summer days as many as thirty-four thousand cars crossed over the bridge. Following one especially egregious fatality, five thousand people signed petitions demanding a new, larger, and safer span.

Among the crusaders for a new bridge was Fred Malkus, white-haired and red-faced, by now the crusty curmudgeon and dean of the Maryland Senate. Malkus noted eroding concrete pilings, a chipped sidewalk, missing metal plates. Even one of the once-imposing pylons at the southern end was gone. Against the odds, Malkus introduced legislation to replace the bridge he'd helped build with a four-lane span so that those who rode the buses and subways on weekdays could drive to Ocean City on weekends.

"This is one we're gonna win," Malkus predicted confidently, "not because they have any great love for us country boys but because the city boys will have a helluva time getting to Ocean City without it." And win he did. Indeed, the new span would be named after him. But it had taken three centuries to bridge the Choptank at Cambridge, and it would be the late 1980s before a new bridge would replace the old. Until then, motorists could look forward to more of the same, times when, on those hot, humid summer days, what would otherwise be a twenty-minute drive from Easton to Cambridge could take forever.

"The Choptank River Bridge affords a traffic convenience as well as a choice fishing spot," said an already outdated brochure. It had, indeed, been a picturesque platform for hook-and-liners whose escape from city streets ended on the sidewalk of this poor man's fishing pier. Day and night ever since the bridge opened, they came to fish, elbow to elbow on weekends.

The big trucks whizzing by brought bursts of air that could blow your hat away, into the water below, or, it could refresh you as you waited for a bite. "If we lived closer," said a beefy Bethlehem Steel crane operator I met on the bridge one summer evening, "I'd be down here every night fishing." Drivers slow to observe the scene—and, occasionally, to throw whiskey bottles, firecrackers, watermelons, tomatoes, and "everything else," according to Bobby Perry, who was tending the drawbridge during my visit.

Despite a dearth of water traffic, the law required bridge tenders around the clock. Three men put in fifty-six hours a week each, including sixteen hours of overtime. They occupied a small "pilot house" fifteen feet above the traffic. It was cold in the winter, hot in the summer, and it shook every time an eighteen-wheeler went by. Inside, the control panel filled most of the tiny space. There was also room for three chairs, a hot plate, a refrigerator, and a TV set.

But the world inside was big enough for the bridge tenders. "I'm very pleased right here," said Charley Wheatley, who at age thirty-four gave up the social work of barbering for this solitary life. "I can't think of a thing I'd rather do than what I'm doing right now," he said. Perry, an ex-Green Beret, would have preferred to be fighting a war, for money or glory. But, for now, all he could do was pass the time reading adventure stories and daydreaming of battles to come.

While workboats and pleasure craft desiring access to upriver only rarely interrupted the bridge tenders' reveries, the Choptank downriver was often full of white sails. They converged on Cambridge especially during the midsummer weekend regatta. But the river also offered opportunities for visionaries like James Rouse, the Easton-born builder of the Howard County "new town" of Columbia and of Baltimore's sparkling Harborplace. Asked to help chart the town's future, he suggested a waterfront development of luxury townhouses as a way to extend the land of the gentry south of its navigable southern boundary.

Postcard view of Cambridge Harbor in the 1940s.

"The Choptank River plays an important role in Cambridge's good life," says the town's chamber of commerce. "Cambridge is a terminus for the quest of a good life. A city of shade trees, lovely homes, well-kept, and attractive lawns and gardens. Here the home is important. In Cambridge, the home is more than a house in which to live. It is an institution that invites landscaping and gardening activities, building and painting and planting."

To enter Goldie Mae Jackson's home, I had to stoop, then climb through a hole in the screen door. Had I opened the door, it surely would have fallen off its hinges. Inside, the flies were buzzing as Mrs. Jackson, a woman in her seventies, and her next-door neighbor watched the fantasy world of television game shows on an old black-and-white set. The faded certificate on the wall recorded the marriage, in 1925, of "Sister Hughes, 20, colored" to the by-now-deceased John Jackson, "25, colored." The eighty-dollar-a-month, two-room unit had a wood stove for winter warmth, a refrigerator that sometimes worked, and the almost overpowering stench of poverty. The kitchen light was broken, the tap water cold, and the back yard strewn with garbage.

Wilmore Stanley, Goldie Mae Jackson's next-door neighbor in the rundown two-family house, had his name on the waiting list for public housing and hoped against hope his turn would come. Until then, he shrugged, "There's nothing you can say because you got nowhere else to go."

Over on Moore's Avenue, people were living in two rows of chicken coops that had been converted years before into eight-dwelling units. Two more families were living nearby in what once had been a horse stable. The chicken-coop houses sat close to the ground. When it rained hard, the water rose through the floors, warping the wood and damaging the furniture. "Everywhere we went to complain, they turned us down," Elois Camper told me. "They kept sending us to this person and that person."

This was the strictly segregated second ward, home to the city's nearly forty-eight hundred blacks—more than 41% of Cambridge's citizens—a place of dilapidated houses on narrow streets without sidewalks or gutters. By 1990, the city's black population would be up slightly, to 44.2%, accounting for 5,093 people still living in the same section of town.

Across town, on a wide street with sidewalks and gutters, a block from the Choptank, lived the landlord of Goldie Mae Jackson and Wilmore Stanley. A distinguished-looking white man with silver hair, E. Haile Creighton, with his family, owned more than one hundred houses in the second ward. He greeted me affably enough at the front door of his large brown frame house, then said, "I have no comment...I can't afford to say anything."

Gorton McWilliams, Sr., owned the chicken-coop houses and the converted stable, along with some twenty other properties in the second ward. I found him edging the lawn in front of his home opposite city hall. The son of a former city commissioner whose own son now held the post, McWilliams blamed the city for any water damage to the chicken-coop houses. The city, he said, had failed to clear a drainage ditch of underbrush. "He's right," agreed the city's public works director. "It hasn't been cleared for years."

Still another second ward landlord was head of the city's less-than-activist human relations commission. Since the panel lacked even the power to investigate complaints, it was hard to get a quorum to justify a meeting. City neglect in the second ward was "a disgrace," declared Robin M. Kirwin, the commission's chairman and owner of fifty properties there. A former packing company executive who had also worked for the State Department in Latin America, Kirwin was regarded as one of the city's better landlords, according to his tenants on Camper Street, which dead-ends behind a baseball park that clearly defines the second ward's northeast limits and separates it from an affluent white neighborhood nearer the Choptank.

"There are a lot of legitimate gripes," said Kirwin, sitting in the back-yard shade of cherry and crepe myrtle trees. "But you get one or two firebrands, you're always subject to problems. I guess maybe they don't believe in working through the system." A white businessman on aptly named Race Street, the white shopping street, put it this way: "The slum landlords run this city. They're not bad people. They say, 'I know it's not right, but it's the system.'" As if to offer further evidence of "the system" in Cambridge, the businessman requested anonymity. "My wife plays cards with their wives," he explained, almost apologetically, "and I'd lose four of my best customers."

The system in this tradition-bound port city of 11,703 people in 1980—and fewer, 10,969, in 1996—continued to frustrate the aspirations of its black citizens decades after the town of Cambridge became a national symbol of racial repression. It was here that Freedom Riders trying to integrate restaurants were arrested in 1962. The following year, voters rejected a public accommodations act and businessmen opposed public housing as "a roundabout way to jam public accommodations down our throat." The Cambridge Volunteer Fire Company closed its swimming pool rather than integrate it.

A year later, in 1967, H. Rap Brown, a civil rights activist and an outsider, led residents in protests that erupted into violence and flames. The fire company refused to enter the burning ghetto or even to lend hoses to its residents. Brown, who left Cambridge after delivering a speech that allegedly fanned the flames, was indicted for arson (charges were later dropped). The National Guard visited Cambridge several times in that tumultuous decade and staged its longest occupation in the entire country here, five days less than one year in 1963 and 1964.

In an extraordinary string of seventeen editorials during those years, the *Washington Post* criticized both black militants and white segregationists and found "the one moderating and enlightening influence" to be the National Guard general whose troops kept the peace under martial law. The chief of police and others blamed outsiders for the town's troubles.

The "outside agitator" theme heard in the 1960s still echoed years later, as some whites continued to wax nostalgic over those quiet days before the civil rights revolution. "It was brought into us," William Wingate, the president of the board of county commissioners who was born and raised in Cambridge, told me in the midst of what threatened to be a new era of black militancy in the late 1970s. Except for "a great rivalry between black and white high schools in sports," he said, race, before outsiders came in to stir things up, was something to which "you didn't pay much attention."

Cambridge, asserted State Senator Fred Malkus, had been "misaccused from the beginning. We were in the forefront as far as race relations were concerned. As far as equal accommodations is concerned," added the man who made sure his county was exempted from the state statute, "whatever equality there is must come out of the hearts of men. It cannot come out of the law books. I got more colored friends than most of the so-called liberals." In his small law office opposite the antebellum county courthouse, Malkus also attacked the press, especially out-of-town reporters like myself. "You fellas," he told me, "all you wanna do is start trouble. You're trying to start a new fire which fortunately is not going to happen. This town, in my opinion, is gonna stay quiet."

In fact, I made my second trip to Cambridge (the first was to cover the national muskrat-skinning contest held there each March) to attend a state human relations commission hearing into race-related problems in and around the Dorchester County seat. The year was 1979, but little had changed in the years following the turmoil of the 1960s.

The legal barriers, to be sure, had come down: restaurants and the pool had long been integrated. But among the town's thirty or so lawyers were no blacks. The town's only black doctor was one of two blacks belonging to the 155-member chamber of commerce. The United Fund had one black board member out of eighteen. There were separate American Legion posts, and no blacks served in any of the county's fourteen volunteer fire companies. There were likewise no blacks among the fifteen sheriff's deputies, and only five on the thirty-six-member police force.

There had never been a black county commissioner, and Cambridge itself, divided into five wards, had only one black city commissioner, from the segregated second ward. "It's a southern town with a lot of old ideas and a lot of older people who want to perpetuate the old ideas," Edward Watkins, the lone black city commissioner, told me during a midsummer visit. Watkins also noted a range of other educational and economic problems plaguing the entire population, but blacks in particular. Fewer than one out of six blacks had completed high school (countywide, one in three students graduated), and, in an area of chronically high unemployment, three times as many blacks as whites were jobless.

The unemployed and the retired passed the time in front of Jones Market, on Pine Street, the main street of the second ward. The congregating spot was across Pine from an "amphitheatre" that had been built with federal antipoverty funds by black youths out of the ashes of the 1967 riots. Consisting of a cinder-block wall, a concrete stage, overgrown grass, and a low brick fence, it stood on the site of a torched school. This ambiguous monument, residents said, was unused except as a dumping ground for liquor bottles and beer cans and as a place to buy drugs.

A few blocks away was another landmark, a 1.4-acre playground named after Charles Cornish, a former second ward councilman whom many of his own people came to regard as an "Uncle Tom" but who had established himself with the city's white power structure. Cornish Park, also erected in the aftermath of the violence, was used by children of the second ward, but it, too, came to be regarded as a monument to white neglect The city spent $10,000 there on landscaping and playground equipment but lavished fifteen times as much on boat slips, restrooms, and showers at Long Wharf Park, which adjoined a white neighborhood and the all-white Cambridge Yacht Club.

Meanwhile, Cambridge leaders fashioned new plans for a downtown shopping mall and proceeded with harbor redevelopment while saying the city could afford only one housing inspector and no large-scale program of low-income housing. And this at a time when the housing shortage had become so acute that the Cambridge Housing Authority, with a waiting list of 200 for its 190 occupied units, bought newspaper space to stop the flood of applicants.

"I've been accused of being lenient" with landlords, said James B. Yates, who as state's attorney had prosecuted black demonstrators during the 1960s and now sat on the district court bench. "But you can't arbitrarily force people out of the place they're living in. They have no place to go." During the tense times in Cambridge, Yates was said to have packed a pistol while prosecuting cases against demonstrators. A judge since 1975, Yates acknowledged having what he called a "pocket bulge" at a time when he said he had received "seventeen or eighteen threats" on his life. But the mild-mannered, pipe-smoking jurist I met seemed to belie his '60s image as a gun-toting lawman.

The racial climate in Cambridge, Yates insisted, was "totally different" from what it had been before. "I've had excellent relations with the blacks," he said. "In fact, I very seldom send anybody to prison, only two in four years, and I regretted doing that." (Subsequently, in 1982, Yates sent a black woman to jail for sixty days for allegedly calling a white assistant principal "honky" during an after-school conference about her twelve-year-old son. "I'm not going to allow anybody to disrupt our schools," Yates said.)

I had met Yates at the High Spot Restaurant, a typical small-town eatery with good food at modest prices near the county courthouse. A few blocks away, in a converted garage on High Street in the second ward, I found another survivor of the '60s. Lemuel Chester was a twenty-one-year old firebrand when Yates had him indicted in 1967, along with Rap Brown, for arson. Now, he was approaching middle age still committed to "breaking down the barriers of injustice," but, he stressed, "through the system." Even Yates, his former adversary, had said, "I've had a very friendly relationship with Lemuel Chester."

Chester's office at the community center he managed bore testimony to his latter-day respectability. On its walls were a Head Start Service Award, a certificate identifying "Lemuel Darnell Chester" as an "Outstanding Young Man of America," a Kiwanis Club certificate of appreciation, and a letter from City Commissioner Gorton H. McWilliams, Jr., lauding him as "one of the leaders and outstanding citizens of Cambridge."

His embrace of the system naturally placed him out of step with the new militancy arising in Cambridge. "My days of radicalism I don't regret one ounce," he said. But in subsequent years, he had become an alcoholic, unable to hold a steady job, "the town's bad boy." His salvation had come through a federally funded "outreach center." Now he was helping others, but his community work hinged on government support. And, fearing the loss of federal monies, he had denied his building's use to a group he deemed too radical. "There was a suggestion people may have to take to the streets. Under our guidelines, that's considered subversive. It could have a negative effect on our being refunded," he said.

What angered him most was his lack of complete acceptance by the

Cambridge establishment with whom he had, by and large, made his peace. In particular, it galled him that his nomination for Junior Chamber of Commerce "Man of the Year" had come from the Bel Air, Harford County, chapter and not from the Cambridge Jaycees, all of whom were white. Tyrone Seymore, a black native of Cambridge who taught school in Baltimore City, had nominated Chester from the Harford Jaycees. A tall man of thirty-six, Seymore lived and breathed the Jaycees' creed with its homilies to God, service, and the free enterprise system. "The Jaycees' my life," he said simply during a summer spent in his hometown. "I believe in everything it stands for. There are young men walking Pine Street who need an organization like this. All I want them to do is open the doors to black people."

The problem in Cambridge was the meeting place. The Jaycees had gathered for years at the Veterans of Foreign Wars building, said to be off limits to blacks. There was nothing in writing; blacks said it was just understood. Determined to break the color bar, Seymore drove up Sandy Hill Road to the VFW post where the Jaycees were meeting. The VFW commander said his post did not discriminate. The head of the Cambridge Jaycees said likewise. "We're all on the same side," said one Jaycee. Then Seymore, wearing a vest decorated with Jaycee patches and buttons, asked for and received a handful of applications to both groups. At the same time, he filled out an application for membership in his hometown chapter. "If I had been allowed to join the Jaycees here when I was younger, I might never have left Cambridge," he said. Then Tyrone Seymore strode into the cool, August night.

The membership cards came, without fanfare, a short time later. Soon, a handful of Cambridge blacks belonged both to their hometown Jaycees (although Lem Chester wasn't one of them; he attended a few meetings but never got around to sending in his application) and to the VFW. Within a year of my visit, the chicken-coop houses had been razed. In their place, two white landlords who owned extensive slum properties in the second ward had built box-like concrete duplexes. Elois Camper had moved from the chicken-coop dwelling into a new apartment. Her brother, James, had joined his cousin Tyrone Seymore in the Cambridge Jaycees.

Change had come, however little and late, across a bridge in time.

On the thirtieth anniversary of the city's 1967 riots, I returned to Cambridge to chart its progress, or lack thereof. Economically, there was no renaissance on either side of town, though some waterfront condos had gone up where fleets of skipjacks once docked and city boosters continued to tout Cambridge as the future Inner Harbor of the Eastern Shore. Over the Choptank arched the new Frederick R. Malkus Bridge, leaving a section of the old span, minus the pylons at either end, to the hook-and-liners. First Chance/Last Chance Liquors relocated to the west side of Route 50 but did not long survive.

The city remained sharply segregated, but there was a new elementary school on the black side of town. There were now two black city commissioners. Lem Chester had served two terms as Dorchester County's first black commissioner. Such political advances had been brought about by litigation and court orders that assured a black majority district in the county and two in the city. Chester was now an addiction counselor studying for the ministry. Together, we revisited the corner where Rap Brown, whom he had invited to Cambridge during the tumultuous times of 1967, had made his fiery speech. The street was quiet but not empty. Kenneth Berry was there with a friend. He didn't know much of the history. "Man, I was two years old. I know there was a riot. I thought it was the late '50s or something." He paused, then asked, "What do you think about the Redskins?"

3

The Vanishing Islands

*B*etween the flatlands of the Eastern Shore and the beaches and cliffs across the Bay lies the Chesapeake itself, its shallow waters and smooth surface creating an illusion of serenity. But potent natural forces are at work, sometimes quietly and sometimes with an unmistakable roar.

The primordial Susquehanna River flooded eons ago to form the Bay; the land today ever so slowly sinks and washes away. Seemingly secure civilizations are eternally at risk in the shifting shorelines of the Chesapeake Bay. The eroded earth often finds its way to other areas in the estuary, contributing to the irreversible process destined in time to fill in the water even as the water eats away at the land.

The Western Shore suffers least from this interchange of land and sea. It is more compacted, its older sediments more resistant to erosion. In addition to geology, wind directions favor the Western Shore. Prevailing west and northwest winds in Maryland generate wave action against the Eastern Shore. Thus, while 13% of the Lower Western Shore has actually been gaining ground, 38% of the Lower Eastern Shore has been losing more than eight feet of it each year since the 1800s.

In the wetlands of Dorchester County, the marsh grass that supports animal life slips away at an alarming rate. Even the terra firma along the earthen shores suffers from the erosive force of nature. Since 1845 Dorchester has lost eight thousand acres of land, nearly sixty-six acres each year. Similar losses have occurred up and down the Eastern Shore. But, most exposed of all, the islands of the Chesapeake Bay fare the worst.

Smith Island on the Maryland-Virginia line has life on it yet, even as erosion threatens its future generations of watermen with the extinction of their homeland. And on Blackwalnut Point, at the southern tip of Tilghman Island, the homeowners have beseeched their government for funds to fight the erosion threatening to wash over their only road to the outside.

But other isles—Holland, Bloodsworth, Barren, Sharps, and Poplar—have suffered the same fate, and no one was able to rescue them from the relentless forces of the Bay. They have been left to wither, like the old ghost towns of the West. But here the signs of civilization were submerged rather than left to crumble. It was, no doubt, folly to sink roots in a land nature could destroy, for who could say where or when the winds would churn up the deceptively calm

Bay waters to tear away at the islands' shores?

Once, each island had been a seemingly secure sliver of land with homes, farms, churches, schools, and stores. Generations were born, lived, died, and were buried there. Now, Holland was all but forgotten, with a few graves and a single house left on it. Bloodsworth, once home to a dozen families, had since 1942 been used for naval shelling practice. Visited by hunters since the last family moved its home and belongings to nearby Hooper's Island in 1916, Barren was little more than a liability to its owner, who had been trying, without success, to sell the remains; it would wind up in the hands of a conservation group. Sharps was but a memory to a dwindling few.

And now Poplar Island, too, its hundreds of years of human history washing away, was almost gone.

During Tropical Storm David, in 1979, the wind-driven waters of the Chesapeake wrested one foot each hour from the shores of Poplar, located two miles west of the Bay Hundred mainland. The Bay swallowed as much as fifteen feet in places, telescoping, according to one conservative estimate, a full year's relentless erosion into one stormy September night.

I visited Poplar the following spring with Kevin Sullivan, director of the Smithsonian Institution's Chesapeake Bay Center, which owned and oversaw most of it. "This damn island has broken everyone's heart who's been on it." Sullivan said as we headed out to Poplar in a Smithsonian launch from Lowe's Wharf Landing. "I suspect it will happen to us, too."

For the time being, however, Sullivan worried about navy planes flying too low and power boats speeding too close, disturbing the ospreys that hatched their eggs on manmade platforms near the water and the great blue herons that nested atop loblolly pines. Poplar was home to one of the largest concentrations of herons on the Eastern seaboard.

This island, where as many as one hundred persons once lived and where Presidents Franklin D. Roosevelt and Harry S Truman fled from the pressures of their office, was home now to a lone caretaker, his cat, a small herd of deer, and battalions of birds. In places, only stands of daffodils hinted at the former sites of human habitation. In time, they, too, would be gone, as Poplar sank inexorably into a watery grave.

Sometimes, on weekends, city people came here under Smithsonian auspices to study the wildlife and sleep at the lodge left over from the island's days as a hunting ground for high-rollers from Washington and Baltimore. "It really gets to be a rat race," said Mike Passo, the caretaker. "On the other hand, it's great they come. Otherwise, nobody uses it and there wouldn't be any justification for even me being here."

Linked to the outside world by only a forty-six-foot boat and a radio telephone, the bearded thirty-two-year-old navy veteran mowed the lawn, maintained the lodge and its electric generator, and, as the one-man Poplar Island police force, shooed away unauthorized visitors—except during storms. "In July or August, a storm came in from the west, with sixty- or seventy-mile-an-hour winds," Passo said. "It went from calm to a full gale, and in fifteen or twenty minutes, it was over. I always dread getting stuck in one. Last year, on four different occasions, we had families drop in to get out of them. One stayed two days.

"The year before last," Passo continued, "there was thunder around 2 a.m. and a weird clanking. A man with three boys in a sailboat had drug anchor and blew into the island. He was a preacher from Pennsylvania and it was a rental boat. Boy, were they terrified when they got in that house."

For years, the crescent-shaped land mass had provided a safe harbor for boats in a storm and had served as a buffer against erosion of the Talbot County mainland. But what in colonial times had been a single, one-thousand-acre island was now in seven pieces, a chain of islands totaling no more than one hundred and twenty-five acres or so. They ranged in size from Coaches at the southern end, with about fifty acres of trees, to tiny islets of a few square yards barely visible at high tide.

The Smithsonian staffers had their own names for the islands and islets. Poplar, for example, was now divided into North Point, the Heron Island, Poison Ivy, and Marshy Islands. Jefferson, home to the caretaker and occasional visitors, retained the name bestowed by twentieth-century politicians. Coaches—Coaches Neck before the island was severed—kept its name of uncertain but long-ago origins. It had once had a Quonset hut hunting lodge, but only the concrete foundation was left. Coaches was also home to the white-tailed island deer, a herd of thirty-two, according to the latest count.

The main island of Poplar, once the largest and a vital center of human life, was now a narrow north-south strip where uprooted trees lay like floating tombstones in the water, fallen from the Bayside banks along with crumbling bricks and bric-a-brac of a vanished world. "Poplar Main" was the fastest-eroding island in the Bay, and this century, scientists said, would be its last.

Since 1847 the western shoreline of Poplar had receded by 2,790 feet. Between 1964 and 1971 alone, 119.7 feet of shoreline had washed into the Bay,

The vanishing Poplar islands in the 1940s.
H. Robins Hollyday

leaving only fifty-four acres on Poplar Main. By the time of my visit, less than half of those fifty-four were left. While residents of Smith clung tenaciously to their land and tried to save their island, here the homesteads and graveyards of generations had already washed away, and no one was left to fight for Poplar's salvation.

At low tide, the flotsam and jetsam of history washed up on shore. The window sills and shelves of Mike Passo's house were filled with them: old bottles that once had contained Dr. Kilmer's Swamp Root Kidney, Liver & Bladder Cure, Dr. Thompson's Eye Wash, and Fink's Magic Oil; a soda bottle dated 1893; and a hollow cannonball from the War of 1812.

On Poplar Main, chimney ruins and a few wooden boards were almost lost amidst the untrampled growth, much of which, I later learned to my regret, was poison ivy. "This is almost primeval," the Smithsonian's Sullivan observed during our tour, just before a jet plane incongruously thundered overhead.

History records that Captain William Claiborne, a Virginian later banished by the Calverts from Maryland, first laid claim to Poplar Island in 1631, the same year he established a trading post on Kent Island to the north. He named it Poplin's Island after a trusted associate. Claiborne gave the island to a cousin, Richard Thompson, whose family and servants were killed by Nanticoke Indians in 1637.

In 1654 the island was sold for ten thousand pounds of tobacco to a Thomas Hawkins. His widow later married Seth Foster, from whom the island briefly took a new name. In 1699 the island was sold again, this time to the former Dutch governor of Delaware. The father of Charles Carroll (one of the signers of the Declaration of Independence) purchased it next, for twenty-two hundred pounds of tobacco and two hundred pounds of sterling silver.

The British plundered the island during the Revolutionary War and the War of 1812. By the 1840s, maps show, Cobbler's Neck—later to be known as Valliant and then Jefferson Island—had separated from Poplar. Before escaping to freedom in 1836, sixteen-year-old Frederick Douglass slaved away within sight of "Poplar Island, covered with a thick, black pine forest," he later recalled in his autobiography.

A map dated 1877 shows only four island property owners: a Captain Howeth, H. N. Sherwood, Captain D. Jones, and the Carrolls, whose estate was over on Cobbler's Neck. But from the 1880s into the 1920s, as many as fifteen families lived there. The Valliants' general store and post office was on the smallest island. The larger island contained a one-room schoolhouse that doubled as a church, a lumber mill, a graveyard, a road, and at least half a dozen farms. Coaches, by then a separate island, also housed several families.

The Poplar Island farmers grew tomatoes, tobacco, watermelon, cantaloupe, corn, and wheat, which they reaped with a steam-driven thresher, which was now said to lie under water one-eighth of a mile offshore. There were horses and oxen to pull the plows. There was no electricity. There were neither cars nor carriages. The people walked or rode on horseback along the road that ran from one end to the other. They sailed to the mainland in log canoes. The men who worked the water reaped good harvests of crabs and oysters in "the Poplar pot," the natural harbor formed by the island chain. Today, rockfish are said to be plentiful near the old wells that have since disappeared under water.

My search for the surviving former residents took me to nearby Tilghman, Sherwood, Wittman, and St. Michaels, and as far away as Cambridge. "It was a beautiful little old island with oyster-shell walks and little white picket fences," recalled Dolores Reese of St. Michaels, whose son, Jan, had become known as "the osprey man" for his efforts to care and account for the birds around Poplar Island.

"We had our own cow and tilled the farm with horses," said Ida Richardson, who was in her mid-seventies when I visited her yellow clapboard house on Mission Street in Tilghman. "A many a tomato plant I dropped [into dug holes] and a many a corn plant I thinned [pulled up]," she said. "It was a right good-sized farm. Had to bring [the produce] over here in a boat." They rented their first house and farm from James Howeth, who lived in Tilghman. It was, she recollected,

a big farm house, I mean that house was built, not like now, and was high off the ground on bricks. We lived next to Harvey Howeth. There was a cemetery on that farm. Then everything began to wash, so they had them moved. Harvey was related to my mother; they were cousins.

I liked it over there okay. Never got bored. If we got tired of doing something, we got in the rowboat and had a race. We used to find a lot of Indian darts and axes over there. One winter, it froze so bad, people walked across the ice, close together and with a rope in case someone fell in. One time, the ice started to run, and they made it back [to the island] in no time. We were satisfied with anything we got at Christmas, toys and oranges and candies. All the families visited. They had a good time there.

We had an old colored fellow used to work for us, used to be a slave. He stayed with us until we moved back here. He could tell you something about slavery. He said you'd go barefoot in the summer if you wanted shoes in the wintertime. I think he was ninety-five or ninety-six when we quit farming and moved down here. I was ten or eleven when we moved over on this side.

My father went over and tore down the house by himself because no one was living there. Kids were just going over and tearing things down anyway. My father built a kitchen on the back of this house with what he got over there about fifty years ago.

She remembered the island church being "just about full," although no preacher resided on Poplar. She recalled, too, a "room full of children" in the schoolhouse heated by a wood stove where she began her education under the tutelage of Joseph F. Valliant, "a right good teacher." He was also the last teacher. The school closed for good in 1918, when he died; at that time he had just one student.

Harvey C. Howeth, Ida Richardson's long-ago island neighbor, had died at the age of eighty-eight just two months before I found his eighty-seven-year-old widow in Tilghman. Nannie Howeth lived around the corner from Ida Richardson in a small white house. The Howeths were married on June 7, 1916, and lived on the island nearly four years before brothers Harvey, Jim, and Charles Howeth sold their farms, "reserving, however, the growing crops for 1919; the burial plot as now laid out to remain forever undisturbed," the deed said, not accounting for the corrosive effects of the Chesapeake.

"I know I didn't like it over there, I know that," said Nannie Howeth in the living room of the house she now inhabited alone. "But if you're gonna marry somebody, you gotta go with them." On her wall were a fiftieth wedding anniversary plate and pictures of Harvey and his mother.

"I don't want to move back there anymore," Nannie Howeth said. She had had three children on the island, the first two twins, and all of them had died in infancy. "I had an awful time over there," she said, fragile from age but still sure of her opinions on the subject of Poplar Island. "I thought it was the worst place I'd ever seen in my life. I was young then, and Harvey was, too. I used to go out with Harvey ducking, hide in the bushes waiting to kill a duck. We had to have something to eat. I thought I'd have it better over here where I was born and raised."

On the mainland, Harvey Howeth had become a housepainter. He continued to miss the island his wife hated. "I have four bunches of Easter lilies in the backyard that Harvey planted over there [on the island] when he was a child," his widow said.

The old-timers still remembered the Valliant sisters, known as Miss Janie (Mary J.) and Miss Hallie (Harriet S.), and their general store where they sold canned goods but no meat. "They were old maids, if you know what old maids were like," said Ida Richardson.

One by one, the families, most of them interrelated through marriage, left. Howeths, Lednums, Sinclairs, Haddaways, and finally, Valliants migrated across Poplar Narrows to the mainland. Their family tombstones fill the cemetery behind the church in Sherwood, almost directly opposite the island.

The spinster sisters kept postponing the inevitable, until at last Captain George Haddaway of the Maryland Marine Police came and got them. In 1925 they moved into a converted schoolhouse in Sherwood bought by their brothers, Lloyd and Hugh. There, Mary Valliant died on July 5, 1933, bequeathing few worldly possessions. Harriet Valliant died less than six months later, leaving a stack of bills from her doctor and the Sherwood general store and personal belongings that brought $151.50 in a Depression sale.

By 1929 Poplar was all but left to the moonshiners. Federal revenuers raided the place that year, arresting five bootleggers, seizing their yacht, and smashing a thousand-gallon still. Mail service to the islands ended in 1932.

Congressional Democrats bought the island where the Valliants' store had been for their Jefferson Islands Club in 1931. According to an apparently tongue-in-cheek brochure, the club "was formed for the purpose of supporting, defending, and advancing the fundamental principles of government enunciated by Thomas Jefferson."

The island was touted as the "playground of presidents" after FDR and Truman visited several times. "The senators did a lot of drinking over there and they used to have a crowshoot," said Perry W. Cooper, who worked at the club as a cook and handyman in the 1930s. I found him watching a televised Orioles baseball game at his home in nearby Wittman, half a mile from where he was born on September 26, 1891. Alice Jane Haddaway, who lived now in Sherwood, had worked there, too, and once spilled peas "down Harry Truman's back," she recalled. "He laughed, got a big joke out of that."

Poplar Main, by then a gunning club belonging to an Annapolis lumberman, was briefly inhabited by full-time residents during the 1930s. "We went back before my mother died," said Margaret Greenhawk, a seventy-year-old survivor

Path along Jefferson Island during the 1940s.

whom I visited in her Cambridge apartment. "It was her hometown, where she was raised. She always did love it. She said she wanted to go back home. My father decided to take her back because she wanted to go so bad, and my husband and I moved over with them. She was very ill. I guess she wanted to die there." They spent two hard winters on the island, and the old lady died shortly after returning to the mainland in August 1939.

A 1942 aerial photo shows four abandoned houses and a fragment of unpaved road, but by then Poplar was a complete ghost island. On Jefferson, the "president's club" the Democrats had acquired burned down in 1946. (The Democrats later established a new Jefferson Islands Club on St. Catherine Island in the Potomac River.) In 1948 the politicians sold their Chesapeake island and its burned-down lodge to George and Marion Bailey, of Cecil County. The Baileys built another lodge, on approximately the same spot, and the picture they painted in a 1950 brochure of life there was enticing, indeed:

> In ducking season, only six gunners are taken at one time, in order that the extensive grounds shall not be overshot. Two men are put to a blind, so that of the eleven blinds only three are shot a day. Bitter days a big boat with coffee and soup hot on its coal fire lies off where it may be signaled if a gunner gets cold, or wishes to return to the Lodge for any reason.
>
> If you are around the house between meals, the steward will bring you bouillon or iced tea or orangeade. In the winter, the bar and lounge fires burn brightly; while in summer, the big screened porch takes every South West breeze from the water a short stone's throw away. Every room looks out over the playgrounds of the gulls and the wildfowl.

Jefferson Island was sold again, after George Bailey's death, to a group of Campbell soup executives. In 1960 there was another fire, an alleged arson for which the caretaker was indicted and acquitted. Having already confessed to the crime, he was represented by Thomas Hunter Lowe of Wittman, later a state appellate judge. "He was so happy," Lowe recalled, "when I sent him the bill, he disappeared." Finally, the third lodge, which stood during my visit, was built where the others had been.

In 1965 a Philadelphia physician acquired the island chain. He later donated all but Coaches to the Smithsonian. "We loved it and went there on weekends and vacations," said Dr. William L. Elkins, "but it became impractical, so I got the

Coaster from one of the incarnations of the Poplar Islands Lodge.

Smithsonian in on the deal, realizing if anyone could stop the erosion, it would take someone like that with some wherewithal. At one time, we talked with [U.S. Interior Secretary] Rodgers Morton. We got up to the highest levels, but what legislature was gonna vote a couple of million bucks to shore up Poplar Island?" The answer was: none.

Government estimates on what it would cost to save the islands ranged from $800 thousand up to $4 million. And there were some, even within the Smithsonian, who questioned the very idea, seeing efforts at saving Poplar as little more than blind, human arrogance challenging nature. "By what right (or to what purpose) should Man seek to mitigate a process as inexorable as the wearing down of the once tall Appalachians, or the extinction of the wooly mammoth, or the demise of some other species doomed by nature?" asked Dr. David Challinor, a Smithsonian official, in 1971.

The battle for Poplar Island seemingly ended then, when human forces abdicated to the forces of nature. Various schemes to use baled solid waste or demolition debris from Baltimore to bulkhead the bayside were discarded as impractical. Other proposals to bulkhead the outer islands by conventional means were deemed too costly.

Even plans to shore up Jefferson, which was not partially protected by Poplar Main to the west, ran into snags when bidding for bulkheading exceeded the $50,000 budgeted for the job. "Our feeling right now is to do what we can to preserve the integrity of Jefferson," Kevin Sullivan told me. "As far as the outer islands, I think we're prepared just to let them go."

So, Poplar Island was rapidly washing away. With the diminishing land, the heron nests were dwindling, too, from five hundred in 1963 to seventy-five less than two decades later. With Poplar gone, some worried, the Bay would have its way with Jefferson and Coaches and, ultimately, Tilghman and the mainland. "Once the island goes," observed the owner of the Bridge Restaurant, within sight of Poplar at Knapp's Narrows in Tilghman, "this goes, too."

"There are some rather titanic forces out there on the Bay, especially with a thirty-mile-an-hour wind," noted Jan Reese, the osprey man of St. Michaels who had gone to Poplar each fall to build wooden platforms for the birds. Tropical Storm David had pushed back the island's sandy beaches, he said. "One of the sand bars on the northern tip of the island got picked up and moved one hundred feet north. That storm did as much damage in one night as three years [of normal erosion]. There's also the ship traffic. There's a ten-mile fetch between the shipping channel and the island. Those tankers carry a lot of water with them when they go past. It's just like blasting with a bomb. The island could go next year or it could last another ten years. I don't know."

"Naught save the alliance and ingenuity of man can avert the catastrophe of destruction, divided as they [the islands] are and attacked on every side by time and tide," said the *Easton Star-Democrat* in a 1931 series on Poplar Island.

Another storm welled up suddenly during my visit. It was not yet dark when Mike Passo raced out to the rickety three-hundred-foot pier at Jefferson Island to pull the moored sixteen-foot whaler marked Poplar Island Security closer to the dock. The sky glimmered pink in the east but elsewhere darkened ominously. Thunder clapped, lightning exploded, and wind-driven rain descended.

Inside the lodge, I watched the weatherman on the black-and-white television announce temperatures dropping from seventy-nine to sixty-four degrees, a severe thunderstorm watch, hail likely, and gusting winds. The storm was moving from across the Bay in a southeasterly direction. "At least it's from the northwest," providing more protection for the island security boat, said Passo. "If it were from the southeast, we'd probably be abandoning the ship right now. It's blowing pretty good out there, probably about thirty knots." A cherry tree swayed precariously at the water's edge about a hundred feet from the lodge. The wind-whipped waters formed whitecaps in the Poplar pot. But soon the storm was over. The cherry tree had survived, and so had the islands, if only for the moment.

Two weeks later, a northwester ripped ashore and toppled the cherry tree into the water. The following spring, the Smithsonian gave up even its part-time presence on the island. It was no longer cost effective, it was decided, to keep Passo there. He was reassigned to the institution's Chesapeake Bay Center at Edgewater on the Western Shore. People at the Center said it broke his heart.

In the fall of 1982, when one small storm ripped five feet from the receding Jefferson shoreline, the Smithsonian put the islands up for sale. The advertisement touted "heavily forested islands together with sand beaches, deep water anchorages, and privacy...a wildlife haven and...an ideal recreational facility for several families or a similar group wishing to enjoy the year-round pleasures of the Chesapeake."

The asking price was $200,000 for the whole thing: $125,000 for Coaches (eighty-two acres, which Dr. Elkins had agreed to sell) and $75,000 for both Jefferson (twenty-eight acres) and Poplar Main (twelve acres). The islands were sold in 1983. A Delaware corporation bought Coaches for $87,500. A dozen men from the Washington suburbs, including a handful of lawyers and one judge, bought the rest for $60,000 cash. Lacking "comparables," the appraisers who established the asking price had included the replacement cost of the lodge and what it would cost to lease such a property, "based on its useful life" of ten to fifteen years.

"And if mother nature treats you kindly at the end of its useful life and there is accretion instead of erosion," said the Easton real estate agent, "you're well ahead of the game." But then again, there was no money-back guarantee.

But then again, who says you can't fool mother nature? A mere 15 years after my 1980 visit, plans were launched to re-create the 1,110-acre island "footprint" of 1847. It seemed downright bizarre. When I revisited the place in April, 1995, there was less than half an acre left of what was now called Middle Poplar, where I'd gotten poison ivy, and half of that was marsh. A half-dozen dying trees held a colony of bird nests, the last dwellings of any kind—human or natural—on the remains of Poplar.

But commerce was at stake, and nothing moves mankind to action more than the market. The Port of Baltimore, accounting for 18,000 jobs, required constant dredging to keep its channels open, and the stuff had to go somewhere. What better place to dump the muck than somewhere in the bay? This time, an unlikely coalition of agencies sometimes at odds with each other had come together over the plan. Environmentalists supported it, too, for here, created with as much as thirty million cubic yards of spoil, was to be a renewed wildlife refuge for the herons and other creatures. There would be both forested uplands and marshy wetlands, but no humans. The recreated Poplar would be owned by the state, which paid its former title-holders in the neighborhood of $500,000 for the vanishing island.

"I've never seen a project with more support and so little opposition," said Ed Sigal, associate director for science of the U.S. Environmental Protection Agency's Chesapeake Bay program. In 1996, Congress approved $15 million to get it going. The Army Corps of Engineers put it out for bids. The total price tag of $427 million seemed just another detail as work got underway at last in 1999.

But after all was said and done, there was still the nagging question of whether humans weren't playing God in seeking to reverse the tides of nature. And there was this cautionary tale to ponder: One nineteenth century owner of Poplar had planned to raise black cats on the island and market their furs to China. But the first winter, the bay froze over, and the eighty cats all scurried across the ice to the mainland. Thus, despite the most industrious and ingenious efforts of man, did nature have the final say at Poplar Island.

4

The World of the Watermen

*S*mith Island is an easy metaphor for the watermen of the Chesapeake Bay, if you believe their way of life is washing away like their land. Pessimists point to the dwindling oyster catches and the disappearance of the Bay grasses that nurture other aquatic life to support their view that the watermen's days are numbered.

But for the watermen themselves, grumbling about the catch goes with the territory and probably has since time immemorial. Crabs are either too plentiful or too scarce, oysters either too small or too tough to find. For the nine thousand or so who earn their living from the water, what matters is the market price, which is ruled by the laws of supply and demand. Whether bivalves and crustaceans thrive or decline, it's one tough way to make a living.

From the fishing village of Rock Hall on the Upper Eastern Shore, to the Patuxent and Potomac rivers on the west and Tangier Sound on the south, Maryland watermen ply the Bay and its tributaries in search of their catch. They crab in the summer, oyster in the winter, and sometimes eel in between. Their workday normally begins before dawn and ends by midday.

Watermen in general are an independent lot, with an accent often incomprehensible to the city ear. Although their ways have carried on from generation to generation, they aren't immune to change, either. To make a living on the water requires not only the strength of an athlete but also the skills of a mechanic, the mind of an accountant, and the spirit of a stoic able to adapt to the vicissitudes of time and tide.

These qualities seem almost inbred among the residents of Smith Island, a place much like everywhere else, but decidedly different. Accessible only by boat, it lies eleven nautical miles west of Crisfield, the crab and oyster capital on Maryland's Eastern Shore. From Crisfield's city dock, island-bound travelers board Frank Dize's Island Belle II (which is also the mailboat) or the Jason I or Jason II, named after co-owner Clarence Tyler's son. These are the boats the islanders themselves ride on their occasional trips to the doctors and shops of the Eastern Shore.

The forty-minute boat ride from Crisfield is a journey across time as well as space. Elizabethan accents are audible, barely, above the drone of the vessel's engine. My first trip, on a windy, rainy January day, was wet and wild, the bow pitching up and down to meet the whitecaps. But on a crystal clear day, the thin treeline of the island is almost visible from the water just outside Crisfield. On the Chesapeake, however, the shortest distance between two points is rarely a straight line, water depths being what they are.

To the uninitiated, the circuitous channel into Ewell, the largest of Smith Island's three towns, seems endless but also acts as a transition: Either side is marsh for miles, with hardly a house or tree in sight. Finally, the passage ends at the Big Thorofare, Ewell's watery main street. The boat stops first at Roy Evans's dock. Charlie Evans, his son, unloads boxes of dry goods and other foodstuffs from the mainland. The boat proceeds to the passenger wharf before ending its voyage in Tylerton. Only the tourist boat goes to Rhodes (formerly Rogues) Point, the third town. At almost any landing, the first dockside view is of stacked crab pots and oyster shells everywhere you look.

On my first visit, the island had approximately six hundred and fifty inhabitants, one-third of them named Evans, with Marshalls, Tylers, and Bradshaws close behind. Compounding the confusion, to outsiders anyway, were four Elmer Evanses: Elmer L., Elmer F., Elmer W., and Elmer W., Jr., who was universally known as Junior Evans.

Despite the confluence of clans, Smith Island is not always one big happy family. Like everywhere else, there are factions and feuds. Ewell is where the money is, Rhodes Pointers tend to resent Ewell's prominence, and Tylerton is accessible from the other two only by boat. They are said to use an even older English dialect there. What unites them all is the water. Almost every inhabitant of Smith Island earns a living from it.

Although part of Somerset County and the state of Maryland, Smith Island has been a world apart since its settlement in 1657. Children are educated through eighth grade on the island itself. For high school, forty or so students take the schoolboat each day to Crisfield, a process interrupted only when the Bay freezes over. Smith Islanders generally feel neglected by their county and looked down upon by many mainlanders, who they feel sometimes lack respect for the watermen's ways and wisdom.

The continuing controversy over the island's mountain of junked cars was a case in point. Sixty or so years ago, a Model A Ford and a Chevy truck made up the island's entire motor vehicle fleet. By the 1970s, there were an estimated one hundred cars that were in working order, and thousands more that weren't. The well-used cars had been barged over from the mainland, driven beyond repair without tags or insurance, and then dumped in the marsh between Ewell and Rhodes Point. There they were left to the elements, an unsightly mountain of rust despoiling the island paradise. The islanders thought they knew the answer to the problem.

"Here's my opinion about the cars," said Gene Somers one morning in the back of Lee Roy Evans's store, a popular gathering place for watermen of all ages. "If they put 'em on the bayside, they wouldn't have so much erosion. It should've been done years ago. But the environmentalists said oil [from the cars] would go in the Bay. It goes in the Bay anyhow, by the tide [sweeping over the marshland junk pile]. They ain't got nothing in the crankcase and it's as dry as this floor. They know it and we know it, but they think we're as dumb as clams."

Almost any evening, big old American cars, doubtless destined for future habitation in the marsh, rumbled back and

Junked cars rusting in a Smith Island marsh.
Eugene L. Meyer

forth along the 1.5-mile "highway" (sometimes under water at high tide) linking Ewell and Rhodes Point. They invariably passed the auto junkyard. They also drove by the island dump, its discarded beer bottles bearing testimony to the fact that although there are no bars on Smith Island, some residents have been known to swig a few now and then.

Smith Island has five miles of road, including the narrow lanes where people live, but it was long a place without street names (until the 1990s, when outside authorities insisted, citing "911" dispatches, as if the Smith Island volunteer fire fighters didn't know where folks lived). In Ewell, you were either "over the hill" (which refers to a barely discernible incline on the low-lying island) or "down the field" (referring to the other landmark, which doubles as a baseball diamond and the site of an annual tent revival each August).

Tourists are sometimes underwhelmed by the island. Frances Kitching, who served meals to mainlanders in her living room and boarded them upstairs, once explained it to me this way: "It's a different place, which they are expecting that.

They say, 'Where can I go?' I say, 'Anywhere you like.' There's no tourist attraction."

There is also no island government, no mayor, no town hall, no police force. There is instead the United Methodist Church, to which all islanders subscribe. With funds raised through the council of ministries from the three small congregations, the church pays for the street lights and the clinic. It's the closest there is to a theocracy in the state of Maryland.

Once, before the churning Chesapeake cut a channel through the marsh, you could walk to Tylerton, but not now. Until a few years ago, the road to Rhodes Point was paved with oyster shells. Then the government put in a new sewage-treatment plant and, after laying the pipes, covered them and the shells with tar. The tar turns gooey during hot summer days, a situation the islanders view as one more example of mainlanders messing up their world.

The worst tar horror story they tell concerns Olivia Tyler, known as Miss Levi. At the age of ninety-two, she got stuck in the stuff while crossing from her home to her general store in Rhodes Point (right down the road from her chief competitor, son Clinton, who ran another store). They say they had to lift her from her shoes.

Despite its tar, dump, and junked cars, Smith Island is scenic. The houses are mostly white, turn-of-the-century, frame dwellings. There's a mountain of oyster shells to behold in front of the small shucking house in Rhodes Point, which also has a marine railway. Half-sunken workboats rest on the shallow Bay bottom.

Just about anytime, the marshscape is a stunning sight. Birds punctuate the Chesapeake sky. In the distance, Tylerton can be seen from the road to Rhodes Point, and beyond it lies the Bay itself, feeding the islanders even as its wind-whipped waters eat away at the island. My favorite time on Smith Island is early morning, when the workboats chug out of the channel from Ewell in the predawn darkness, a flotilla of fishermen following the water as they have here for generations. Sunrise in this setting is almost worth keeping watermen's hours to see.

William Smith Dize was a little late getting started one midsummer morning when I went along for the ride. His brother-in-law, Junior Evans, was already at work culling soft-shell crabs from his floats, and all other workboats were gone when Dize and sons "Smitty," ten, and Martin, four, boarded the Miss Sally. It was not yet 5 a.m.

The forty-foot workboat moved quickly from its mooring through the narrow channel from Smith Island into Tangier Sound. The CB radio inside the small cabin crackled its own version of the "Today Show."

"Quite a little crab out there," a voice said.

"I been seein' more than I been seein'," came the reply.

Billy Dize had one hundred and fifty pots to pull, rectangular wire-mesh traps laid out in six rows of twenty-five each and located by red markers bobbing on the surface. Normally, he had a hundred more, "but it ain't worth it right now," he said. "The price just ain't that good."

Male crabs, the desirable "jimmies" that are sold for the steamed-crabs-and-beer crowd, were bringing only ten dollars a bushel, compared to twelve dollars two weeks before.

"I guess you gonna bait crabs as long as you live, ain't ye?" the CB radio voice said as the sun rose over Chesapeake Bay, a reddish-purple glow of water and sky.

Billy Dize had almost always baited crabs, ever since his father's cataracts forced him to drop out of school on his home island of Tangier, just across the state line in Virginia. "I was thirteen years old," he recalled. "His eyes got so bad, he couldn't do it on his own. He done everything in his power to keep me in school, but I had to quit to go with him." "A waterman's ambition is not to retire," Junior Evans had said, but bad eyes had ended the Chesapeake career of one Dize—and started another's.

It is a path taken by many on the water. The best education for a waterman, they will say, is to be found on the water, not in the classroom. But, often, they want more for their sons, the way Billy Dize wanted more for Smitty, just as his father had for him. "I holler at him for his own good," he said, "make it as hard as possible when he goes with me, so he'll think it over before he quits school."

He had spent three years in Washington a decade before, selling seafood on the Maine Avenue waterfront. There were fond memories of those days and of nights spent on the 14th Street beer-joint and go-go strip, and not so fond ones of tear gas on the Mall in the age of antiwar protests. Washington "was all right," he said, "but it wasn't as good as on the water."

Except this morning, it wasn't so good on the water, either.

"I ain't been out too far, but I ain't caught much yet," the voice on the CB reported.

On the Miss Sally, the hydraulic winch that helped Dize hoist the metal crab pots failed, its oil hose sprung an irreparable leak, and the boat's engine twice overheated. After a while, he had to pull the pots the old way, by hand.

Fifteen of the pots were badly bent out of shape, a condition he blamed on clam dredgers who shared the same waters. Before hard times, he said, "you'd throw the old pots away. Now, everything's so expensive, you keep 'em as long as you can."

From each pot, Dize dumped the contents into a worn rubber tray, then tossed the jimmies into a wooden basket and the sooks (female crabs) into a big barrel bound for the crab-picking plant. Along with the crabs came an occasional flounder, bluefish, and toadfish and an abundance of sea nettles, also known as jellyfish, which sting. "You know when you go to the dentist and he gives you a needle? That's the way my arms feel right now," Dize reported. It was 7:30 a.m.

At the age of thirty-one, he had a weathered face and a burly and bulky body. Only his longish blond hair and his "Play Boy" tattoo with the skull and cross bones gave him away as a Chesapeake child of the '60s. "I'll tell you," he said, "the way I feel sometimes, I ain't very young."

The young on board were William Smith Dize, Jr. (Smitty), who helped steer the boat and pack the baskets, and Martin, whose mind was on a milkshake almost the entire trip. "Daddy, I want to drive," Martin said during a lull in his milkshake reverie. "Marty, you leave it alone," his father said sternly.

"Well, it's gettin' hot now, my sideburns are sweating," a voice over the CB radio said at 9:20 a.m.

"It's getting hotter than fire," Billy Dize agreed.

"When am I gonna get a milkshake?" Martin said.

By 10:30, three fifty-pound boxes of fish bait were empty, and Dize cleaned up the boat and himself and headed for Crisfield.

Seen from the land, she was a dowager past her prime, shrunken in size, her shopping district half shut down. From the water, though, Crisfield bustled with commercial life. The crab houses lined both sides of Somer's Cove, the harbor's main street. What began before dawn on the water ended here, at land's end.

Inside the cove, Billy Dize pulled the boat alongside a parking area where refrigerated trucks waited to take the hard-shell jimmies to Baltimore and Philadelphia. Dize's catch was fourteen bushels "and a piece." The man on shore counted out just under $150 in bills and handed them over.

Dize brought the Miss Sally around the city dock, to the Metompkin Bay Oyster Company, where owner I.T. Todd was waiting to weigh and record his sooks. A mechanical hoist lifted the two barrels, with a combined gross weight of 280 pounds. The net weight would be computed and the week's sale added up at the end of the week. If last week's price held, Dize would get $17.54 a pound.

He would need it. Miss Sally swallowed $26 worth of fuel for the one day's work, and the winch would cost $150 to repair. "We're working from week to week for nothing, just about," he said. Nonetheless, there was money enough to buy Martin his milkshake over at Nancy's Place on Crisfield's Main Street.

The crabs bought at dockside are steamed in a big cylindrical pot—twelve hundred

Main Street, Crisfield, Md.

Postcard scene of Crisfield's Main Street early in the twentieth century.

pounds in twelve minutes—cooled overnight, and then moved in a wheelbarrow to the room where Metompkin's thirty-six crab pickers sat four to a table. A fan kept the air circulating over the crab pickers, invariably black women. It is seasonal work, in which a good picker could gross as much as $300 a week. In the winter they collect unemployment, as the oyster-shucking men do during their off season, keeping Somerset's unemployment rate always among the state's highest.

The automators of industry had tried to perfect a crab-picking machine. But all they had to show for their efforts was an expensive contraption that noisily shook one hundred pounds of crabmeat an hour but couldn't distinguish between the succulent lump meat and the rest of the product. The stuff was packaged as "Maryland Deluxe Crabmeat." It doesn't taste the same, so the pickers weren't worried. Not even machines could completely replace their dexterous hands.

The fastest picker in Crisfield worked for I.T. Todd. She was Mary Elizabeth Ames, also known as Miss Liz. "I love it, I just love it," said the fifty-five-year-old woman. "I make a decent, honest living. I just come in and be quiet and keep my mind on what I'm doing. Most of the times, I sing hymns…'How Great Thou Art,' 'Trust in God.' I trust in Him, and the crabs, they follow."

First, she pulled the two large claws for cracking later. Then, crab in her left hand, knife in her right, she went to work. Off came the crab back, discarded in a bucket. The knife scraped the insides, first the eggs, then the lungs they call "dead man's fingers." Then the other claws and backfin were discarded and, finally, the lump and little meat chunks were extracted from the core.

She quickly filled the six cans in front of her, then took them to another room to be weighed and recorded. Between 7 a.m. and 3:30 p.m., she picked fifty-five pounds, for a gross income of $63.25. Nobody else came close.

She had quit school in fourth grade and "picked potatoes and skinned tomatoes" to help raise her nine brothers and sisters when her mother died. At nineteen, she had become a crabpicker. "In other words," she said, "I just been a hard worker all my days." The fruits of her labors included a modest, pink-shingled house on the outskirts of Crisfield, its walls filled with homilies to home and God. Her dining-room table was covered with a lace cloth "a white lady made and gave to me," a Bible, family photos, and several trophies won at the annual Labor Day Crab Derby. In 1966 she had come in first in crab picking. She was proud of her trophies but prouder of the children she had sent to college, her daughter who taught first grade in Salisbury and her son who was a policeman in Syracuse, New York. "I did it all with the help of God and these fingers here," she said. "No help whatsoever except for Godamighty and these hands, and it all came from crab picking."

Her granddaughter had tried crab picking and didn't like it. Her daughter was "better than [she] was" at it but wanted something more. So Miss Liz was the last of her clan to earn a living in what was, to many, dirty, demeaning work. But not to her. "I'm just so happy to get up in the morning and get my clothes on and get to my job," said Miss Liz. "I love it to death. I've had regrets, even shed a few tears, but this job is pay enough for me, thank the Lord. I can't think of nothing else."

Billy Dize and Liz Ames did not know each other, but both knew I.T. Todd. "About as fair as it is round" is how Dize described him. "About as fair as they come," said Miss Liz.

Ira Thompson Todd, Jr., was the last baby born on Holland Island before its residents surrendered to the Bay and, their land washing away with each storm, dismantled and moved their homes to the mainland. His father, I.T., Sr., had been a commercial waterman, crabbing, pound netting, and oystering in a two-masted bugeye below Calvert Cliffs between Cove and Cedar points on the Western Shore. When the military declared his fishing grounds off-limits during World War II, the senior Todd acquired an interest in an oyster-shucking house. It was located on Metompkin Bay on Virginia's Eastern Shore. He kept the name but moved the business.

I.T., Jr., had gone to college to study accounting, but the war changed his plans, too. He returned home to run the family oyster business. Gradually he bought out the other partners and expanded into crabs. From a dozen employees, Metompkin had grown to employ seventy-five during the peak period in the fall, when crab picking and oyster shucking overlap. It was among the largest of

Crisfield's dozen crabmeat plants. Billy Dize was one of sixteen watermen who regularly brought their catches to its docks.

"It's a business that lends itself to individual operation," said Todd in the second-floor office of the eighty-year-old building that had once been a lumber yard. "You've got to have that personal touch with the crabber and so forth. They look for it. You can't operate this business by remote control."

The business had been good to Todd, who was now sixty-two. He lived in a red frame house in a nice section of town, right next to the widow of the late Maryland Governor J. Millard Tawes. He had sent one son through law school and another to learn medicine, and, now, he was getting ready to retire "whenever it gets convenient for me."

Like a waterman's son or a crab picker's daughter, Casey Todd had followed his father at an early age. He'd worked weekends and summers, standing on a box when he was small to pack soft-shell crabs for the city markets. Now, at the age of twenty-five, he was the newly installed president of the Metompkin Bay Oyster Company.

He had been sent to law school in case the seafood business ever went bad, but Casey Todd, it was always understood, would someday manage Metompkin. "If I don't come in the business," Casey Todd said, "what's taken generations to get would go down the drain. When you sweat blood over something like this, you'd like to see it carried on."

Not all the watermen of Smith Island bring their catch to Crisfield. Those who scrape the shallow grassy bottoms around the island for peeler crabs often sell their harvest to brokers from as far away as New York City's Fulton Fish Market. Almost paternally, the scrapers watch over the crawling creatures soon to shed their shells inside wooden floats. After acquiring their new "soft shell," the crabs are to crustaceans what filet mignon is to steak, a much-sought-after delicacy. Boats come to the crab shanties on Smith to pick up the fresh soft-shell crabs, tightly packed with seaweed inside cardboard boxes. The boxes are then shipped to Crisfield, where huge refrigerated trucks wait to take the freshly packed food on overnight trips to the major markets.

Staying as close to home as he does, the scraper's daily routine differs drastically from that of his hard-shell-catching counterparts. So do his problems. One of the diciest, for many years, stemmed simply from history and geography: the Maryland-Virginia state line. It was not only that Virginia's laws were more lax, allowing, for example, the catching of the succulent sponge (pregnant) crabs that were often sold in Crisfield. It was that arbitrary state line itself Smith Islanders couldn't abide.

It had been battled over for generations between the governments and residents of the two states, ever since that trader from Virginia, William Claiborne, laid claim to Kent Island in 1631. It was a border war lasting more than three hundred years and fought sometimes with gab and sometimes with guns. The "oyster wars" of Chesapeake Bay, they came to be called. They ranged from the Potomac clear across the bay to Pocomoke and Tangier sounds. In the middle of it all was Smith Island.

It wasn't always so. Over the years, the line had changed three times. The original line under the charter of 1632 granted by Charles I to Cecil Calvert crossed the Chesapeake from the mouth of the Great Wicomico in Virginia to the Pocomoke River across the Bay. That boundary was almost immediately disputed by a Virginia Colonel Edmund Scarborough, who tried to tax Maryland settlers in Somerset County.

Officials of both states convened at George Washington's Mount Vernon estate in 1785 and, drawing a new line from Smith Point at the mouth of the Potomac, gave twenty thousand acres to Virginia. Virginians settled ever farther north in the 1830s, moving into marshes south of Tylerton now uninhabited. They claimed "squatters' rights" and paid taxes to Virginia, even though they were in Maryland. Their claims led to the arbitration of 1877, which gave even more of Maryland to Virginia, and to a 320-foot adjustment on the southeastern side of Smith for Johnson Evans, who wanted his store at Horse Hammock to be in Virginia and his home to be in Maryland so he could dredge for oysters on both sides of the border. The line had become a ragged zigzag that placated Virginians and appeased Johnson Evans but settled nothing.

Although the store is long gone from Smith Island, the line isn't. And while markers have mysteriously disappeared from the creeks and channels, it remains just the same, a border that had prevented generations of Smith Islanders from following the crabs in their own back yard, where the rich eelgrass harbors the primest of the peelers.

"My God, that crab don't respect lines," said Davey Laird, an island waterman for twenty-seven of his forty-two years. "That crab goes where he wants." Indeed, as the crabs migrated south in late fall and then north in the early spring, Virginia watermen could crab in the months Marylanders could not.

Open warfare over the line raged well into mid-century. When Junior Evans was a teenager, Virginia police pursued Smith Islanders, allegedly engaged in illegal oyster dredging, clear up to Tylerton.

"There were twenty-five or thirty Smith Island men with rifles behind every pole" aimed at the interlopers, Junior Evans recalled. "They came to when they seen the rifles. Then they turned tail and left." Evans recalled hearing the

Virginians' leader say, "You let me out of here, you'll never hear anything from me." It was around the same time, Smith Islanders recall, that one of their own had his engine shot at by the Virginia Marine Police.

Since the early 1960s, peace had prevailed as Smith Island crabbers, scraping the Bay bottom with a metal-framed net for peelers, continued to work in their domain. When the eelgrass grew thicker below the line than above it, the crab scrapers worked there anyway, without fear of harassment from marine police based on Virginia's faraway Eastern Shore. That was before Peter (Juney) Crockett took the job.

The domain and tools of the Smith Island watermen. Eugene L. Meyer

Crockett had quit his post as town cop of Tangier Island to take the state job, which offered better benefits. On most mornings, Crockett sat in his patrol boat just off South Point enforcing the law. What his omnipresence meant for Marylanders straying beyond the half-mile or so he allowed them below the official line was a tow to Onancock, Virginia, and a stiff fine plus court costs.

"One boy got a $250 ticket for being over the line, trying to make a living," Billy Dize had told me, indignantly. "They come over the line, we don't say nothing. The difference is if we get caught in Virginia, we get towed and stand a chance of a $250 fine and losing the boat. If they get caught in Maryland, it's only a $25 fine, that's it. That ain't right."

"The main problem, it's not even being towed, but sometimes it's the only place you can get crabs," said David Laird inside his crab shanty one early fall day. "This time of year, it's the only place you can get crab. The only thing, God it's been hard on a lot of people. Sometimes, if that's where the crab is, you have to catch 'em. I don't know how to do nothing else. If I can't catch the crabs, ain't nobody else gonna pay my bills."

The weather, not the law, was the major topic of conversation one late September morning, as chilly northwest winds blew twenty to thirty knots, turning high tide to low and driving the crabs deep down in the mud. Only three scrapers ventured out where twenty-five to thirty normally go, at the lower limit south of Tylerton.

Wes Bradshaw, thirty-seven years old and beefy with bleached blond hair, steered his small, flat-bottomed boat through the predawn darkness down Shanks Creek. With hand signals passed down through the generations, he communicated from a distance with Davey Laird and Frederick Marshall, the other watermen. Drawing an index finger across the throat signaled "ain't nothing here," Bradshaw explained. Moving one hand around in a circle meant "a few in here." Fingers motioning inward said "all the crabs you want." It was when they were well into Virginia waters that the men used the last sign, if only once or twice. Juney Crockett was nowhere to be seen, and so the watermen ventured well below South Point, the unofficial line the Virginia lawman had drawn.

"He'd make us leave," Bradshaw said, as he picked through nets thick with eelgrass, some crabs, and occasional shrimp, oysters, and fish. "But it doesn't look like old Juney's coming up here today. He probably figures nobody's out."

Crockett, it so happened, was having his boat bottom painted for the oyster season, which began in Virginia the following week. So the Smith Islanders had a free, if not a fruitful, day. "If you're not up there," Crockett confirmed over the telephone, "they'll go across the line."

If the line was an arbitrary act of governments, then, the Smith Islanders reasoned, it could be changed. By going to court in Maryland, they had already abolished the county lines extending into the Chesapeake that had kept watermen from working up and down the Bay in their own state. That was back in 1971. Now, negotiations as delicate as any international treaty talks had failed to achieve an informal settlement creating a "neutral zone" in which Smith Islanders could crab. So, they voted to take things one step further. They marched off to federal court.

So concerned was the state of Maryland about the outcome of the suit and its effect on other baywide fisheries that it joined on the side of Virginia against its own citizens. "Nobody has any real problems with the crabs," explained William (Pete) Jensen, the director of Maryland's tidal fisheries. "Everyone's looking beyond this decision if the residential barriers come down."

And down they came. In June of 1982, U.S. District Court Judge D. Dortch Warriner in Richmond ruled that Virginia had no legal right to bar any

Working the Bay led to heated feuds—even violence—in the 1980s.
Eugene L. Meyer

Maryland watermen from crossing the line "to engage in his livelihood of pursuing his quarry, subject only to reasonable, nondiscriminatory rules related to those Virginia imposes on its own citizenry." The following October, a federal judge in Baltimore signed a similar order allowing Virginians to crab in Maryland waters, and the deed was done.

No sooner had the ban on commercial crabbing across state lines been lifted than two Somerset County watermen were shot at and injured in Pocomoke Sound, inside Maryland. Their alleged assailants were four men who pulled alongside in a Virginia boat and opened fire.

The Marylanders weren't even out crabbing. They were tonging for oysters.

The war between Maryland and Virginia over the bay heated up again a few years later, this time over dredging for crabs—illegal in Maryland, but legal in Virginia in the winter months. The Old Dominion made Marylanders pay more for a dredging license. The Maryland watermen, from Somerset County and Smith Island, challenged the practice and once again won their case in the federal courts.

For Smith Island, however, the picture was less than bright. Population declined, from 650 when I first came to visit to 347 by the turn of the century. Some of the men I'd met and written about had found other more secure jobs, working in the new state prison in Princess Anne, or piloting tugboats. Inevitably, these career moves meant moving, too, to the mainland. The dwindling population led to the closing of Tylerton's school, the only one-room schoolhouse left in the state, in June, 1996.

Smith Island's future, if indeed it had one, seemed to lie in tourism. Here and there, a bed and breakfast opened up. Janice Marshall, a Tylerton native, joined the trend, even as she and other women organized a crab-pickers cooperative to meet stringent state standards. In Ewell, Charlie Evans sold his store in 1997 to an outsider, who sought official sanction, despite Smith Islanders' long-held intolerance for liquor sales, to sell beer and wine. Meanwhile, the Smith Island Center, an island museum, opened with state funding and local support. Smith Island even had a Web site on the Internet.

Heroic—and expensive—efforts by the Corps of Engineers in 1994 had seemingly stopped the erosion on the bay side with ten white mounds of plastic bags, each one hundred feet long, five feet above the water, and filled with dredged spoil. But there was another more subtle threat: Rising sea level that could well sink Smith, much of which stood barely a foot above sea level, within a matter of decades, or years.

5

Annapolis-by-the-Bay

*A*cross the Bay, the Western Shore suffers not from isolation. Geographically and culturally, it is close to the modern mainstream. Inland just a bit lies megalopolis: the Baltimore-Washington corridor, city scenes, and suburban sprawl.

Accessible as it is, the Western Shore should look, from the water, like Condo-City-by-the-Bay. It doesn't. Mostly, from Havre de Grace at the mouth of the Susquehanna to Point Lookout at the mouth of the Potomac, its coastline is uncluttered.

The army's Aberdeen Proving Ground prevents development along its thirty-mile shoreline near the head of the Bay. Its red-striped sentry boats keep pleasure craft beyond the range of the booming guns on shore. Near Baltimore, the jagged industrial skyline of Sparrows Point seems out of place. Farther south, the Steuart Petroleum Company's off-shore liquefied natural gas dock near Cove Point is another aberration, looking like the empty set for a science-fiction film about intergalactic war.

Unlike the Eastern Shore, the Western Shore of the Chesapeake Bay does not have a sharply defined sense of itself as a place apart.

Annapolis, the sailboating state capital on the Western Shore and also the seat of Anne Arundel County, is another story. It is places apart. It is at once many thriving worlds. It's a tourist trap, a seat of learning and of government, a place to live and to work, a bedroom suburb for metropolitan Maryland, a place to commute to and from, a burgeoning "region" expanding beyond its borders with new shopping centers and subdivisions.

"For the commuting worker, the Annapolis region is increasingly an alternative to residential locations in Montgomery, Prince George's, or other suburban Maryland or Virginia counties," city planners have noted. "The city's role as a 'bedroom suburb' for workers in Washington and Baltimore seems to threaten its sense of community as a place where one both lives and works.... Should the city encourage luxury waterfront condos catering to wealthy households outside the immediate Annapolis housing market?"

The question and the warning reflected market forces that, in the 1970s, were changing the city's demographics and spurring new growth around its fringes. There, along roads like Forest Drive, billboards sold the present ("Now Leasing—Annapolis Roads") and heralded the future ("Coming Soon—

Georgetown Plaza Shopping Center"). "Forest Drive used to be a two-lane road," Frank Walker told me, motioning to the highway that now had four lanes. He remembered when the Parole Shopping Center was a vacant field, Hechinger's was a "drive-in thee-a-ter," and Montgomery Ward "used to be a little store and a bar where they sold farm feed in back."

Docked sailboats in Annapolis. Gary Cameron, *Washington Post*

To hear the man talk, you'd think he was an octogenarian recalling the turn of the century. But Walker, who lived in the house his grandmother had built on Forest Drive, was twenty-five, and the year he was talking about in late 1978 was only 1961. The outskirts of town were still growing twenty years later, while the population of the city itself remained remarkably stable.

In the city's center, diverse populations coexist on a seasonal basis. The middies of the Naval Academy and the classical scholars of St. John's College are present but not omnipresent most of the time. The tourists are weekend day trippers, mostly, who appear in the spring, summer, and fall. After the October sail and powerboat shows, the boaters leave to make way for the lawmakers, who recess in the spring to make way for the boaters.

The legislators occupy the capital, its hostelries and watering holes, from mid-January through mid-April. For ninety days—no more, no less—they pontificate, procrastinate, and legislate. They are an unlikely band of city slickers, suburban hustlers, and country gentlemen which includes more than a few lawyers, and it is not unfair to say that vested interests have a way of running rampant. Every session of the General Assembly has its share of "snakes,"

Navy midshipmen at cutter drill pictured
in an early twentieth century postcard.

seemingly harmless bills with hidden beneficiaries.

Seeking to influence legislation with their numbers, people rally on the steps of the State House, built in 1772. Here, where the Continental Congress met for a year and George Washington resigned his commission as commander in chief of the Continental army, history lurks behind the day-to-day doings of democracy in action. Citizen groups seeking media exposure compete with more discreet lobbyists representing special interests. These spokesmen (a few are women, but mostly it's still a man's game) wine and dine the lawmakers at lunch and dinner, and the organizations they represent contribute to campaign coffers to underscore their clout. Roll call votes often tell the tale.

When the General Assembly is in session, the lobbyists and the lawmakers might as well be in Timbuktu, for all they have to do with the rest of Annapolis. It is a self-contained world that has traditionally extended from the State House and nearby buildings down Main Street as far as Fran O'Brien's, the favorite after-hours retreat until a devastating fire in the midst of the 1984 General Assembly, or just a bit farther, around Compromise Street to the Hilton.

In the warm months especially, Annapolis is a sight to behold. Strollers crowd the City Dock and Main Street on up to Church Circle and the State House. Pleasure craft ply its harbor and fill its marinas. Sailing-school students in tiny sloops and Naval Academy plebes in blue-hulled yachts glide by the private docks of waterfront condominiums.

When freighters are anchored offshore awaiting entrance to the port of Baltimore, foreign seamen come ashore to buy all the bluejeans that Britches Great Outdoors, the Annapolis outlet of the Georgetown haberdasher, can supply.

At one time, more than thirty freighters anchored for nine miles, from the Bay Bridge south past Thomas Point, dwarfing the tiny sailboats that navigated around them on weekends. As many as eight launch companies sprung up to serve the floating population. Among the first to sense the monetary possibilities was Tim Peregoy, a slight, mustachioed man who converted an oversized workboat into a seamen's shuttle service. At the peak of Peregoy's business, his boat, the Tradewind, was making five runs a day, seven days a week.

Under Coast Guard rules, the Tradewind could carry up to twenty-nine passengers on the rivers but only fourteen on the Bay. One late summer day, when I rode along, seventeen Asians descended to its deck. Peregoy wouldn't budge the boat until three had climbed back up the ramp of their coal freighter, the Bombay-based Maratha. "They know better," Peregoy told me. "They always try to get away with it."

The foreign seamen seldom were rowdy in Annapolis, I was told. Peregoy's passengers seemed true to form. "I fancy badminton," said Sipiao Carvatho, the twenty-nine-year-old chief officer. Thus, he planned to look for a good badminton racket ashore. His purser was looking forward to "a good walk on land." He would also buy two pairs of bluejeans, although he had already acquired ten in Newport News. "It's in fashion now," he explained. "It's about four times the price in India."

If the Eastern Shore is in a time warp, then the Western Shore—around Annapolis, at least—is a link to today. Other places along the Western Shore march to different drummers, but Annapolis, if not quite in the fast lane, is still close enough to breathe the exhaust. Behind its facade of restored townhouses and chic shoppes, the city teeters precariously between the best and worst of both worlds.

While many seeking escape from mean city streets or suburban sameness might find it a quaint and restful place, it has, by Chesapeake Bay standards, a highly charged, go-go atmosphere. The people and the planners alike revere the town's past, but Annapolis seems to be lurching forward to a pricey future.

"I think I was part of Washington discovering Annapolis," said Philip Merrill, owner of the *Annapolis Evening Capital,* who lives on the Severn River, outside town. "As people bought a condominium, I bought a newspaper. I own the largest business in town but can't afford to live there." Merrill, who is also the publisher of *Baltimore* and *Washingtonian* magazines, could, of course, live in Annapolis proper, if he chose. But many people can't. "The success of the historical movement, which really made Annapolis, has spawned a lot of other problems," he told me one afternoon in his Washington office, just thirty-seven miles and forty-five off-peak minutes from his riverfront home. "The historical preservation people are like someone who overwhelmingly won an election and doesn't know what to do. If the consequences of success are all single bars and saloons, then Annapolis is not a living city anymore. I want real people, businesses. There should be something besides my newspaper. There should be working people and work for them to do. Economic forces drove the watermen away from the City Dock, and rising prices may drive out the marine business. The historical movement doesn't care about sailmakers."

It is, in some respects, an insoluble dilemma, where the marketplace plays such a major role. Since 1952, a group known as Historic Annapolis has largely kept the developers at bay while helping to restore three hundred buildings, saving the old market building at the City Dock, and managing thirteen vintage properties. Winning battle after battle, the preservationists have kept out-of-scale hotels and office buildings away from the eighteenth-century historic district. Amazingly, downtown Annapolis still closely resembles an 1856 overview on display in the magnificent William Paca House, which has been restored and is maintained by the preservationist group.

Pat Kohlhepp, the public affairs director for Historic Annapolis and a former writer for the *Evening Capital*, took me through the historic house and grounds that once belonged to the Revolutionary War governor and Declaration of Independence signer. Inside, the fourteen-bedroom house had an antiseptic look. But it was no mere museum, I learned. It was available to rent, at $1200 a day, for conferences. Weddings and fashion shows were also held here. There was, in addition, a "Protocol Room" that had been used by the State Department for a reception honoring Chinese officials.

After a walk through the extensive back-yard gardens, we strolled around the town, past the old houses once inhabited by black working-class people but now restored to upper-income chic. The historic district's population hadn't changed much in two hundred years—it was twelve hundred then, it's three thousand now—only the people. And the very success of Historic Annapolis in limiting the growth had led to premium prices on what real estate there was.

"We're becoming more and more a bedroom area for Washington and Baltimore professionals because they can afford the real estate," Kohlhepp said. "Money's been poured into the town. Property's more valuable, and it's more costly to live. I don't have the answer to it. Gentrification of Annapolis comes up all the time. What are your choices? With uncontrolled development, Annapolis would lose its character. Our link with the past is too important to turn our heads and ignore."

And yet, the past that was being "preserved" here was, like the past of

Oxford, across the Bay, somewhat artificial. What bothered my tour guide most were the touristy trinket shops near the City Dock. "This plastic Annapolis is the part that upsets me," she said. "People who come only to the City Dock area, eat ice cream cones, and throw trash around. The day trippers are not putting anything into the town. They're not staying in hotels for a few days. They're just shopping in these boardwalk-type places."

For sure, Annapolis was no Williamsburg: John D. Rockefeller, Jr., whose philanthropy had restored the colonial capital of Virginia, had looked first at the Maryland city with similar thoughts in mind. It would have meant the demolition of many buildings that did not fit the colonial theme. Annapolitans opposed his plan to turn their city into a museum village. "Even in its sleepy state," said Kohlhepp, "it was viable and had a commercial center."

Annapolis was sleepy no more. And if its commercial center remained viable, it was also, well, different. The supermarkets, the hardware stores, the mom and pop stores that once served the residents of downtown were gone, replaced by trendy specialty shops and fancy restaurants that catered to outsiders. To see a movie, to shop for groceries, to buy a wrench or whatnot, now required a trip to the shopping centers on the city's outskirts, which were booming. Or crossing the Spa Creek Bridge to Eastport.

The old downtown area around the City Dock, once known as Hell Point, had lost its rough edges, but Eastport, across the creek, seemed still to be fighting a losing battle to keep its working-class character. Annexed to the city in 1951, Eastport was in the grip of a double-edged "renaissance," its real estate rocketing, its poorer people leaving. It was, for now, beyond the pale of the city's historic district ordinance, which meant high-rise hotels and condominiums could sprout alongside the restored homes the architects referred to as "Annapolis vernacular."

"Everyone says, 'What's in Eastport?' You'd be surprised," said Pat Kohlhepp, referring to the houses she described as "modest but charming." The watermen who used to keep their boats at the City Dock were also there, but in dwindling numbers, as sailboat marinas and yacht yards took over the Spa and Back Creek waterfronts that define the Eastport peninsula.

Among the Eastporters most strongly bemoaning the changes were relative newcomers from elsewhere who, by reason of their residence dating back ten or fifteen years, qualified almost as old-timers in the community. I found a slew of them at the home of Erik Dennard, an artist, and his potter wife, Kimi Nyland, opposite a black church on Chesapeake Avenue.

"The boats are a large part of what's happened," explained Dennard, a jovial,

Drawbridge across Spa Creek connects Eastport
to the rest of Annapolis. Eugene L. Meyer

fortyish Texan whose accent had been muted by years spent elsewhere. "Eastport used to build boats. Now it just holds them. Simple little seafood places where you could buy fresh food now have to support themselves with a good restaurant. Housing prices here have doubled, tripled, quadrupled, or more in eight years. It seems like a lot of upper-middle-class people are getting houses to be near their boats, part time. Billions of dollars in boats surround this peninsula."

Dennard had come to Annapolis from Europe in 1965, an era ago. "It was a small town. There were skipjacks at the dock. You could buy a dozen oysters from them and a fifteen-cent beer nearby. Fleet Street, from the dock to State Circle, was mostly poor people. It would take two hours to walk up Main Street because you knew every person you saw. Now, it takes ten minutes. It's sort of been taken out of the hands of Annapolitans. Annapolitans don't go downtown much, unless they work there."

Don Quick, a bartender turned psychiatric worker, said he avoided downtown Annapolis "like the plague. I automatically rule out downtown for lunch because of prices and crowds. I'll drive all the way out to Parole or go to the Eastport shopping center."

"Where they charge Eastport prices, not downtown prices," Erik Dennard interjected.

"Everybody's from out of town," complained Quick, who himself had come, originally, from Long Island, New York. "All the businesses, one by one, they dropped out. The shoe store. The jeweler. You don't even know these new people."

Mary Crawford, another member of Dennard's circle of friends, sold real estate in Eastport, "where the working-class people lived and all that good stuff."

She had bought her home here three years before for $55,000. She estimated its present worth at triple that amount.

"We've got a lot of D.C.'ers down here," she said. "It takes them maybe fifteen or twenty minutes more to get to work. We have a lot of yachtsmen who'd been making the commute for years who are now living here. Maybe twenty-five or thirty percent of those living in Eastport are real Annapolitans." As for herself, why, she'd come here twenty years ago, from North Carolina.

"The kids of Eastport are gone," Erik Dennard said. "This used to be a complete community of poor to upper income. The poor can't afford to live here anymore. They can get a good price for their house and then move to a nicer home on the outskirts of town." He still liked Eastport and Annapolis. "Even with all the changes," he said, "it's one of the best places in the world to live. It had to grow because of its history, its location. It's probably been handled pretty well. And much of the credit goes to Historic Annapolis."

To the painter, a recovering alcoholic, Annapolis was "the best place in the world to get drunk in, and the best place in the world to get sober." In his former phase, he had sometimes frequented Marmaduke's, an Eastport bar that mirrored the changes in town. It used to be, Dennard recalled, "a rowdy bar with morning-drinker types. Watermen hung out there a lot, to swap lies and fishing stories. Nobody spoke more than two-syllable words, and drinks were cheap. Now, it's the blow-dry crew."

While covering Annapolis, the state capital, I had lived in the blow-dry end of Eastport. The sun rising over the Bay awoke me each morning in the third-floor condominium bedroom at Horn Point. And, from time to time, I had made the Marmaduke's scene. It was strictly business, of course. Marmaduke's, in a sense, was still a working-class bar, only the work and the class were different.

The patrons—invariably white, bright, and sophisticated in the ways of the sailing world—were young adults who moved easily up and down the East Coast, from Florida to Annapolis to Newport and back. Migrant workers.

"We get a lot in here, all they do is crew out," the bartender told me. "Some race for the owners. They're [like horse] jockeys, walkers, and trainers, all in one. Other guys rig boats or scrape them. We also get sailmakers and yacht brokers. In winter, they're all gone, to Florida, where they do the same thing."

I had wandered over to Marmaduke's late one spring afternoon in search of a skipper and a chartered boat with which to explore the Chesapeake. A special feature during the season now was Wednesday night video cassettes of the afternoon's sailboat races. Another feature was the bulletin board at Marmaduke's. It was plastered with help- and job-wanted ads, often scrawled on napkins.

"Caribbean, Florida, Bermuda, Chesapeake, Points North, Gulf Coast, West Coast," began one notice that tried to touch all bases. "Crewman for Hire. Local & Long Distance. Deliveries and Charters. Reasonable Rates." An "Intelligent, Adventurous Young Woman" wanted a "position aboard sailing vessel cooking for crew for the Annapolis-Newport Race." The phone number and address were in Devon, Pennsylvania, an upper-crust suburb on Philadelphia's Main Line. One job seeker wrote that any potential employer could find him "around Marmaduke's."

One of the Marmaduke regulars was an Australian named Mike Perry. As co-manager of an Annapolis boatyard, Perry had a special porthole on the world. These maritime drifters, he explained, "are like priests to these [sailboat-owning] people. They must be highly intelligent, mechanical, and be able to deal with very rich people, socially and business-wise. They could easily make a lot of money."

Not all were white. Perry proudly told me about a black youth he had taken under his wing at the boatyard. He was twenty and commuted daily to Annapolis "from the worst slum in Baltimore." Perry was teaching the young man the ropes, he said, and the kid could have a future working with boats. He was good. Shortly after my visit to Marmaduke's, I tried to find Perry and his protege. Both had left the boatyard. True to their transient trade, they had moved on without a forwarding address.

I returned to Marmaduke's one winter evening, seeking respite from the whirlwind legislature. It was one of those typically hectic times in the General Assembly. The chief executive was an honest and amiable enough fellow named Harry Hughes. He would later win reelection in a walk, but this year he was having problems with the lawmakers.

His gasoline tax, which we reporters glibly termed a "major cornerstone" of his supplemental spending and revenue-raising package, was in deep trouble. So was his race-track consolidation bill. In an evening session, the lower chamber, known as the House of Delegates, was approving a watered-down version of the governor's proposed levy on trucks.

Down at Marmaduke's, to my delight, they couldn't have cared less about the whole business.

"Harry who?" asked Suzanne the bookkeeper. "With the warm weather, we get rid of these creeps," she said of the State House gang, "and the people will venture back into Annapolis asking, 'Are they gone yet?' Right now, it's a very odd time of year. It's not the summer crowd yet. It's sort of the winter leftovers."

Be that as it may, I asked the Marmaduke patrons what they thought of the state's sunset law, which was of urgent concern up around State House Circle.

"What's that?" replied Bobby Leonard, who had moved to Annapolis from Bethesda, a Washington suburb, to be near his boats.

Well, surely they knew of Harry Hughes's gasoline tax and of his budget problems.

"When did this happen?" said Suzanne, shocked at the news.

"I don't know anything about it," said her friend, Linda, who had joined the conversation.

Well, then, had they ever been to Fran O'Brien's, the politicians' after-hours place?

"Not if I can help it," said Suzanne. "My God, I'm not safe there! My girlfriend and I went in there once. It took us maybe two seconds: we sat down, we were hit on. My God, it's terrible. They have no shame at all. Legislators. They're terrible—no class whatever. One of 'em said, 'What are you doing for the next fifteen minutes?' I said, 'Whatever it is, it won't be with you.' My God, they have no shame!"

The talk down the bar was of sailing towns on the California coast. "I've Got the Crabs," read one of many t-shirts in evidence. Legislative anarchy may rule the State House, and the governor may be beyond political salvation, but in Eastport, where skippers outrank politicians, life just sails right on.

It still does at the turn of the new century, though Marmaduke's passed into history in 1998, to be replaced by a Ruth's Chris Steak House. Denizens of Eastport mourned its passing, but in a defiant act of rebellion, staged a mock secession from Annapolis. The Maritime Republic of Eastport spawned banners, pub and "paw" crawls, its own currency, anthem, and motto, stunning in its simplicity: "We like it this way." Of the 200 maritime businesses in the city of Annapolis, 173 called Eastport home. Annapolis proper had its politicians, its upscale shops and restaurants, its "Ego Alley" along City Dock, a spectacle of flashy boats flaunted by their immodest owners. Across Spa Creek—playfully renamed the Gulf of Eastport—there was change, to be sure, but somehow a sense that the Republic would survive.

6

Life After Slots

The Casbah sign was rusty and falling down. Almost all the neon letters that had spelled "Stardust" were out. The Wigwam was now a bakery. The Desert Inn sign heralded a hobby shop. Aqualand by the Potomac River Bridge was a marina and a campground, and the Crystal Door, too, was gone, although its building at Bel Alton now housed the VFW.

Along U.S. 301, which was a major north-south highway before I-95 existed, the crumbling old signs seemed strangely out of place. New shopping centers and office buildings had sprouted on the strips that skirt the towns of Waldorf and La Plata. Farther south, surviving motels advertised double-room rates as low as $15 a night, while some that didn't make it had been turned to other uses, like the antiques flea market near Pope's Creek, which itself would soon vanish.

The visible reminders of Southern Maryland's heyday as "Little Nevada" were fading fast. By the summer of 1999, the Stardust was newly demolished, the 301 Ranch, the Spring Lake Motel, the Desert Inn, and Earl's Truck Stop were also gone. Yet, once, for a period of nineteen years, from 1949 to 1968, these and other venues made Route 301 one raucous, round-the-clock casino. And understandably so: Maryland was the only state except Nevada with legalized slot machine gambling. The one-armed bandits that sprouted throughout Anne Arundel, Calvert, St. Mary's, and Charles counties surpassed tobacco as the region's cash crop. The gross take in Charles and Calvert was even more than the counties' budgets. Then, the bubble burst. The slots were outlawed by the state. An era of gaudy prosperity, of easy money for the county coffers of Southern Maryland, had ended.

But what a time it was. When Naomi Smith married in 1959, she and her husband checked into the Heidelberg Motel in Charles County, and then he checked out. She sent him out for a hamburger, and he didn't return until morning. Instead of celebrating their nuptials, he was gambling across the street. "He ain't never won nothing but me," she told me, still married to the same man decades later and working as a bookkeeper at the Waldorf Motel, another former slot haven that had survived.

In my travels, I had occasionally encountered the ghosts from that bygone era. Writing about a small-town political feud in 1977, I'd listened to one side accuse the other of fronting for "the slot machine interests." On another occasion, I'd tracked the tale of seventeen 1939-vintage machines trucked from Calvert County to National Airport, where they were to be flown to California at a time when it was against the law to transport even antique one-armed bandits across state lines.

It sounded so quaint. Indeed, it's hard to imagine a time when the twenty miles of U.S. 301 from the Prince George's County line to the Potomac River were, as a 1955 pulp publication put it, "a wide-open strip." B.W. Von Block, writing in *Man's Conquest*, also described it as "Felony Row...one of the most tawdry, squalid, and sordid stretches of autobahn I've ever seen...razzle-dazzle neon squalor set in the middle of Maryland tobacco fields."

Charles County, with its major arterial highway and its proximity to the nation's capital, received national notoriety. But the phenomenon extended beyond the well-traveled roads to almost every grocery, tavern, drug store, and filling station.

At one time, Southern Maryland slots grossed $18 million a year. License fees accounted for one-quarter of Charles County's annual budget and sharply lowered taxes throughout the region. Charles County had 2,350 machines—one for every thirteen residents. The other three counties had 2,300 more. Maryland, according to the IRS, had twice as many business establishments with slots as the state of Nevada.

Contributing to the coffers and the controversy were casinos built on piers jutting from Virginia into the Potomac, which, under the original 1632 land grant of Charles I to Cecil Calvert, is entirely within Maryland up to the low-water mark. So, from Jones Point off Alexandria to Coles Point near the river's mouth, the Old Dominion played host to gamblers galore during Maryland's short-lived legalized slot machine era. Colonial Beach, already established as a down-river resort, boomed bigger than the rest. Casino signs at piers' end welcomed gamblers to the "Free State" of Maryland. The nickname stemmed from Maryland's antipathy to Prohibition, but the spirit was the same: The good, if not necessarily the righteous, life was part of the Maryland tradition.

It seems so long ago, but it was only yesterday, a short, sweet and sour span of time, when slots ruled from Colonial Beach on the Potomac River to Chesapeake Beach and North Beach on the Bay's Western Shore. With the banning of the one-armed bandits, many communities plunged into a financial abyss. Some, like the adjoining "Twin Beaches"—Chesapeake and North—of Calvert County, lingered for years in the depths of economic despair. Others, more out of the way, regained their former status as sleepy small towns. Benedict, on the Patuxent River, seemed to recede along with the oysters washed away by storm-driven torrents of freshwater. Its place in history as the port from which British soldiers marched on Washington in 1814 remained secure, but its fling as a river gambling town faded quickly. Benedict's historical plaque recalls the British invasion but not the slots.

The slot machine era isn't popular history in Southern Maryland, despite its central role for two decades in the peninsula's economic, social, and political life. Scour the Bicentennial history of Charles County, published in 1976, and you will find nothing about it. Walk into the library in the quiet county seat of La Plata, as I did one weekday, and you may find a lone file folder on the subject with nothing inside.

To say that slots remain controversial in the counties south of Washington is to engage in understatement. The legalization of the machines, which had long operated illegally in those parts, led to a sort of localized civil war, pitting an aroused clergy and citizens against both businessmen and politicians. Fifteen years later, the wounds were still there, tender to the touch. The price of peace, it seemed, had been mostly to avoid the subject—like religion or politics at the dinner table.

"There were a lot of strong feelings, a lot of strong feelings," remarked Walter (Jessie) Bowling, who with his sons farmed six hundred acres of mostly tobacco adjoining Gilbert's Creek, a Potomac River tributary. "I was for running 'em out, and I hope they never come back," Bowling told me in the living room of his hillside home, whose front windows gave an unmarred view of snow-covered countryside. Slot machines attracted "a criminal element," he said. This was a familiar refrain, although one tavern owner told me when the slots went out, drugs came in.

The one-armed bandits, said Bowling, were "a false premise on which to base an economy. A lot of our budget was based on slots, and when the state pulled them out, we had a hard way to go." Without them, he noted, the county's economy was now booming, as a bedroom community for Washington. Instead of tawdry roadhouses, there were suburban tract houses, a profusion of shopping centers, and, on one three-and-a-half-mile stretch of 301, nine fast-food restaurants. Sin strip had become "eat street."

The Lost Cause resurfaced in the 1980s, under the benign auspices of the Maryland Committee for the Humanities and Charles County Community College. With a $4,000 state grant, project director Susan Shaffer sought to recapture this chapter in the history of her native county before all its participants had passed from the scene. She conducted twenty-eight taped interviews, collected stacks of pictures and papers, and prepared a slide show and panel discussion to bring the bygone era back to life.

On a chilly, autumn night, nearly one hundred people came to the community college campus, a complex of modern buildings tucked in the country a few miles from the county seat of La Plata and the formerly infamous Highway 301. One-time protagonists rehashed old arguments. The issues of morality and criminality were again raised and again went unresolved. It was, given the explosive topic, a rather polite encounter.

"The biggest problem with the panel was, we didn't want anybody lynched," Susan Shaffer said afterward. "You're dealing with a raw subject."

Indeed, her preliminary research foreshadowed the way the evening went. "Virginia people, who lived with Charles County machines, are far more willing to talk about them than the natives of Charles County," she wrote in a summary of her interviews. "Prostitution was a difficult topic to pursue. The sheriff of the County (who also had slot machines) felt that it only existed in isolated cases. This needs considerably more study.... However, even the anti-slots people could not (or would not) cite any cases that they had heard about. Finally, a general conclusion might be that the slot machine people have tended to be much more helpful in this study than those who opposed the machines."

The evening's moderator was John T. Parran, Jr., a former Charles County state senator from Indian Head on the Potomac River. During the slot machine era, he had tried unsuccessfully to assuage the opponents by advocating strict regulation of the industry. He managed, somehow, to tiptoe through the evening of nostalgia without recalling his own central role in the fray.

Parran had also played a major role in the post-slot period, chairing the Tri-County Council for Southern Maryland that grew out of gambling's demise. "We said to the legislature, 'You're taking revenue away from us. What are you gonna do to replace this, to help us rebound?'" Parran told me later. "The state gave us some road programs, built the Solomon's Island-Lexington Park Bridge, gave us money for St. Mary's City [Maryland's first colonial capital] and General Smallwood State Park, improved Cedarville State Park. It started a whole new approach to Southern Maryland's future." That approach, as evidenced by road signs on major highways directing motorists to "Historic Southern Maryland," was tourism. But there was no museum of slots.

Also at the community college was the Reverend Andrew Gunn, a Yale- and Oberlin-educated minister who had led the anti-slots crusade. "My life was threatened," said the minister, blaming slot machine forces also for the burning of copies of a Waldorf newspaper opposed to gambling.

Parran paid tribute to the preacher's political prowess. "Gunn completely outmaneuvered us," he said. "My opinion is the other counties without gambling had rather powerful religious groups opposed to it. They [the legislators] could've cared less, but it was a matter of voting for their own political necks. It was the undoing of senatorial courtesy" (a General Assembly tradition in which senators yielded to each other in matters affecting their respective jurisdictions).

In addition, Parran noted later, Southern Maryland's legislators had told their colleagues from the Eastern Shore, where slots existed under laws allowing gambling for charitable and fraternal organizations, "'You're outlawing them here. You've got them over there.' They all denied it, naturally. The Legions and VFWs are where most of them existed, as far as we knew."

As far as I knew, from a visit to one VFW hall on the Eastern Shore, they still existed years later. Then, in September 1984, state troopers seized 160 slots from twenty-four fraternal and veterans posts on the Eastern Shore. Two Eastern Shore prosecutors refused to try the cases, which were dropped. Reform-minded legislators sought to standardize gaming laws in the state, a hodge-podge of legalese that seemed to exempt any group with a charitable purpose. In the end, only a bill legalizing slots for Eastern Shore charities passed, and that was vetoed by the governor.

It was but a temporary setback: Slots in Shore fraternal lodges would be legal-ized by the General Assembly in 1987. Five years later, as many as fifty clubs were grossing $30 million, with half of their $5 million profit going to charity, as the law required. Soon, slots came to Delaware racetracks, and pressure grew to allow the one-

Slot machines seized in a 1984 police raid.
Edward G. Owen, *Maryland Independent*

armed bandits as well at Maryland tracks, which feared the competition. Maryland Gov. Parris Glendening resisted. The slot interests bided their time.

In Charles County, meanwhile, cash payoffs on electronic poker games briefly replaced those that once flowed from the slots—until a grand jury probe resulted in the arrests of seventeen persons, including several who had been active in the slot machine days. The machines and their proceeds were seized, a parade of remorseful residents entered guilty pleas, and the president of the county commissioners, whose store had three machines, served thirty-three days in jail, then quietly resumed his executive duties in the courthouse, one floor below the prosecutor.

But the great gambling scandals of the post-slot era were yet to come. This night at the community college, the Reverend Gunn easily mustered some of the old righteous indignation that must have swayed an earlier generation of lawmakers. He told tales of families destitute from one member's gambling. He also asserted that prostitution and other sordid vices flourished along with the one-armed bandits, and he suggested links between Southern Maryland gambling and organized crime.

Asked for specifics, Gunn said, "I do not have detailed information."

"You have no information, directly," the questioner said.

"Yes, it's all hearsay," the preacher replied.

The interrogator was Walter Hendrix, former slot machine mogul at Colonial Beach and now a robust seventy-four. Hendrix was recognized but not identified from the podium, although he had been a leading figure in the industry in both its legal and its "bootleg" days.

The audience at the gathering was asked for a voice vote on whether slots should return. "The chair is in doubt and the meeting adjourned," Parran proclaimed, diplomat to the end.

A few weeks later, I found Walt Hendrix cutting timber on his 408-acre farm several miles from his waterfront home at Colonial Beach, Virginia. The farm had been two-and-a-quarter acres larger, Hendrix said, but he had given some land to the local Methodist minister. Hendrix, it turned out, was a regular churchgoer and a former treasurer of the church men's club. Not exactly the sinful stereotype.

He had come to Washington in 1929 from Columbia, South Carolina, to operate a sightseeing bus. Soon, he had a delicatessen on Rhode Island Avenue NE with pinball machines. After repairing the machines for another company, he went to work for himself in 1942. "I was in the coin machine business—juke boxes, pinball, slot machines," repairing and then distributing them "wherever I could bootleg 'em in D.C., Virginia, or Maryland," he recalled. Colonial Beach was among his locales.

"We had 'em bootlegged in Charles County," he said. "I got a call one time that the grand jury was in session, had to get them out quick. When the grand jury was over, they went back in."

When Southern Maryland counties, by referenda, legalized the one-armed bandits in 1949, Hendrix had his bootleg slots and he had a steakhouse in Northeast Washington. He quickly conferred with Walter Green, his Hyattsville attorney, about operating slots legally on the Virginia side of the Potomac River. "Walter said he thought we could operate them out over the water," Hendrix said.

They talked it over with Rudolph Carrico, an attorney in La Plata whose wife later became a Charles County commissioner. Carrico called Patrick Mudd, the clerk of the county court, who issued the permits. "They suggested a one-inch crack in the pier" from the Virginia shore, Hendrix said.

Hendrix had his slots on the pier extending from the New Atlanta Hotel, owned by someone else. "After the first weekend, he [the hotel's owner] said, 'How many [machines] can you get me next week?' By the following weekend, we had doubled the size of the pier. They drove down, hell, they were from New York, all the way up to New England, and from Richmond, from all over the country. On weekends, we had people standing three and four deep. At the end of Colonial Avenue, I also had the Little Steel Pier. Hurricane Hazel took that away in 1954."

The boom times along the Virginia shore of the Potomac did not last. Four years after Hazel and at the behest of the Old Dominion, the Maryland legislature passed a law allowing slot machines on the river only if they could be reached by foot from the Maryland shore. Colonial Beach, in Hendrix's words, "went down hill hellfire." Hendrix responded by opening the Crystal Door seven miles north of the Potomac River Bridge.

When slots were banished from the Maryland side as well, Hendrix hung onto the place, along with three farms he still owned in Charles County. He retired in 1975 to enjoy some of the property he'd bought with the proceeds of Potomac River gambling.

The three hundred machines he sold in 1968 were "still around," he said. Of this much, he was sure. "I wouldn't go anywhere where there was one," he said. "If they got raided the next day, they'd say I'd turned 'em in. I wouldn't do that, though."

Resplendent in his Browning Rifle cap and gray moustache, he told me where to see deer and wild turkeys on the way out, extended an invitation to deer hunt with him someday, and said, "Well, take care. Everything I told you I can back up."

On my way home, I stopped briefly at Colonial Beach. There, sitting out over the river, was a club called Little Reno, the reduced remnant of a football-sized casino once run by Delbert Connor in competition with Hendrix. Connor had passed away in December 1982, leaving the sanitized, smaller place to his widow.

There were occasional bookings of the "new" Glenn Miller and Guy Lombardo orchestras, offering echoes of a glorious past, but it was really just a glorified bar with three pool tables, eight video games, and a snack bar. An inoperative one-armed bandit sat atop the cigarette machine. And over in one corner of the establishment was a computer terminal and a cashier selling Maryland Lottery tickets.

"It is a very-high-volume terminal," said Martin Puncke, a state trooper in Charles County during the slot machine days who was now the director of the Maryland Lottery Commission. He said Little Reno took in about $17,000 a week, compared to a statewide average of $7,000. "It is the only one we have on the Virginia shore. It's been there ever since the lottery started." In due time, off-track betting and Keno—both conducted under the legal protection of the Free State—would also flourish here, at pier's end in the Potomac.

"Oh yes," said barmaid Ouida Register matter of factly, "when you come inside the door, you're in Maryland."

The Desert Inn, the Crystal Door, and the Casbah were all gone, but somehow the Little Reno, embodying the spirit of the slot machine days, lived on.

Like Colonial Beach, the adjoining towns of Chesapeake Beach and North Beach on Chesapeake Bay in Calvert County existed before the era of legalized slots but fell on hard times afterward. Before the one-armed bandits and the Bay Bridge, city dwellers had flocked to these Western Shore resorts for summer vacations. After the bridge opened, the slots kept them coming for another fifteen years, until the machines were outlawed. Then the Twin Beaches became year-round residences for commuters or retirees, with all the amenities of ghost towns.

Chesapeake Beach was the ill-fated dream of Otto Mears, a Colorado railroad builder who wanted to build Coney Island and Monte Carlo on the Chesapeake Bay at the turn of the century. Many streets were platted, but only a few (such as Mears Avenue) had been built. A grand clubhouse overlooking the Bay burned down in 1922. A race track was built but never opened. Its grandstand was torn down to build the boardwalk, which was swept away by storms in 1929 and 1933.

To carry the crowds from Washington, Mears built the Chesapeake Beach Railway. A pier extended into the Bay for the steamboats from Baltimore, Annapolis, and Norfolk. The mile-and-a-half boardwalk five hundred feet offshore was lined with booths and shops. The clubhouse "is lighted throughout with electricity" and "entirely surrounded by double verandas which afford cool shade at all times of the day," a brochure said. There was more: a bandshell and

Visitors enjoy Chesapeake Beach's sand
and pier during the resort's heyday.

dancing pavilion, carousel, "Scenic Railway or Roller Coaster," a casino, picnic areas, and a beach bottom of fine white sand with water "clean, pure, and briny."

Chesapeake Beach was touted as "Washington's Only Salt Water Resort," presenting "attractions not offered by another resort this side of Atlantic City." Lots for summer cottages were sold there, but it was the area directly north that became the major residential section of the shore resort. Starting in 1910, small summer bungalows to house the vacationers sprung up "at the hustling little city of North [Chesapeake] Beach," where, a real estate ad said, "the living expenses are for the grocer and not for the doctor." It was, the 1912 advertisement asserted, "a well-regulated, high-class seashore resort."

A one-mile trolley linked North Beach and Chesapeake Beach, and, although the Beaches were never quite what Otto Mears had envisioned, they nonetheless attracted many vacationers of modest means seeking relief from the sweltering heat of the cities.

The railroad that brought Washingtonians to the Beaches—as many as 350,000 a year to this working-class vacation spot—went bankrupt in the Depression. Buses replaced the trains, but travel declined. During World War II, gas rationing discouraged day trippers. The Beaches fell on harder times when the opening of the Bay Bridge in 1952 lured away the families to Ocean City. But a faster crowd came with the legalization of slots in 1949.

The cynical view is that the "slot interests" took what they could from the two towns but never put anything into them. Then, when the one-armed bandits were outlawed, the towns were left for dead. "When the slots went out, it hit North Beach more than Chesapeake Beach," North Beach's attorney told me. "There were nicer houses and more undeveloped property in Chesapeake Beach." So North Beach in particular gained a reputation as a run-down refuge for motorcycle gangs, alcoholics, derelicts, and other ne'er-do-wells from Washington, D.C., and nearby Prince George's County.

By the 1970s, sections of Chesapeake Beach also looked bleak: The amusement park was closed, its once-ornate buildings in shambles, and the old railroad station was shuttered. The Chesapeake Beach Hotel Company long ago had sold its property to Chesapeake Parks Incorporated (CPI), the corporation that continued to own the old amusement park land, the Rod 'n' Reel Restaurant, and a marina on Fishing Creek. But the amusement park's real legacy, some said, was a war between self-interest and the public good.

The closed and dilapidated North Beach pier
in the late 1970s. Eugene L. Meyer

With the intermingling of corporate and town interests, home rule took on new meaning: The inheritors of the slot machine mantle were the sons and grandsons of others who had once worked for the amusement park, and they were the natural town leaders. Conflict was inevitable: Several town council members had past or present associations with "the Park," as CPI was known, or with Union Vending Company, the once-dominant slot machine firm that shared owners with CPI. The town's lawyer had represented both CPI and Union Vending. The town accountant also worked for both firms.

Until his death in 1963, the local manager for CPI was the unpaid mayor. His son-in-law, also a CPI official, succeeded him briefly. (And his son, Gerald Donovan, who worked at the Rod 'n' Reel, would become mayor as well, in 1983; he still held the job in 1999.) From 1964 to 1973, William (Buster) Fortier, who had purchased property from "the Park" but had no other direct connection, was the town's chief executive. His father had cut hair and his mother had sold groceries on the old boardwalk while he had hustled newspapers to new arrivals. In town government, Fortier, a lean-looking man with a crew cut, was followed by a local manager for Union Vending. Then, a controversial coin toss brought to power a Paul Bunyonesque figure named Hugh W. Ward, Jr., a land developer and ardent critic of the "slot interests." Ward also had his supporters.

What divided the town most was land—especially the undeveloped parcels along all those platted "paper" streets never built—and what to do with it. As mayor, Ward had inherited a zoning application from a developer who wanted to build high-rises on the amusement park land. Ward balked at the plan. He also opposed deeding over the paper streets to CPI, another part of the plan.

Litigation, naturally, ensued. The voters then ousted Ward and returned Fortier to office.

"This town grew from a wilderness and ran its whole course in seventy-five years," griped the six-foot-five-inch, 285-pound Ward. "Now, what you're seeing is the politics of decline. They're so busy milking the dying cow, they're too busy to worry about resuscitation."

While Chesapeake Beach was mired in small-town politics, North Beach was staggering steadily downward. Over the years, the small summer houses had been winterized, and the old people stayed on in retirement. But, once touted as "the most delightful summer resort on Chesapeake Bay," North Beach had become Skid-Row-by-the-Bay. It had hit rock bottom when I first visited in 1977, and more than a few residents wanted the slots back.

"This ain't no Ocean City," observed Albert (Pop Brown) Glickfield, a controversial Washington nightclub figure during the 1940s and 1950s who had come to North Beach "to find peace of mind." Glickfield, who had also run clubs in New York and Montreal, landed in North Beach during the slot machine era after numerous run-ins with the law over his operation of after-hours "bottle clubs" in the District of Columbia.

In his new locale, Pop Brown ran a small Marlo furniture store (his son had started the chain in 1955), acquired real estate, and owned a bar called Mother Brown's, where, he recalled, there had been "plenty of action with slots."

He was nearly eighty when I first met him in the corner furniture store. "I don't know how people find this town, but they find it," said Pop Brown. "It was a boom town. Now, there is no work here at all. You get what you call a lot of welfare and retirement and stuff like that. Ever since the machines moved out, it's been the same. Today, the state comes in with the [lottery] numbers, and I personally think they're robbing the public [with unfair odds]."

The slot machine era had given the town two decades of prosperity. Freespenders from Washington and Baltimore had jammed North Beach hot spots owned by Pop Brown and by gambling barons Charles E. Nelson and Joe Rose.

Nelson, one-time head of a $6-million-a-year Washington numbers syndicate, had his collection office over Uncle Billie's Arcade, which he owned along with Uncle Billie's Restaurant, Uncle Billie's Pier, and Uncle Billie's Bingo. Nelson's North Beach Amusement company was counted as one of Calvert County's largest slot machine distributors. Nelson, who resided on a 105-acre farm in Ritchie, near the Capital Beltway, sold his North Beach interests in 1962, his widow told me. "It was good," she said. "There was plenty of people around at that time. We just wanted to get out."

Joe Rose owned Rose's Musical Bar, Rose's Arcade, Rose's Casino, and Rose's Snack Bar—side by side on Bay Avenue—until a suspicious fire destroyed all four in 1951. Just north of town, in Anne Arundel County, was Rose Haven, a yacht club development he began in 1947. In Anne Arundel, only nickel slot machines were legal; Rose was fined $500 for "keeping gaming tables" because four of his machines took quarters, dimes, and fifty-cent pieces. To cushion the loss when slots were banned, Rose proposed for northern Calvert County a ten-thousand-seat dog-racing track with pari-mutuel betting, but nothing ever came of it.

A fire also consumed the Reef Restaurant, at the end of the town's pier, which was further damaged by a 1955 hurricane. What remained was off-limits to the public "By Order of Police Department," according to a hand-painted sign. There were no marinas and no seafood emporiums left, just a few stores: a small supermarket that used to be a casino, a High's, a bowling alley, a bakery, a gift shop, and Franchi's Restaurant, an oasis of niceness all but surrounded by decay.

"It used to be so nice," said Alba Franchi, a native of the Italian Riviera who had first come to North Beach to vacation with her late husband in 1932. She first spent summer weekends at the Beach, then moved here full time in 1959, and somehow kept their restaurant going through it all. "I wish with all my heart they fix the beach like it used to be and make it nice again," she said. "People can still come out without the slots. Is near the city. Is near the water. But now, there is no pier, no place to fish, crab, no restrooms, no place to change. It used to be so nice."

Opposite the eroded beach and shortened pier were several vacant storefronts, one-time gambling spots. And in what used to be Ewald's dry goods store on Bay Avenue, there was Nice & Fleazy, a used-furniture-and-junk store aspiring to "antiques and collectibles" status. There were, in addition, no fewer than six bars and two liquor stores in this tiny town on Chesapeake Bay. And while hard statistics on the town's alcoholism problem were lacking, officials said that a "great proportion" of the patients admitted to the county hospital with alcohol-related ailments—aching legs, bad backs, bursitis, chest pains—were from North Beach. Drugs were also epidemic, I was told.

None of this seemed to bother the town's third police chief in little more than a year. "It's all blown out of proportion," the chief assured me. A few years before, it was widely recalled, a former police chief and his deputy drew guns on each other in the middle of the main street. It was the embarrassing theft of a police car in front of the town hall that led to the departure of another police chief and one of his deputies.

It was little wonder that the problems plaguing North Beach persisted, as life's losers were irresistibly drawn to it. One of the havens for the down-and-outers was Ye Ole Anchor Motel, also known as the Tiltin' Hilton, a converted warehouse owned by Pop Brown and located across from Mother Brown's, which advertised "Liquor to Go" and now sold school supplies and groceries along with whiskey by the gallon.

An eighteen-year-old girl stood in front of Mother Brown's. With her at midday were four youths eighteen to twenty-two, all with the same complaint—nothing to do but drink. Inside Mother Brown's, the Anchor Motel manager said North Beach "ain't all bad."

"There is a totally new administration" protested the motel manager, whose view was not shared by others in the store. He was referring to the recent mayoral election of a well digger who had previously presided over the town for four years. "You got to give the new administration a chance," the motel man insisted. "It takes time. I think the Beach is getting a bum rap. A lot of nice people are moving in, taxpayers."

Around town were a few "For Sale" signs and two dozen or so newly built homes, modest in price and appearance, mostly selling to families with job ties to the Washington area. "There is an awful lot of renovation and new construction intermingled with existing slums," said J.D. (Denny) Murray, a Calvert County developer active in North Beach. "There is an awful lot of pride among the people who live here. With a little tender loving care, it could be a dynamite community."

Five years later, I returned to the Beaches. Denny Murray had more new housing on the drawing board for North Beach, but he and a partner were actively developing the old Chesapeake Beach parkland with attractive bayfront homes. The upscale houses were bringing a new breed of resident to the old community. They were almost invariably professionals who commuted to such Washington area suburbs as Gaithersburg and Silver Spring, Maryland, and even McLean,

Virginia.

The streets of "Chesapeake Station" bore names like Arcade Court, Bandshell Court, Carousel Way, and Dentzel Court, the last after the man who designed Chesapeake Beach's wondrous merry-go-round. The houses came in three models with names harkening back to Otto Mears's Colorado days: Silverton, Durango, and Ouray, three of the towns he had connected by rail, were now labels for single-family homes overlooking the Chesapeake Bay and adjoining a "Private Beach" posted "No Trespassing."

Mayor Buster Fortier had turned into an able grantsman, obtaining $10 million in government loans and grants for his town. At the same time, the old train station had been turned into a museum, and the Rod 'n' Reel next-door was no longer owned by CPI but by the Donovans, who had formerly just worked there. The population of Chesapeake Beach had grown 50.7% in a decade to 1,408 in 1980. "Chesapeake Station" and other development on Hugh Ward's 240-acre bayfront farm promised more growth: By 1996, the population more than doubled to 3,118.

"Everything looks good," said Fortier from his modern deck home overlooking marsh and bay. The spry septuagenarian was nearing the end of what he said was his last term with a sense of satisfaction and accomplishment. (He would quit a few months early, in disgust over petty bickering in the town government.) His successor was Gerald Donovan, who drew bigger crowds to his Rod 'n' Reel each Sunday with high-stakes commercial bingo. "I guess you could say we're pro-gambling people throughout Southern Maryland," he said. Development, for one thing, was a sure bet: By the late 1990s, there remained just one undeveloped piece of waterfront left in Chesapeake Beach. An eighty-unit seventy-foot-high apartment house was proposed to fill the gap, a development Donovan welcomed.

"I mean it's going to be beautiful," said the Chesapeake Beach mayor-entrepreneur. "I think this is called progress," though, he acknowledged, "Some people don't like it."

North Beach, meanwhile, also had a new mayor by the early '80s. W. Alan (Buck) Gott was a building contractor whose campaign platform openly addressed the town's social and economic ills for the first time. "My ideas and issues are pretty progressive, compared to what a lot of people are used to," he said. "You drive into our town, on Bay Avenue, you see the worst of it, where you find the derelicts, the drop-outs. I don't mind if people see it, so they can come back and see it [changed] four years from now. My intention is to rebuild the sand beach, the piers, to bring people back in. That will create a demand on the private sector that will lead to rehabilitation of some of the deteriorated buildings."

Gott stirred the citizenry with talk of remaking North Beach into a "family-type resort" he planned to promote "from Maine to Florida." He hired consultants as a first step toward redevelopment, remodeled and expanded the old town hall, and, taking his cue from Buster Fortier at Chesapeake Beach, sought and obtained state and federal aid. Backed by the town council, Gott also ordered a crackdown on public drinking and on homeowners whose yards resembled the county dump. In 1984 the town had its First Annual Bay Festival, or BayFest, and eight thousand people came. A year later, the *Washington Post*'s trendy Home section featured the North Beach "renaissance" as its cover story. There would be resistance. In a close election in 1986, the voters ousted Buck Gott—who would soon be indicted and convicted of mishandling town funds— and returned his predecessor, the well-digger, to office. Older residents on fixed income breathed easier, but not for long.

Like a pincer movement, the forces of change were attacking North Beach from all sides. While Chesapeake Beach was revitalizing itself to the south, Rose Haven to the north had lately become Herrington Harbour, a restaurant-motel-marina complex with 650 boat slips, the largest on the Bay. In North Beach proper, Christopher Cohl, thirty-three, a relatively new arrival from metropolitan Washington, ran a clothes store that sold the latest in designer jeans. "A lot of people around here are commuting to Annapolis," he told me. "People are moving out of the Annapolis area because it's getting too busy for them. They're starting to look at the north end of Calvert County." At North Beach, in fact. There'd soon be another new mayor with fresh ideas, and even talk of parking meters.

For a while, the commercial district remained decidedly downscale, but someone with the perspective of the years could see the future coming into sharper focus: the Anchor (renamed the Twin Beaches Motel) was closed, shops had filled the empty storefronts facing the beach, and Nice & Fleazy had achieved antiques and collectibles status, expanding from a corner of the old dry goods store to fill the entire building. The town had grown, too. The population of year-round residents had almost doubled in a decade, to 1,504 in 1980, and the number of houses had increased by almost one-third. By the mid-1990s, a thousand more residents would call North Beach home.

The town was rebuilding on a solid foundation of folks who had endured the worst and were ready for better. They remained divided on the pace and direction of renewal, but they agreed on the need for change. They lived blocks back from the waterfront in neatly kept homes, complete with outdoor decks and back-yard barbecues. Along with the derelicts, these families called North

Beach home. But, unlike earlier generations, they didn't come to North Beach for vacations. With a sandy beach almost in their front yards—and with a newly rebuilt and policed pier soon to come—at least some of the good folks of North Beach drove to Ocean City to get away from it all.

And for year-round diversion, there was a bus that regularly took them from the Twin Beaches all the way to Atlantic City, the new Monte Carlo by the sea, where they could gamble legally to their hearts' content.

7

Pride in Tobacco

*I*n the rolling countryside of Southern Maryland, tobacco springs stubbornly from the rich, sandy soil.

In spring, the seeds are warmed and nurtured by a white plastic or cloth cover, often held down by old tires or cinder blocks. Transplanted seedlings sprout leaves on their stalks through the summer. In autumn, plants are cut and hung on wooden spikes in drafty old barns to die slowly, the four- to six-week process known as "air curing." Then, in "down weather," when the humidity is high enough to keep the leaves from crumbling, the stalks are taken down from the barn rafters and the leaves are stripped, tied, and placed on flat baskets to be trucked to market.

In Southern Maryland, it is a never-ending cycle, this tobacco-growing business. It has been part of life here since colonial times and likely will remain so for generations to come, despite price fluctuations, urban encroachments, occasional outbreaks of blue mold, and various campaigns against the "killer weed" in public places and private use. In Southern Maryland, the crop and the culture of tobacco endure.

While more and more land is planted in houses instead of tobacco, the crop and culture survive on the very edge of suburbia, half an hour or so from the nation's capital. In the Prince George's County seat of Upper Marlboro, as elsewhere on the Southern Maryland peninsula, the tobacco is auctioned for two months each spring. This old community on the Patuxent's Western Branch houses the government of the state's second most populous county, yet it retains much of the look and feel of a sleepy southern town. "Upper Marlboro...has been a tobacco town since it was founded in 1706," says the Works Progress Administration Guide to the Old Line State, published in 1940. "All the townsmen know and talk tobacco; and many business buildings display prize leaves during the sales."

When I first arrived in the town known to locals simply as "Marburruh," the WPA tobacco mural still hung in the vintage 1936 post office (which has since become the town's branch library—with the mural still on display). But county workers were less interested in golden leaves than they were in Golden Arches, in the hopeful pursuit of which they were circulating a petition. Years later, a McDonald's replaced a tobacco warehouse at the edge of town. But back then there was no fast-food in the vicinity. For what most people considered a decent lunch, I had to drive past the tobacco auction buildings to Route 301, a divided four-lane highway that was once the main road from Baltimore to Richmond. There, in a shopping center, I found the Marlborough House, a restaurant possibly named after a landmark tavern-hotel razed in 1957 in the town itself. The new place, since twice renamed again, had good cooking, modest prices, and a waitress who grew tobacco on the side.

She and her husband had grown tobacco on their eight acres for nearly twenty years. The previous year, they had made $3,000. This year, they were hoping for $8,000. Like many Southern Marylanders, they raised tobacco as a sideline—and a tradition.

"Ever strip tobacco?" I heard a woman at another table ask her male companion.

"Uh uh, and I ain't gonna," he replied.

"You don't know how to strip tobacco," she said, with an air of superiority and finality. "You ain't from Merr-lin."

Some of those who are and do belonged to the Maryland Tobacco Growers Association, a farmers' cooperative with headquarters in southern Prince George's County and five satellite stores that sold feed and farm equipment and, after the markets closed, unsold tobacco. Its members were substantial growers, wealthy good old boys who, in the words of one outsider, "look like hayseeds."

They gathered together once a year shortly before the auction season starts. The meeting I attended was held in the Plantation Room of the Martha Washington Motel, on Route 301 in Waldorf, Charles County. Those present included four charter members of the organization, which was formed in 1919. Copies of the *Leaf*, the group's newsletter, were circulated. Door prizes included half a ton of lime, an International Harvester toy tractor, and a seventy-five-foot section of lawn hose.

In this meeting of forty prominent tobacco growers, Ronsil lighters were passed out and free cigarette samples were at every place setting. But hardly anyone smoked. They were concerned, nonetheless—almost obsessed—with efforts to ban outright or even reduce the use of tobacco.

"No one has established tobacco smoking is directly linked to cancer," asserted T. Jack Cross, the group's general manager. "The Tobacco Institute and all forces are enlisting support to spread the word and combat this American Cancer Society program.... We're having enough problems with labor and weather. We don't need this harassment. If everyone would go home and write their opposition to the American Cancer Society, it would be a big help."

"I stopped smoking eight years ago, as a nuisance thing," he later confided to me, somewhat sheepishly, "but I believe it's a free country... I'd be opposed to anything detrimental to tobacco, naturally."

"You know," said Y.D. Hance, a Calvert County grower who also happened to be Maryland's secretary of agriculture, "now they want to kill smoking and chewing tobacco and make marijuana legal! I'm a smoker, but it offends me when regulations are being passed to make me sit in the back of the bus, and that's what we're talking about." Y.D., as he was universally known, grew tobacco on land said to have belonged to the original Lord Calvert and was the state's first agriculture secretary, testimony to the power of the tobacco growers in Annapolis. Hance, Jack Cross said, approvingly, was "someone that talks our language."

The language in Southern Maryland is spoken by judges, lawyers, county commissioners, and just plain gentry, who lived on the rolling tobacco farms while their tenant farmers did the hard manual work of raising and stripping the crop. If this arrangement sounds a bit feudal, it is. But it's an arrangement that worked.

It had been that way for three hundred years on the peninsula. This is the land of "hoags" and "doags" and occasional deer crossing the unpaved back roads. South of Marlboro, the old families still reign over the land along the Patuxent River where once boats stopped to load their tobacco and take it, packed in hogshead barrels, to Baltimore for sale to the highest bidder. Rotted pilings are all that's left of the old tobacco wharves in tiny towns like Nottingham on the river, but the families remain.

Sasscers, Clagetts, Duvalls—the old names abound from Upper Marlboro south along the river and in the old church cemeteries dotted with Confederate crosses. These are the stewards of the land, and any attempts by government to take over the task have been fiercely fought. "They have enough land on the river and they're not using it," said one Peter Wood Duvall, Jr., a tobacco and soybean farmer whose family came to nearby Anne Arundel County in 1653. "I don't think we have feudal estates. We just happened to have lived here a long time."

Of the same mind were Robert (Bobby) Clagett and his wife, Bradford (Brad), who built themselves a Williamsburg reproduction house on a hill overlooking the Patuxent and a panorama of marshland, tidewater, and undeveloped land unchanged for centuries. Clagetts were largely lawyers in Marlboro, not farmers, but Bobby Clagett built his house on 270 acres his father had acquired in 1956 for $18,000 and easily settled into a life that encompassed both law and the land.

Yates Clagett, his twelve-year-old son, was responsible for growing, hanging, and stripping a "burden" of tobacco (a three- to four-foot stack of the stuff, weighing one hundred to two hundred pounds and ready for market), but it was the Clagetts' sharecropping family that handled the rest of the twelve-acre crop of tobacco and twenty acres of grain. For supplying living quarters, gas, and fertilizer, the Clagetts reaped 40% of the proceeds. For his 60%, the sharecropper supplied the farm equipment and the manual labor that not even a newfangled stripping machine could really replace.

Bobby's cousin was the chief promoter of a National Tobacco Museum to display the tools of the trade. But before the project could succeed, Hugh Clagett, an engineer by vocation who owned a tobacco farm with his brothers outside Upper Marlboro, died, and the project seemed to die with him. "After his death, there was no one person who wanted to pursue it," his widow, Kathryn, told me.

The living museum is to be found in the fields, stripping rooms, curing barns, and auction warehouses of Southern Maryland, the five counties in which are located all but a few of the state's tobacco-raising farms.

One day before market, I met James Garner, fifty-one, whose grandfather had built most of the barns below Croom, in Southern Prince George's County. Garner was at work in his stripping room. There the leaves are pulled from the stalks, separated by quality, and then bunched into "hands" of several leaves each. Spread out like fingers, they are tied at the stem end with a single leaf of the same grade. Typically, the stripping room was beneath the barn, where the dampness seems to last, and there was a radio to keep him company and fluorescent lighting "to bring out the color features."

A fourth-generation tobacco farmer, Garner was delighted to report, "The tobacco's right soft now. It's as good as it's been yesterday. The humidity's been one hundred percent this morning, so it's right soft now, except the stem." The only thing he fretted about, he said, was clear weather with northwest winds, which caused the leaves to become too dry to strip and market.

Garner produced about twelve hundred pounds of tobacco on fourteen acres, along with one hundred acres of grain. His wife worked as a registered nurse to supplement their income. "My son would also like to work a small crop of tobacco if he'd have the time," said the farmer, a John Deere cap planted on his head. But his son hadn't the time, commuting back and forth to a Bethesda engineering firm.

A few miles away, Bernard (Bud) Johnson continued at the age of sixty-seven to raise tobacco on five acres, stripping eight thousand pounds a year. His wife was a schoolteacher, and they lived in a large, new, brick house built next to the old dilapidated family home in which he and his eight brothers and sisters had been raised. The three other surviving brothers had left the farm—one went to the government, one to the ministry, and the third to the undertaking business up in Washington.

Johnson's stripping room was eighty feet long and had cinder-block walls, which the old farmer said kept the moisture in. "I pick up help now and then," he said, but mostly Johnson's tobacco crop was a one-man operation.

"I just like to see things grow," he said, steering an old pickup truck over winding country roads to a barn he shared with several other men. While it rained heavily outside, the men removed the unstripped stalks of tobacco from the rafters. Among the helpers was John Brooks, night supervisor at a county youth detention center in nearby Cheltenham. "I love tobacco," he said. "I just wish I could make a livelihood out of it."

Making a living is on everyone's mind at the tobacco markets, where Maryland farmers, who by choice receive no government subsidies, gather to learn their fate. Marlboro had three of these cool, cavernous buildings. Edelen Brothers, Planter's Warehouse, and Marlboro Tobacco Market were all on a slope rising to Route 301. On market days, the buildings are filled with long rows of stacked tobacco. In the Edelen Brothers warehouse, an old poster for Lucky Strike "greens" hung on one wall. "With Men Who Know Tobacco Best, It's Luckies 2 to 1," the sign said. "It's Toasted."

Across Old Marlboro Pike were rural houses, some dilapidated, and, behind them, a black enclave known as "Sugar Hill" where families lived for

Roger and Marge Hyde strip tobacco in Brandywine, Prince George's County. Eugene L. Meyer

generations without amenities such as indoor plumbing. Down the road toward the train tracks was the Gieske & Niemann plant, where the bought goods were packed for shipment. Once Prince George's was the leading tobacco county, but no more. Subdivisions have taken their toll on its farmland, and in the 1987 agricultural census, fruits and vegetables were a larger cash crop in the county. St. Mary's County produces the most tobacco now, with the Hughesville market showing the largest volume. Nonetheless, Marlboro holds its own.

Before business begins, market day is a social event in Southern Maryland. Mary Thomas, a middle-aged woman who had no tobacco for sale in the Marlboro Tobacco Market, went anyway because she always did. "My daddy raised tobacco, and I've raised tobacco ever since I was a little kid," said the short, heavyset woman with long, dark hair. "I helped my aunt strip tobacco, too. I also worked as a waitress, cook, and bartender, but I always stripped tobacco. We had a place of our own with five acres of tobacco, but we sold it two years ago when my arthritis got too bad. It's a good life, though. The country is a good life. Wouldn't trade it."

The auction is a moving event: Two parallel lines of men in motion are divided by a row of tobacco. On one side the auctioneer, who follows the markets from state to state, chants prices by the stack. A man following him notes the high bid and buyer on each. Across the way is a line of men representing foreign and domestic buyers. The men feel the leaves and raise their fists to bid. During sales in the first few rows, the large room is filled with the sweet smell of the leaves. After awhile, the aroma is buried under a storm of tobacco dust, enough to make you sick.

Along with bidders from the domestic cigarette companies are others, representing European buyers. Starting after World War I, Maryland's fast-burning aromatic leaf became especially popular in Switzerland and, to a lesser extent, Germany, Belgium, and Luxembourg. The demand grew after World War II, so much so that since 1950, or thereabouts, the Europeans have heavily subsidized the Maryland Tobacco Improvement Foundation, which is headquartered on the University of Maryland's experimental tobacco farm outside Upper Marlboro. About one-third of the Maryland crop annually goes overseas, where it is the dominant strain in what are regarded as high-quality cigarettes. The rest is blended but not dominant in American tobacco products.

Tobacco brought $1.20 a pound at my first auction, in 1977. The price jumped to a whopping $1.80 four years later. There it remained through 1982. At a time when prices for other crops were dropping, tobacco looked like leafy gold to many farmers. New siding went up on old barns, and throughout Southern Maryland, new barns, costing as much as $15,000 to build, rose on agricultural land. "Everybody's raising tobacco," observed Bobby Clagett, and, indeed, on opening day in 1983, the number of young farmers compared to those in prior years was high.

The result: depressed prices and depressed farmers. With supply projected to reach 37.5 million pounds, the demand had dropped. Farmers in caps that said "Pride in Tobacco" milled around, helplessly, as the prices sagged to around $1.60 a pound in Upper Marlboro. The season's best prices come on opening day, it is said, so a whole year's worth of work is determined within the space of a few tense minutes. Glumly watching the procession move down the rows, an old Anne Arundel County farmer noted, "When you see 'em just keep on walkin', it's a good sign, the market's good. When it's slow like that, it's a bad sign."

"I'm gonna have to take what they give me," his companion, from Mitchellville in Prince George's County, said. "There are gonna be a lot of sales at the courthouse," he added, wryly. The season's average price would be $1.51 a pound, and the next year's prices would be lower still. The average price for the 1998 crop sold in 1999 was $1.62.

The buyers began their work at Planter's, then moved to Edelen Brothers and finished up, by noon, at the Marlboro Tobacco Market, where bids went as low as $1.30 a burden. Representatives of foreign buyers, I heard later, were prepared to bid up to $1.80 a pound but found no reason to do so.

Basket burdens of tobacco loaded on a truck for delivery to the market. Eugene L. Meyer

"When you get up to $1.50, you're in big money," said a sarcastic farmer's wife with three young sons in tow. "Ain't no way we can buy the fertilizer, the gas," she said in disgust. The day seemed to hit a new low when the newly crowned Southern Maryland Tobacco Queen, a seventeen-year-old dimple-faced blond from Calvert County, had her purse stolen.

Watching the proceedings with an air of detachment were men in jackets and ties. They are the tobacco company managers the farmers call "the big shots." They direct their men on the floor how high to bid, but they do not follow the line, and before long they disappeared from the dusty scene.

At the side of the building, far from the high-rollers, I talked with the men who hauled the stuff from the auction floor to the packing plant. They were mostly minimum-wage workers like Homer Bohannon, who drove the truck. "I been in the tobacco business for twenty-five years, and I'm poorer than a sonovabitch," he told me. "There's no money in the manual end of it." After the markets close, he said, "if you're lucky, you get on unemployment. Otherwise, you play poker or shoot crap."

The industrial revolution had come at last to the tobacco-packing plants in the 1970s. Fresh from the auction floor, the tobacco had been packed in barrels for shipment south. At Gieske & Niemann, the Marlboro packing plant that had been in business since 1858, coopers were in great demand to build three hundred hogshead barrels a day, and migrant workers were needed to pack them. Then, in 1975, along came the "dump packer," a Rube Goldberg contraption that appears to eat the tobacco leaves at one end and spit out a packed load ready to be shipped at the other. Thus are as many as 250,000 pounds of tobacco handled in a single day. When I first visited Gieske & Niemann in 1977, the plant manager said, "The coopers are gone. I've got but two, and they go around to these folk festivals."

Gieske had further reduced its migrant work force, from three hundred to thirty, by packing tobacco "green" rather than recurring it as in the past. "We're hiring a lot of local people now," the manager said. "We're rapidly reaching a point where we won't have to bring any people in." Consequently, some of the migrant living quarters had been demolished and others were vacant: small, spare single rooms with bare cinder-block walls.

Gieske's lingering migrant workers lived according to the unwritten rules of the Old South. The seven whites lived in a pleasant, white, frame building with air conditioning, a large living room with color television, communal kitchen, indoor bathroom, and individual bedrooms. The blacks, meanwhile, lived without air conditioning or other amenities in the gray cinder-block buildings. Their communal toilet and shower were in another cinder-block building behind the packing plant. The fifty-nine-year-old black night watchman told me the housing segregation was by "personal choice."

"It's just the design that's been followed over the years," explained the plant manager. "We're not committed to furnish anything. Years ago, you had [discrimination]. Now, we have a black foreman. We're an equal opportunity employer."

When I returned to the plant six years later, the cinder-block buildings remained but almost all their doors were covered by wooden boards or padlocked. There was no more housing segregation at the packing plant. "We have all local people now," the plant manager said. "We've had nobody staying here for two years." Within a few years, Gieske & Niemann would also close, as tobacco buyers trucked the Southern Maryland crop to the Carolinas for packing and shipping.

Farther down the Southern Maryland peninsula, near the line dividing Charles from St. Mary's County, I found a part of the tobacco culture more resistant to change. At the Farmer's Tobacco Auction Warehouse in Hughesville, Wednesday is Amish-only market day. It wasn't the people so much as their rigs: Horses and trucks just don't mix well.

Feeling too "crowded" in their native Lancaster County, Pennsylvania, eight Amish families had led the way to Southern Maryland in time for the 1940 spring planting. They came, too, to escape the Pennsylvania school laws requiring attendance beyond the age of fourteen. Maryland requirements were more lenient, although they were later tightened, promoting special legislation in 1967 for the Amish. Today, as before, Amish children attend only grade school, attaining enough formal learning, it is believed, for a farmer and his wife.

Eventually, one hundred Amish families had migrated to the swampy area southeast of Washington. They soon turned it into impressively productive farmland. In time they grew tobacco, and, in recent years, acres of tomatoes for ketchup.

Shortly before six in the morning, the procession of steel-wheeled horse-drawn wagons starts up Route 5. Their Amish drivers stand atop the stacked baskets of tobacco, a cash crop that signifies some accommodation to the world around them.

Amish tobacco farmer uses horse power to get to Hughesville market. Eugene L. Meyer

From Pitt's Donut Shop, observers have counted as many as forty-eight tobacco wagons heading up the road. Midway through the market season, I counted ten by 7 a.m. and then drove to the Hughesville warehouse.

There, Amishmen helped unload each other's flat-bed wagons and chatted in Pennsylvania Dutch-accented German.

Warehouse officials told me the Amish tobacco always brought the highest prices. A non-Amish bystander explained why. "All this tobacco is stripped the same length and color," the man said. "They separate the grades better, and they don't put a whole lot of chemicals down to make weight. It don't cost them as much to raise because they use horse manure. In two years, that land is rich. When they plant tobacco, I mean it just keeps on growing. It will grow anything you put on it."

An Amishman informed me his people grew better tobacco because they cared most about doing a good, painstaking job, while others paid more attention to making a profit. He also expressed uneasiness over any outsider's efforts to portray his people in pictures or print. Inevitably, he said, the portraits drawn had displeased its Amish subjects. "You're not getting anything out of me," he said and laughed.

A few nights earlier, however, I had met another Amishman who, although he drove a horse and buggy and looked the part in his plain garments, patriarchal beard, and straw-brimmed hat, seemed to crave contact with the outside world. One night a week, he regularly ate pizza, drank coffee, and conversed with outsiders in a small restaurant near the donut shop. He spoke in low tones, as if imparting secrets. Often what he said was funny in a wry, country way, and he knew it, judging from his laughter.

How many children did he have? "I got eight too many." What's so special about Amish tobacco? "They put a little bit of horse manure on it, to give it special flavor." Why do they call his kinfolk's shop a notions store? "You got a notion you want it." Why would Amish use tractor engines for belt power, to thresh wheat in the barns, but not for plowing the fields? "It's just like the parents make a line with the children, too."

And so it went with this Old Order raconteur, late into the night. He was not, he insisted, a farmer. "I got less than two acres," he said. Nonetheless, he kept two cows, three horses, and fifty chickens and had a vegetable garden large enough to feed his family. By trade, he was a blacksmith and a carpenter who built mostly tobacco barns for "English." Getting to work was no problem. Although he would never drive a car himself, he rode in the truck of his non-Amish employees to the job site.

"If I wasn't so tired, I'd sure like to ride home in your buggy," said a young woman who worked at the pizza place to the Amishman out on the town, "but I got to get home faster."

Some people, even more than the Amish, refuse to accept change for its own sake. Francis M. Gasperich was one. He and his father had always grown tobacco on their farm near Annapolis until 1974, when Gasperich went into the business of tree surgery. In 1977 he finally took his three-year-old crop to market, packed, as if in a time warp, in hogsheads.

If the ritual of tobacco growing has remained constant over the years, the marketing of the product has changed with the times. Before 1938 all Southern Maryland tobacco went to the "hogshead market" in Baltimore. The five "basket" markets were established during the Depression to lower hauling costs and hasten payment to the farmers. The hogshead market hung on for years, however, until the building was razed for redevelopment of the city's inner harbor. A new structure eventually rose in southern Prince George's County in 1971 to replace the old, at a cost of nearly $1 million. But by then the tobacco farmers had committed themselves to the basket markets closer to home.

Although every other tobacco farmer in the state had long ago abandoned the old way, Gasperich hadn't. He and his ninety-year-old father, Francis G. Gasperich, packed their five acres of tobacco into ten five-by-three-foot barrels they made themselves. The elder Gasperich, who had come to Maryland from his native South Dakota in 1922, had first sold tobacco on the hogshead market in 1933. His son's first sale there was in 1947.

That the state tobacco inspector's post, created for the hogshead market, had been vacant for years didn't matter a bit. Nor did the fact that there hadn't been a hogshead market since 1973. The state was obliged under an archaic section of the Maryland Code to provide personnel and a facility for a hogshead market. It was also required to store the hogsheads indefinitely should the sellers reject the price.

"The tobacco's not vulnerable in a barrel," said Gasperich. "If you're dissatisfied with the price, you don't have to haul it home. You don't have the pressure of the basket market. We've held a tobacco crop [in storage] for four years when we were not satisfied with the price."

Somehow, the overwhelming advantages of marketing in hogsheads instead of in baskets had been lost on Maryland tobacco farmers—except Francis Gasperich, that is. So, were it not for Gasperich, the obsolete-when-built Maryland Tobacco Authority Warehouse in Cheltenham would never have seen a leaf of tobacco. Were it not for Gasperich, four state employees would have been elsewhere one spring day in 1977: Agriculture Secretary Y.D. Hance and aide Dick Carter at their desks in Annapolis, James Johnson inspecting eggs in Parole, and Donald Mackall at the state print shop in the nearby Tawes Office Building.

It was apparently the last hogshead market in the state if not in the entire country, although in Maryland the law affecting the handling of hogsheads is still on the books.

The ritual followed a carefully prescribed procedure and was performed in one corner of the building, otherwise full of Prince George's County voting machines and discarded government files. The full cask was weighed first. Then the three state employees detailed to the job removed the barrel (except its bottom) from the tobacco, which sat like a compressed golden-brown cylinder.

James Johnson, the egg inspector with fourteen years' experience in the hogshead market, poked an upright "breaker bar" into the cake of tobacco at six locations, one more than the law required. At each point, an official of the Maryland Tobacco Growers Association extracted a bunch of leaves. One bunch per casket was marked and sealed, for later inspection by prospective buyers. The empty barrel was then weighed to determine the net weight of the tobacco, and the cake was placed back within the cask. The ritual was repeated for each of the ten hogshead barrels.

"I'd rate this very good," said the association inspector. "It's handled well. It's uniform. It should bring just about the top price."

There was, as it turned out, just one bidder. The price was slightly higher than in the loose-leaf basket market, but it was an all-or-nothing offer, and Gasperich turned it down.

"I kept the tobacco there for two or three years, then took it down to Wayson's Corner and sold it on the loose-leaf market," the farmer-turned-tree-surgeon told me later. "They had me over a barrel."

By 1999, the hogsheads remained history, but machine-baling of tobacco was replacing hand-tying of the leaves. Tobacco was still Southern Maryland's cash crop but shrinking—8,000 acres compared to 23,000 in 1981—as suburbia continued to sprawl and farmers found more lucrative and less laborious ways to make a living. The last season of the century, I followed Roger Hyde, Prince George's last fulltime tobacco farmer, from the stripping room floor to the market in Waldorf. He was losing hanging barns to houses, and the price was lower than expected. But it wasn't anti-tobacco litigation that was affecting his income; it was the prior year's drought, resulting in a lower quality harvest.

8

Military Maryland:
A Tale of Two Bases

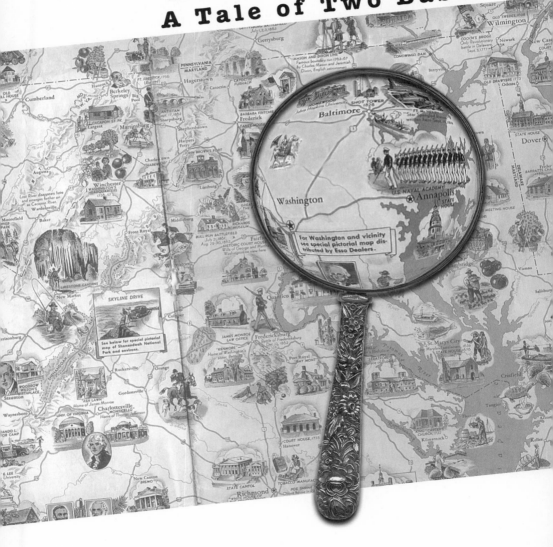

The new commander-in-chief made his first presidential departure from Andrews Air Force Base on an unseasonably warm February morning. Nearly one hour before the president's flight, the blue-striped National Emergency Airborne Command Post, a Boeing 747 jumbo jet, left for Nebraska, where its crew members were based. Another NEACP craft would fly to California, to be near the president. Except for a small press pool traveling with the president, the reporters and camera crews would leave here twenty minutes early on a commercial jet.

On a clear day, controllers in the 156-foot-high tower designed by I.M. Pei could see the presidential helicopter ascending 200 feet over the White House. But today the Washington Monument was barely visible through the clouds. The Marine chopper carrying the first family and California-bound staff arrived at 9:52 a.m., depositing its passengers some fifty feet from the nose of Air Force One.

While the black-bereted air force security police and their German shepherds looked on, the president was met and escorted by Brigadier General Archer L. Durham, the Andrews base commander, from the chopper to the boarding ramp of the big jet. They chatted about the weather, and the base commander lauded the president for an "outstanding speech" to Congress the night before. The president and first lady waved for photographers, then disappeared into the craft.

In the control tower, Dick Jones heard the president's pilot say, "Air Force One is ready."

President Kennedy greeted at Andrews Air Force Base.
U.S. Air Force

"Air Force One is clear for takeoff, runway to the right," the air controller replied. Durham and Lieutenant Colonel Jim Sweeney, the base protocol chief, saluted, the plane taxied, and, at 10 a.m., the commander-in-chief was airborne from Andrews.

Andrews AFB commander and protocol officer salute Air Force One, the presidential plane. Joel Richardson, *Washington Post*

History is made regularly at this forty-nine-hundred-acre base in the Southern Maryland suburbs ten miles from the White House. In this high-profile setting, the mechanics for Air Force One wear special light-blue uniforms instead of regular fatigues, and even routine jobs like refueling the president's plane are considered "elite" details.

The self-styled "Aerial Gateway to the Nation's Capital" is among the most dramatic datelines of our time, a pastiche of presidential comings and goings, of heroes' homecomings, of triumphant and tragic arrivals and departures. Unforgettable images come quickly to my mind: The American hostages from Iran, descending from Freedom One, jubilant; a disgraced Richard Nixon and a defeated Jimmy Carter leaving official Washington behind, their families in tears; Vietnam POWs, home at last; the Pope and his ecclesiastical entourage.

My first impressions of Andrews were those of a detached observer, as I passed through the terminal or ventured onto the base for a special occasion. There had been a brief visit in the mid-1970s, to interview returning POWs about their imprisonment. Later, I stood on the field and watched a casket containing the remains of a murdered CIA agent arrive. In December 1980 an early-morning ice storm made my trip to Andrews slow and treacherous, but I got there in time to board Air Force One for a presidential Christmas in Plains, Georgia. This is the Andrews most Americans know, but there is more than meets the television camera's eye, as I discovered during a three-week tour around the base.

"Our mission is diverse, unique, and exciting," gushed the official welcoming letter to Andrews Air Force Base. "Being so close to the capital, you can almost feel the pulse of the nation," added the base "intro" fact sheet. "You may see or even participate in events and operations that directly affect the course of world affairs."

Altogether, 26,000 active duty personnel, civilians and military dependents work or live here. Those fortunate to find a residence on this military reservation live in 2,300 units that range from the tree-shaded luxury of Command Lane to the trailer-park impermanence of Flower Village, across the base.

In this military society, where a "homesteader" is anyone assigned to one place for more than two years, I found Robert B. Starkey, a civilian who had been around since the start. At sixty-nine, Starkey reigned as deputy chief of civil engineering, which in his case meant maintenance and construction. The sign outside his office across the base from the presidential wing contained his name in large painted letters under a removable metal plate identifying the colonel who currently wore the official title of chief.

"When a full colonel comes in, you just don't go and tell him he's O.J.T. [on-the-job training], you know what I mean?" said Starkey, who had often served as teacher to such men.

Starkey had gone to work building the base in 1942. "It was just a country area," he said, "mostly forest, Maryland jackpine, with chicken houses and grape arbors." Camp Springs, where Union forces had been stationed during the Civil War, was in the general vicinity. Smack in the middle had been Meadows, a crossroads community of a dozen or so homes, a general store owned by Robert M. Hardy, a garage, and a church where the old paths of Pennsylvania Avenue and Allentown Road converged. The church is still there, used as a base chapel and numbered "Building 3715." The old cemetery—its tombstones etched with old Southern Maryland names like Duckett, Beall, and Duvall—is also intact. So is the old Meadows public school, converted into a military school for nuclear and chemical warfare preparedness. The rest of old Meadows is gone from the scene.

But just south of the base, the Meadows Market and Restaurant recalls the former town. Nearby is Tucker's Restaurant, which still draws customers from Andrews, although not as many as when the main entrance was at this end of the base. "You're in Meadows," said Blair Tucker, whose father opened the place in 1952. "This is it." Next-door, the Andrews Field Motel, which once catered to the military, now counted truckers among its primary clientele.

Down the road lived Russell Richardson, a tobacco-chewing Southern Marylander approaching seventy-five. Richardson had worked at Hardy's Store in Meadows—had lost his job, in fact, to the war effort that wiped out the town. "Sometimes I wish they hadn't made it history because the airplane noise is terrible, but I guess that's progress," his wife, Annie, said, in a conversation punctuated by jets flying over the house that the couple had called home since 1931.

It rained heavily during October 1942, making the base-building chore even more difficult. But it was wartime, and the workers pushed ahead, finishing in June 1943. There were four small runways, squadrons of pursuit planes, 892 military, and 200 civilians. The base commander was a mere captain.

One veteran recalled a "relaxed atmosphere" that allowed all personnel to be off base "from retreat to reveille." German prisoners of war did KP and clean-up details. Two POWs were bakers in the PX coffee shop in which a POW artist, the veteran said, "was put to work painting scenes of air combat on the empty walls. He was good. I watched him working through more than a few breakfasts. Somebody with a more discerning eye took a closer look at his chef-d'oeuvre and discovered that his mural showed a disproportionate number of allied warplanes being shot down. The artist was banished."

In January 1946, army air corpsmen at the base protested what they regarded as foot dragging on demobilization. "1,000 GIs Here Hoot Down C.O.," headlined the *Washington Daily News*. After the war, plans called for converting "Andrews Field" to civilian use, but it never happened.

It had been known first as the Camp Springs-Meadows, Maryland, Fighter Command Station. It became Andrews Field in 1945, named after a World War II flier who died in a plane crash over Iceland, and Andrews Air Force Base in 1950. To provide access to the base as the war drew to a close, the Army Corps of Engineers built the Military Highway from Washington. It is now called Suitland Parkway.

In the late '50s and early '60s, the presidential plane (which had used Andrews only occasionally) moved permanently from Washington National Airport, and new buildings sprouted to support the growing air force mission on the western half of the base.

Military people move in and out almost as often as the "distinguished visitors" (known also as DVs) who put Andrews on the map. Civilians can be found working almost everywhere on the base. Like Starkey, they stay on and on while military men and women come and go. They are where they are mostly by choice, and many are retired from the service and receive a pension that supplements their civilian pay. Others are spouses of military men assigned to the base.

The base commander at the time of my visit was Brigadier General Durham, the third-ranking resident of Command Lane, after a pair of two-star generals. From his plaque- and plant-filled office, Durham kept "an eye on the flightline," which extends for more than nine thousand feet across the base.

Apart from the presidential fleet—two Boeing 707s alternately known as Air Force One when carrying the chief executive—the view from Durham's office encompassed the "doomsday" jumbo jet, one of four strategically deployed planes (each officially designated a National Emergency Airborne Command Post) from which a nuclear counterattack could be directed from the air. Crew members wore beepers and moved to the front of the line at the Freedom Dining Hall, where they ate together at reserved tables near the door. At the sound of an alarm that sounds like a basketball buzzer, they dashed to their "alert vehicles" and returned to their craft.

Downfield from the NEACP craft and Air Force One were several smaller passenger planes that carried government movers and shakers, ranked codes 2 through 6 (in descending order of official importance). For the dignitaries, foreign and domestic, a special VIP lounge awaited with leather couches and chairs, a console color TV. Air force art adorned the walls, and soft drinks and coffee were served, but not in Styrofoam cups.

"We're very unique," base commander Durham explained. "We're event oriented."

"No list?" an incredulous Lieutenant Hugh F. Oliver asked the South Korean military attaché in the VIP lounge prior to the departure of President Chun Doo Hwan. "Just let anyone on the airplane?" There was, as it turned out, a list, which appeared at the last minute. But there was some anxiety about the receiving line as the visitor went from a U.S. helicopter to the Korean plane. The Koreans didn't wait for General Durham to greet the departing dignitary as he emerged from the chopper.

"I told them three times to wait," said a chagrined Lieutenant Colonel Jim Sweeney, who was in charge of dampening such diplomatic "brush fires," as he called these minor crises on the tarmac.

As the Korean's ritual departure progressed, the wind whipped the temperature to ten below zero on the flightline. "You'll have to take your equipment out," Captain Clemmer L. Montague told a wire-service photographer as the two approached a black-bereted guard and his dog. "They'll want to check it for gunpowder."

"I'm familiar with that procedure," the photographer said as the dog sniffed his camera bag and found nothing. The cameraman then proceeded to "the pit," an enclosed area in which he would remain confined during the "ramp freeze."

Behind another security fence, a hundred or so Koreans waved flags and banners. A small group of embassy children, including one warmed by a mink coat, was ushered out to the Korean Airlines airplane ramp to see their president off. All of this was dutifully recorded by Korean reporters and camera crews.

I asked the protocol chief overseeing it all what his happiest moment was. "When they all leave," he said.

Aerial view of Andrews AFB, site of triumphant and tragic arrivals and departures, and of annual air fair, pictured here. U.S. Air Force

This is Andrews, a high-powered mini-city of fifty missions and two worlds where the work is often glamorous but the life often difficult. The official pronouncements are true enough: Here an enlisted man might find himself working on a presidential inauguration, and it was indeed considered a career steppingstone for an officer to be assigned to the base. But there is another, unofficial, side to life at Andrews. It is, in some ways, more a mirror of nearby Washington than of sleepy Southern Maryland. Like Washington, Andrews can be a professionally rewarding place—"where the action is"—but for a financial and psychic price.

The high cost of living and the high-pressured atmosphere combine to make

Andrews about as desirable an assignment as, one officer suggested, the missile base at Minot, North Dakota. From the lowliest enlisted airman to the highest-ranking senior officer, the story is much the same. At Andrews, a sense of community comes from the shared experience of working in what is regarded as a hardship post. Off-base bars that often bind servicemen (but dismay the locals) are almost nonexistent in the Andrews area. Even on base, the officers' club is little more to many than a place to cash checks.

For members of this scattered military "community," life inside is like life outside, only more so: Andrews is more transient even than Washington, with transfers occurring as regularly as summer, when most of the shifts occur. Washington prices strain civilian budgets, but military families on essentially fixed incomes say they are hit harder.

Listen to Lieutenant Colonel Ronald Bowen, not yet forty, with the choice job of special assistant to the head of the Air Force Systems Command, the weapons procurement agency headquartered at Andrews: "The Washington area is a place where an up-and-coming officer has to come sooner or later to get to the top, and professionally it's been good for me. But my blood pressure is probably extremely high and my backside emaciated." And, despite his officer's pay, his wife's part-time job as a nurse, access to the base commissary, and other fringes, life for Bowen and his family, who lived off base, had become "a hand-to-mouth type of operation...I honestly don't see how an enlisted man could survive."

Many can't. First Sergeant Ronald D. Shusta, an older enlisted man who was almost a father figure to the young personnel in the base supply squadron, told me he received several requests each month for hardship transfers based on the cost of living. "They want to know, 'How can I get out of here?'" Shusta said. "I just look at them and say, 'You can't.'"

"They say if you can survive in this area, you can survive anywhere," said Sergeant Helen Gibson, who lived with her husband, an amateur boxer, and two children in a second-hand trailer on the base. For Gibson, a stock clerk, survival meant collecting food stamps and cashing them in at the commissary.

"We asked for Washington State, not Washington, D.C.," said Lois Rice, a mother of three and the working wife of a sergeant who also held down a second job. "This is a hard area." She should know. She also ran Family Services, a base office staffed by twenty-eight volunteers who helped the uniformed needy. Among other services, the office lends dishes, dishpans, and even beds to the newly arrived and the hard pressed. "We got two calls today from people moving off base; they don't have enough money to buy beds," said a weary major's wife.

Those in trouble often flocked to the chaplain's office, where eight ministers spent more time counseling than preaching. Whatever spiritual problems afflicted other bases, Doug Jones, the head chaplain told me, "the primary need here is financial." And from that need, he suggested, spiritual problems—family feuds, in particular—flowed.

Among those seeking to stem the tide was Lieutenant Colonel Jerry Singeton, a former fighter pilot and Vietnam POW who had become a Southern Baptist chaplain. Since arriving the previous August, he had counseled seven or eight people a week, a caseload twice as large as he'd had at the larger Sheppard Air Force Base in Texas. "When I was first told of this assignment, I wanted very much not to come, just because it's a very busy, pressure-intensive environment," he said. "By comparison, down there the general pace of life is somewhere around fifty miles an hour. Up here, it's a hundred miles an hour. Just being in this area puts added stress. It's still not the kind of place I want to establish our family permanently. But it's good because I get a magnified view of the kinds of problems air force families face."

The biggest problem for many was housing. There were only 2,301 units on the base for the 5,000-some military assigned to it. In the early 1980s, there was no base housing set aside for the 744 airmen. For the 1,325 officers, there were 390 units. There were 1,696 units for 2,774 noncommissioned officers. The 215 trailers ("Security Patrolled") parked in a remote corner of the base were open to all ranks. By the mid-90s, things were hardly better. There were long waiting lists for all types of on-base housing, which is classified by the budget year built, as in "Fiscal Year 64 housing."

Most were forced to find housing on the private market. For enlisted personnel, that meant places like Andrews Manor, an apartment complex adjoining the base ("So-o-o convenient," said the classified ad) where brochures from three furniture rental firms could be found in the office and 45% of the tenants were military. For officers—most of whom had little equity for down payments because of frequent moves—there were the subdivisions of southern Prince George's and Charles counties. An additional "variable housing allowance" paid to service members to take into account regional differences was second here only to that received in the Los Angeles area.

Real estate firms near the base boasted of their air force connections, of the number of agents who were either retired military or service wives. "We talk on their level," said a retired air force lieutenant colonel in charge of the Camp Springs office of Coldwell Banker-Routh Robbins Realtors, in the Andrews Manor Shopping Center opposite the base. "It's the camaraderie of belonging to the same organization, like Italians moving into Little Italy or Chinese into Chinatown."

The camaraderie at Andrews, like other aspects of life here, was often defined by distance. Social life could be as close as the Best Western State Inn (across Allentown Road from base chapel "1"), where the Kitty Hawk Lounge catered to the military, and men's room graffiti included scrawls such as "Married cpl. wants guys for three-somes. We come here Friday or Saturday nights. She takes guys to cars for sex." Or socializing could require substantial travel throughout the area.

"It's a fractured environment," explained Major William Campbell, an Air Force Systems Command public information officer who has, like fifteen hundred base personnel each year, since moved on. Campbell himself commuted from a Northern Virginia suburb. "The first social function, I had to drive sixty-five miles one way. You just don't have office parties." When base banquets beckon, he said, "you have guys changing in the base gymnasium and in cars because it doesn't make sense to drive home, suit up, and drive back."

In this environment, base clubs are different. Among the largest in the air force, they also have unusually high percentages of retired military as members. Active military members comprised a bare majority of the O Club roster of 5,452, with the rest divided between retirees, civilians assigned to the Defense Department, thirty-one widows, and fourteen local politicians, who enjoyed its hospitality for free. The NCO Club had nearly as many retired as active air force members.

"Last year, when it came time to elect officers [who must be active members], we had an awful time," the NCO Club president told me. Most of the members of the Officers' Wives' Club also had "associate" status because their husbands had retired, and, of those whose husbands hadn't, a majority lived off base.

I met the president of the Officers' Wives during country and western night at the O Club. Dorothy Curto and her husband, Sal, lived on base. While many others came here to work and then went home, the Curtos were home and, as Dottie Curto told me, "We're a big family. I think people on the outside don't understand the military, which is too bad. We are 'them.'"

On base, however, life could be a bit sheltered. At the NCO Club, bingo—promoted as the central feature of "adult games" night—was big, and "variety dancers" did a bump and grind but, unlike their off-base counterparts, never stripped. During the O Club happy hour, draft beer was an enticing thirty-five cents, and new and vintage music shared the jukebox.

The world beyond this comfortable cocoon can be "like another planet," a lieutenant colonel's wife who works on base as a legal secretary said at the O Club, her frequent retreat. "You meet very interesting people on the base. Off the base, you meet weirdos, people coming up to you asking directions in foreign languages.

Living at Andrews, I shop mostly on the base. I'm afraid to leave it. Outside, it's very crime oriented, very scary, and the people you're afraid of are afraid of everyone else. On base, it's very unpressurized."

But hostile, outside forces keep intruding at Andrews. Several hundred base children were bused to four public primary schools in surrounding towns, while several hundred more attended two county schools on base. Shortly after my visit, the Prince George's County School Board voted to close one of them, Andrews Elementary, as part of a countywide consolidation.

"I'm sure you will enjoy Andrews and the Washington area," the base welcoming letter had promised. "Though there may be some adjustments required for those not accustomed to metropolitan living, the benefits of an assignment here cannot be matched."

Lamented one officer who knew of both the benefits and the adjustments, "It's another world beyond the fence." And the fence seemed to get smaller and smaller all the time.

At U.S. Army Fort George G. Meade, the troops have never looked to the fence for protection. Instead, it was all that stood between them and a honky-tonk strip known as Boomtown. Andrews is the president's base, but Meade, midway between Baltimore and Washington, calls itself a "people's post." And while Andrews's high-profile mission garners it fame in peacetime, Meade comes to life only in war.

Peace can be hard on camp towns, Boomtown included. The army base that kept it going is now a shadowy, slumbering giant with a historic past and an unpromising future as long as peace prevails. Even the hooker population is in decline.

"I wish we had more [hookers]. It would be good for business," the owner of the Patio Lounge along the Boomtown strip told me. "It used to be every summer new faces showed up when the reserves and the national guard came here. Now, you don't see the hookers, the reservists, or the national guard." A few years ago, he added inside his bar with its "Draft Beer / Not People" sign, he could at least count on military payday to boost his business. "Payday now, you might as well forget it," he said. "It's just the same as any other day."

Up the block, the man presiding over the Teddy Bear Arcade, bustling now only with local teenagers, agreed. "The base is empty," he said. "They got mostly civilians working over there."

In fact, twice as many civilians as military work at Meade. In the early 1980s, that meant some 16,100 civilians to 8,400 military serving on the 13,500-acre base. At the century's end, the civilian majority was even greater—21,850 to 8,800 in uniform—while the base had substantially shrunk, to 5,415 acres, as 8,100 were transferred to the Department of the Interior. Military downsizing.

"They always call us the 'sprawling' army base between Washington and Baltimore, always, 'sprawling.' It doesn't sprawl," insisted Dunbar MacNemar, a civilian employee who grew up in adjoining Odenton and entered the army here in 1942 after spending two summers as a five-dollar-a-day helper building barracks at Meade for his generation of warriors. "They can't even fire artillery anymore. There's not enough space."

It was, today, a sleepy place where "terminal colonels" were sent before they retired; it was the last duty assignment for four recent post commanders. At Tipton Army Airfield, privately owned single-engine planes appeared to outnumber the military craft. I saw few of either taking off or landing in several weekdays spent at Meade. But even Tipton would be turned over to civilians in 1999, as Anne Arundel County took ownership. The shelling range was likewise quiet. And even at rush hour, traffic flowed easily along the streets named after otherwise anonymous soldiers killed in World War I.

The "temporary" buildings raised during World War II to last five years have lasted more than fifty, but their paint was peeling and some of their windows were boarded. "Building will be demolished in the near future," said the faded, stenciled letters on the siding. Day and night, many buildings went unused. The millennial goal was to tear them all down by 2001, and demolition was proceeding apace. But 300 remained on the cusp of Y2K. There is an almost eerie, ghost-town quality about the place. It looks like an empty Hollywood set for a 1941 service comedy. A ghost post.

It wasn't always so. Shortly after the turn of the century, the future site of Fort Meade was platted as the site of a new town midway between Washington and Baltimore. Developer Richard Respass envisioned a city of ethnic communities, each self-governing. Streets were surveyed for the Irish, Italian, and Polish sections. An inter-urban railroad was planned to link "Respass City" with Washington, Baltimore, and Annapolis.

Located near the Annapolis Junction, Odenton was first of all a railroad town, named after B&O Railroad president and nineteenth-century Maryland Governor Oden Bowie. In World War I, Congress chose the area for one of sixteen cantonments across the country where those drafted into the American Expeditionary Force were trained. In this Maryland locale, the government acquired ninety-four hundred acres, including four thousand planted in fruit trees.

In the middle was the train station known as Admiral, now the site of the commissary.

The rolling countryside of Camp Meade (named after Civil War General George Gordon Meade) was "in many respects an ideal place for training troops," a 1918 construction report remarked. But the sandy roads were unfit for trucks, and construction materials were carried to work sites by half-full horse-drawn wagons.

"In the first lot of men," the report said, "the commanders of the various units took the opportunity to get rid of all their misfits, and we were sent mental deficients, foreigners who couldn't speak a word of English, fruit dealers for plumbers, barbers for foremen, etc. The division commander, however, did not allow these transfers to stand."

World War I postcard depicting barracks and army personnel at Camp Meade.

The first winter, temperatures were zero to twelve below on many days, causing pipes to freeze. The camp was completed nonetheless, by December 1917. It had room for 40,550 enlisted men and 1,535 officers. Before the war ended, 103,000 soldiers trained there, and 800 died on base in the great flu epidemic of 1918.

Myrtle Phillips had been married only three days when her husband, Roy, went to Meade from Maryland's Eastern Shore. She recalled years later, at age eighty-six, that long-ago time when she traveled to camp to see her husband off to the Great War. "It was people going and coming and loving each other," she said.

After World War I, Meade was considered for inclusion in a "National Capital Forest," to extend from the District of Columbia halfway to Baltimore and eastward to Annapolis. President Coolidge established the Meade National Forest within the base's bounds in 1925, one of four such conversions of military land, then canceled the whole deal two years later.

Civilian Conservation Corps workers of the New Deal encamped at Meade beginning in 1935. Soldiers were trained in tank warfare and schooled in baking and cooking. Between the wars, Meade's status rose from camp to fort, but, since a Fort Meade already existed in the Dakotas, it was named Fort Leonard Wood. This infuriated Pennsylvanians, who claimed General Meade, a hero of Gettysburg, as a native son. Pennsylvania politicians attached a rider to the 1929 military appropriations bill. Thus, the place became Fort George G. Meade by an act of Congress.

"Before World War II, the soldiers were looked down upon in Odenton," said Dunbar MacNemar, whose father had been a country doctor there. "The railroad track was kind of the dividing line, and the civilian population discouraged soldiers from crossing it. If they did, they would be run back to the base."

After the draft was passed in 1940, 6,191 acres were added to the base and a massive building program began as war threatened. On round-the-clock shifts, 18,000 workers completed one new building every fifty-three minutes. Altogether, 3.5 million were mobilized here, and 200 separate units passed through the base between 1940 and 1946.

Among the soldiers was Richard G. McQuay, a twenty-year-old draftee from Baltimore inducted in 1942. Three days after being inducted "you were on a troop train that came right in Rock Avenue" to the post, he remembered. Discharged from Meade in 1946, he worked at the post off and on from 1947 as a civilian. The tracks that brought him into the base were still there, but seldom used.

Glenn Miller also trained at Meade, in the star-studded Special Service Unit. So did the French Women's Army Corps. During the Battle of the Bulge, replacement troops moved rapidly through and on to the front. The wartime population peaked at 69,746 military and 3,296 civilians.

Boomtown came into being along Annapolis Road, at the northern edge of the post, in 1940. "Everybody was trying to jump over the fence to get that beer before they left good old Fort Meade for parts unknown," said McQuay, who wound up in Europe with the 15th Army. "I was one of the guys who didn't go over the fence, probably because I didn't have the dough. I used to watch 'em. There was action going on there all night long."

There was the time five hundred airborne troops, small but feisty, took over

Newly inducted draftees pass through Fort Meade in 1952 before leaving for basic training. Henry Rohland, *Washington Post*

Boomtown to protest what they said was watered down beer. They held their position for two nights, so the story goes, until the officer who trained them was recalled from leave in Annapolis to calm them down.

At their wartime peak in 1943, Boomtown businesses averaged $1,000 a week. The business dried up with the war's end: A penny arcade built in 1942 for $35,000 went on the market for just $3,500. But when the Korean War erupted in 1950, Meade was back in business, and so was Boomtown.

The cycle of boom and bust continued, through the peacetime years of the 1950s and the Vietnam war of the 1960s and 1970s. Social issues affecting the country came to Meade, as well. The base was the last in the military to maintain a racially segregated public school in the 1950s (due to the resistance of the Anne Arundel County School Board to integration). Discrimination in off-base housing became a federal case a decade later, with the government declaring segregated apartments within seven miles of Meade off-limits to military personnel. In the 1970s, actress Jane Fonda was arrested when she visited the base to protest the war in Vietnam, and an underground newspaper, *Highway 13*, flourished.

In 1957 the National Security Agency, a joint civilian-military intelligence agency, located first in a three-story building and then in an adjacent nine-story one, just off the Baltimore-Washington Parkway. Its thousands of employees came and went without making a visible impact on the Fort Meade scene.

The last armored cavalry division left the base for Texas in 1974. "After fifty-five years, the rumble of tanks is no longer heard at Fort Meade," says the sign at the Meade museum. In 1983 the 76th Engineers also departed, for Fort Drum, New York. There would be more departures.

Unlike Andrews, there was no base housing shortage (though by 1999 there were short waiting lists for family and bachelor quarters). "The day I arrived, I was offered housing," said a public affairs officer who found Meade a rather boring post with "no combat units, certainly no divisional ones."

Small units with special missions—military intelligence, a medical battalion (later disbanded), the U.S. Army Field Band—were now the order of the day at Fort Meade. Recruiting for the volunteer army for eleven states was—and still is—run from Meade, even though none of the recruits trains here. One of the most active units administered reservists. The base was the 1st Army headquarters, in charge of all reserve units from Virginia to Maine; but that command would later move to Fort Gillem, Georgia. Overall, Meade ranked as a "Class D" post.

But if war ever came again, Meade would spring to life. As many as 249 units from all over the Northeast would mobilize and embark from the post—as, in fact, 42 active duty, reserve, and National Guard units did during the Persian Gulf War. For the time being, though, the post commander told me, "the young, unattached population has gone down, there's no question about that."

Over at the old officers' club, which opened for business in 1941, when the base was bustling, a colonel in the military police paused to give me this assessment of modern-day Meade: "There's a difference in an installation that is predominantly headquarters versus a troop installation. The headquarters guy is normally screened. We don't have the troop that is substandard, from an educational, developmental standpoint. From an MP's standpoint, this means fewer problems."

Until a few years before, county and military police shared patrol duty along the Boomtown strip. There was no longer any need for that. "Community relations are cordial," said the post's community relations man.

When Fort Meade marked its fiftieth birthday in 1967, the local chamber of commerce took out a full-page ad in the post newspaper declaring, "Odenton is moving ahead with Fort Meade.... Walking together, both Odenton and Fort Meade can confidently expect a great future." The Odenton Chamber of Commerce I confronted wasn't so bullish. "Meade is no longer what it was," said Mike Davis, its president. "We don't have the military-type atmosphere of the '50s and '60s." As for Boomtown, he said, "There's no such thing anymore." The camptown had become so tame, in fact, that the Super 170 Drive-In on the east side of the base had stopped showing X-rated movies, a former staple. Fast-food chains seemed to thrive, and enterprising Korean store owners had moved in where masseuses no longer trod. Overall, Davis said, Odenton was "not decaying, but we don't have the growth. It's almost stagnation."

"Before, everything was good; we had a complete line of men's and ladies' fare, a constant trade," said the manager of Sid's Department Store ("Military Accessories...We Buy Old Gold"), which also served as a pawnshop and a dry cleaner. "Dry cleaning is the main business now," the manager said. "There used to be four or five dry cleaners on the strip. Now, there are two of us left. Business-wise, we've more or less adjusted to it."

As for the future, the manager said in the nearly empty store, "The only prospect I see of this place ever building up again is if there is another war."

Still, the ghosts of old wars lingered.

At the outbreak of World War II, several hundred enemy aliens were interned behind brick walls that still stand at Fort Meade. Later, Meade became a prisoner-of-war camp where Germans and Italians worked at patching and pressing GI clothes. Some got to take college extension courses under the auspices of the Johns Hopkins University in Baltimore.

It was the first and last war in which large numbers of foreign prisoners were interned on our shores. The POWs came first in mid-1943, after the defeat of the Afrika Korps. Successive waves followed the Normandy invasion and the final assault on Germany in 1945. More than thirteen thousand wound up in Maryland, at Meade and in eighteen other camps across the state—from Camp Somerset, near Westover on the Lower Eastern Shore, clear over to Green Ridge, near Flintsone, in Allegany County.

Most of those who waited out the war in the Free State passed through Fort Meade, which also had the nation's prisoner-of-war records center, staffed in part, after mid-1944, by Italians, whose country had switched sides. After a nest of Nazis was found to be tampering with the letters at the postal center in Texas, Italian prisoners at Meade helped handle all POW mail entering the country. Meade was also an interrogation center for newly arrived prisoners. One who talked, U-boat prisoner Werner Drechsler, was later hanged by fellow POWs at Camp Papago Park, Arizona, in March 1944.

My postwar tour of Fort Meade took me to the small Fort Meade post cemetery, which is also the burial ground for thirty-four German and two Italian POWs. They are the only World War II prisoners of war buried in Maryland. Every year, I learned, delegations from the Italian and German embassies arrive here two weeks apart to pay homage to their fallen countrymen.

Werner Henke was the only officer and the first prisoner to die here. A naval captain, Henke was shot while trying to escape on June 15, 1944. The last, Heinz Saack, a twenty-three-year-old private, had died of tuberculosis on July 4, 1947. In between were five suicides, one the day after Germany surrendered. Of the thirty-four Germans who died, twenty-seven died after their country had lost the war.

I drove to Meade to watch the Germans revere the dead on a gray, blustery November day. It was a Sunday morning, and the Germans were met at the graves by Colonel Barton M. Hayward, the post commander.

Silently, the military detachment of six marched two abreast inside the post cemetery. They laid a wreath by the tombstones, then stood at attention. In German, Commander Ulrich Fricke, the assistant naval attaché, memorialized more than those buried here. He spoke of soldiers who died on battlefields and in prison camps, but he also spoke of civilians whose race, religion, or convictions condemned them to death, and of all victims of war and violence.

The Germans in uniform saluted and stepped back. Then Colonel Hayward and the delegation from the German embassy retreated to the officers' club—built when Hitler's forces were surging across Western Europe—for champagne and lunch.

9

Yesterday's Interstate

*L*ong before surfaced highways, a dirt road linked Baltimore and Washington. The General Assembly voted in 1906 to pave it, an unprecedented use of tax monies fiercely opposed by the Eastern Shore interests. In 1925 State Road Number 1 became U.S. Route 1 in the new federal numbering system and part of the highway reaching from Calais, Maine, to Key West, Florida.

In time, Route 1 became the bane of travelers, a crowded, dangerous highway, its shoulders cluttered with billboards, its traffic slowed by crossings and curves. The new roadways that came, eventually, to replace it—the Baltimore-Washington Parkway in 1954, I-95 in 1971—were widely regarded as progress in an era when Americans were highway-hungry. But the old road was more than a bottleneck to be unclogged. It was a way of life. So what were regarded as traffic and engineering decisions to build new roads to bypass the old had scenic and social side effects.

It happened all over the country, as first the "parkways" of the 1940s and 1950s and then the interstate highways of the 1960s and 1970s marched across the land. They bisected cow pastures and cornfields, created new cloverleaf commercialism and left towns along the old alignments to wither away. For some cities, the new highways created "growth corridors." But for Baltimore and Washington, they mostly meant faster passage between the two cities and a way to bypass old Route 1.

U.S. Route 1 sign pointing the way from Sylmar to Washington. Eugene L. Meyer

Bypass-bound one Thanksgiving weekend, I renewed my acquaintance with the Maryland segment of U.S. 1. Returning to Washington from New York, I faced the unpleasant prospect of traffic jams leading to and through the tunnel bypassing Baltimore. But there was another way. The Baltimore Beltway was more roundabout but promised to be quicker in the long run. I planned to leave I-95 north of Baltimore, circle the city, and then rejoin the interstate southbound.

As luck would have it, tunnel traffic was backed up for miles at the other end, as well. So before reaching I-95 southbound, I exited the beltway one ramp early and found myself on old Route 1. It was a misty night, and the highway had an eerie quality. The road was almost empty, a forgotten byway. As I journeyed southward, my way unimpeded by other cars or trucks, I passed vintage motor courts and roadhouses of another time. I promised myself a more leisurely return trip to recapture this ribbon of forgotten America, yesterday's interstate.

With stops along the way to plumb the highway's history, my return trip from the Pennsylvania to the District of Columbia line took a week and then some, with the 33.8-mile segment between Baltimore and Washington consuming all but a day. Once, before the new highways came through to change the landscape and the lives of the people passed and bypassed, this was the corridor through which traveled most north-south interstate traffic. The Main Street of the East Coast, they called it.

In its heyday, the old highway was cursed as "Bloody Mary" for the large number of traffic accidents on it (forty-four people were killed in one year shortly before the parkway opened), and as "Billboard Lane" for its surfeit of signs. In 1934 no fewer than 1,099 billboards marred the roadscape between Baltimore and Washington. "Every known device is used to induce tourists to stop and buy sandwiches, hot drinks, cold drinks, liquor, cans of jam, used cars, and even tombstones," said the Works Progress Administration's *Guide to the Old Line State*, published in 1940. "Clotheslines hung with gaudy tufted bedspreads vie with the neon lights for attention."

The neon lights are long gone from Route 1, and so are most of the billboards. But roadside relics remained in abundance when I first revisited the highway. They included abandoned motor courts (Contee Motel, McClain's, Ridge Rest Cabins) and old-fashioned gas pumps that no longer pumped, with gas prices missing or frozen in time (32.9 cents at the Beltsville Garage). Behind a liquor store in College Park, I found half a dozen cottages used only for storage. A discarded "MOTEL" sign rested upside down against one of the surviving stone structures. In places, the highway cultures of different eras co-existed side by side: Golden Arches ("Over 23 Billion Served") and Little Taverns ("Buy 'Em by the Bag"). Gone was the dog-shaped building ("One Spot Flea Killer"), but surviving were the One Spot Grocery and a small black community nearby also known to some as One Spot. Another survivor: the neon soldier signaling Vets Liquor in Beltsville. Most of the neon was out. At night, only his eyes lit up.

Route 1 in Maryland begins in a place called Sylmar, as Old Baltimore Pike. It ends eighty-nine miles later as Baltimore Avenue, in Colmar Manor at the District of Columbia. In between, it's variously known as Belair Road, Washington Boulevard or Avenue, Baltimore Boulevard or Avenue, and as just plain Route 1.

At Sylmar, a border crossing missing from most maps, State Line Road marks the Mason-Dixon line between Maryland and Pennsylvania, even as it bisects the tiny village of half a dozen homes. A rusted railroad sign signals a grade crossing, but the right-of-way I found on either side was completely overgrown by grass. A former alignment of U.S. 1 came to a dead end at an abandoned grocery.

Here, there was little to distinguish U.S. 1 from other rolling country roads. Its two lanes were flanked by fields and a few houses but no motels. Fifty miles south lies Baltimore. Philadelphia is almost equidistant in the opposite direction. Early in the motoring age, construction of U.S. 40, a widened version of the colonial King's Highway near the Chesapeake shore, largely spared this stretch from development. The farmscape here is broken only by a rough and narrow passage across the Philadelphia Electric Company's Conowingo Dam over the Susquehanna River. So poorly maintained was the road over the dam, built in the 1920s, that, soon after I traversed it, trucks were barred from crossing, and the entire roadway was eventually closed to all traffic for safety reasons and repair.

Below Conowingo, I paused at a roadside meadow, where the producers of a religious revival readied themselves for an evening performance under the big tent. Seventeen miles south of the dam, a bypass appears seemingly out of nowhere. It takes the impatient traveler around the Harford County seat of Bel Air. Once, before U.S. 40 was widened, before I-95, and before the Bel Air bypass, touring motorists drove straight through town on old Route 1, and, sometimes, as I did, they stopped.

An era in highway travel began by chance just north of Bel Air in 1921, when Felix N. Irwin, who did not like to farm, left for Chicago to sell cemetery plots. A doctor and his wife, driving their touring car from Boston to Washington for the cherry blossoms, stopped by the Irwin farm a mile from town. It was a time when interstate auto travel was still a novelty, and places to stay were few and far between. Maye Irwin, Felix's wife, couldn't refuse their request to pitch a tent on her property. When Irwin returned from Chicago, his cemetery venture summarily buried after two and a half months, he found a field covered with tents and carpenters busily building a grocery store on his property. In her husband's absence, Maye Irwin had not been idle. An entrepreneur above all, Felix Irwin quickly saw the possibilities.

"Oh boy, he got busy," said Maye Irwin, a gracious and gregarious if fragile woman of eighty when I stopped at the white farmhouse she still called home. "He didn't mind working on the farm then." She laughed at the memory.

By the time Irwin died in 1969, at the age of eighty-four, the family owned and operated three motels on old Route 1 in Maryland, their fates closely intertwined with change along the old highway. Their story is part of the story of a nation transformed by cars.

They had come out of the North Carolina mountains, with little formal education, from a backwoods life in rough-hewn cabins. Felix Irwin had worked in his father's water mill, hauled produce by wagon over the mountains, contemplated mining in West Virginia, tried farming in South Dakota and logging in British Columbia. After three years as a lumberman, Irwin, a frugal man who saved his wages, returned to North Carolina to marry Maye on January 28, 1911. She was not yet thirteen. He was twenty-three.

Irwin bought a store near home, sold it, and bought another one in nearby Virginia. It was the second decade of the twentieth century, and Irwin soon joined a migration of a thousand Southern families, many of them Tar Heels, to Harford County, Maryland. Like the rest, he was lured by the reports of a friend who preceded him of cheap land, rich soil, and money-making markets.

"He didn't like a farm to work on himself," Maye Irwin said. "He didn't want to do the milking of cows. He used to say, 'I'll use my head, not my back.'" So he hired men, often others from North Carolina, to work the farm while he went into real estate. In 1919 he bought a farm he did not sell, the 210-acre Major's Choice, where his widow lived in their 1834 farmhouse.

What was to become U.S. 1 was then "the Conowingo state road," according to Irwin's description in a 1920 booklet published by the local newspaper. "Few farms are as ideally located as this one," said the advertisement touting the place he was then trying to sell. And, indeed, for the motor court business the Irwins later pioneered, the locale couldn't have been better.

After Maye Irwin allowed the Boston doctor to pitch his tent, he returned with six other cars. Five farmhands, who lived in a former slave house on the property, converted a chicken coop into a luggage building. The tent charge became fifty cents a night, but soon there were also four corrugated tin cabins, with "just enough room for them to put their pad mattresses on the ground," for a one-dollar nightly fee.

A dozen wooden cabins sprung up, later increased to twenty-three. To the grocery store was added a restaurant with twelve hotel rooms upstairs—one even had a private bath—and nine gas pumps were installed out front. There was a recreation building, where you could throw balls at likenesses of cartoon characters Maggie and Jiggs; a stream-fed swimming pool; three outdoor barbecue spits that could roast five hams at once; a dollhouse on the lawn; and, by the early 1930s, pony rides, a small zoo, a driving range, archery, and miniature golf. Del Haven Hotel and Cabins, it was called, and it boasted "Complete Hotel Service. Deluxe Gas. Heated, Electric Lighted Cabins (Running Water)."

They came by the carload to this unique stopping place on Route 1, in their Overlands and Essexes and Pierce Arrows and Model Ts, from as close as Baltimore and as far as Wilmot, South Dakota. For a room in the 1930s, they paid from $1.50 for two to $4.00 for four people per night. At first there was a central bathroom. Later, individual bathrooms were installed in each cabin.

Not all the transients were tourists. During the depths of the Depression, there were the Bonus Marchers, World War I veterans out of work and on their way to Washington to ask for help. "I was so sorry for them," Maye Irwin said in her soft southern accent, "and they wouldn't have shoes on their feet goin' to Washington. They'd come up and they'd want to chop wood, you know, to get a sandwich, and I said, 'You get a sandwich, but you don't have to chop wood.' We'd give 'em every old shoe, clothes, and they certainly did appreciate it."

It was, as Felix (Bud) Irwin, Jr., and his sister, Felicia Irwin Jackson, recalled, a "family-managed" business. The five daughters were waitresses and maids. Bud Irwin "did everything," including washing the pool on Mondays. None received a salary or allowance. That was Felix Irwin's way. "We're all family," he would tell Bud. "Anything you need, you get out of the cash drawer, but don't spend it foolishly." They rarely spent it, foolishly or otherwise.

Despite the Depression, business at the Bel Air cottages boomed. But an improved U.S. 40 threatened to take away much of the north-south traffic. Since most of the cars were Washington-bound, the Irwins looked for a new location south of Baltimore. What they found were ten acres of weeds and briars and the Revolutionary War-era Rhodes Tavern said to have been visited by George Washington. The property was also on Route 1, in Berwyn, just above the future route of the Capital Beltway. To Maye Irwin forty years later, it was still "the new place."

The property had an "old-time well with a bucket," she said. The tavern had "an old-time fireplace to bake bread and cook in, and down in the cellar was where they kept the slaves. There was one place for them to put their chin—the boys destroyed that when they cleaned the cellar out—and chains to lock their feet."

By 1937 they had turned the site into the Del Haven White House Cottages, with fifty brick units. It was one of the largest, fanciest motor courts in the country.

"This was a big deal then," said Bud Irwin, who managed the place from 1947 to 1957. "No tourist court in the U.S. then had as many units, brick construction, ceramic tile bathrooms, carports between the units." Sadly, or perhaps just inevitably, the cottages were closed by 1999, left forlornly to decay behind a twisted chain link fence, while the historic tavern was shuttered. A few hundred feet south a new Holiday Inn, owned by Florida interests, had opened by the Beltway entrance ramp.

A picture postcard of the Del Haven White House Cottages in Berwyn in their 1940s glory, and a recent photograph of its historic tavern. Eugene L. Meyer

The American Automobile Association's Northeastern Tour Book for 1941 called the Bel Air Del Haven "one of the better camps of northeastern U.S." and the Berwyn Del Haven "among the finest in the northeast." The AAA book neglected to note a feature common to both places and to most other establishments on Route 1 in the Free State of Maryland: They were racially segregated.

"We didn't have a restroom for blacks" at Bel Air, Bud Irwin said. "The sign said 'White Only.' There was carry-out food only for blacks. At College Park [Berwyn], we didn't have 'White Only' signs, but we did not rent to colored. That was another reason we left the 'No Vacancy' sign on. We never accepted black. I'm not saying this with any pride. It's just the way it was."

Catering to whites only, the Berwyn motel did exceedingly well. "I was there from 1939 until I was married in 1947," Felicia Jackson said, "and during the summer months, it was filled through reservations."

Times changed. Felix Irwin "could see the economic obsolescence" of the Bel Air complex "coming fast," his son said. He sold it in 1941 to a brother, who in turn sold it outside the family after World War II. The Bel Air cottages continued in operation until the 1960s, when they were replaced by a small shopping center called Del Plaza.

Times changed, too, at the other Del Haven. The opening of the Baltimore-Washington Parkway in 1954 had brought a sharp decline in Route 1 traffic, and old motels were undergoing a new era of modernization to compete with the latest generation. Bud Irwin, by then president of the Maryland Motel Association, got the word from AAA. He would have to add a restaurant and room phones or be dropped from the book. His father balked, but Bud Irwin pushed ahead, building a restaurant where the gas pumps had been. When it came time to pay his father's $220,000 bequest to twenty-two grandchildren in 1975, he was forced to sell the restaurant.

Anxious to be on his own, Bud Irwin teamed up with a friend who was dissatisfied in his father-in-law's lumber business. The two men went into real estate. One of Bud Irwin's first sales was the Royal Pine Tourist Court, a ten-unit motel dating from the early 1940s and located midway between Berwyn and the University of Maryland on Route 1. At the time, the youngest of the Irwin daughters had just married Ed Sims, an Alexandria man with plans to take his bride and his law degree to California. To keep them at home, Bud Irwin gave the couple the down payment on the Royal Pine. "I wound up with practically no commission because it was in the family," sighed Bud Irwin, still slightly bitter two decades later.

The Ed Sims I met was a tall, athletic-looking man of forty-nine. He was busy managing the Del Haven White House Cottages—jointly owned by the six Irwin children—and expanding the old Royal Pine into a 115-unit Best Western. "You have to work a little harder at it now," he said, seated in a chair on the motel's front lawn. "You can't just sit there and wait for business. You have to go out and promote.... I hate to think about it, but I guess I'm one of the old-timers on the road."

Bud Irwin paid tribute to his brother-in-law as a "really good operator," so good he wanted him to run a 240-unit motel Irwin planned to build at the intersection of Route 198 and I-95 near Laurel, the largest Route 1 town, located midway between Washington and Baltimore.

"There will be no other motel within sight of I-95," Bud Irwin beamed. Then, sounding remarkably like his father describing the Bel Air location nearly sixty years before, he added, "It is one of the number-one sites on the East Coast."

They are an independent breed, these motel men and women. Take John T. Baltzell, for example. He opened the original thirty units of Colonial Plaza, opposite the Del Haven White House Cottages, on Pearl Harbor Day, December 7, 1941. When I first stopped by, in 1977, he was eighty years old. In 1941, he happily recalled, he had been a Pathé newsreel cameraman assigned to the White House. It was a career that began in the Harding era and ended in 1943, when he was fired "because I was here [at the motel] when I was supposed to be in Pittsburgh on a story."

Over the years, Baltzell had filled his ten acres with more buildings, to accommodate church, school, and scout groups that came from around the country to tour the nation's capital. More than one hundred people could camp in "dormettes," tiny, tent-shaped closets with cots located inside the skating rink Baltzell built in 1958 and closed in 1963 when construction of a Capital Beltway ramp blocked the entrance. For regular overnighters, rates were comparable to other motels, but groups were charged only three or four dollars per person.

"We are fully aware that we are not a Hilton Hotel or a Holiday Inn," Baltzell wrote group leaders. "There have been many offers to buy Colonial Plaza, all refused. We realize that if we sell, our 'pet' dormitories will be quickly replaced by a group of high-rise apartments or a multistory motel with sky-high rates. Our low-cost, budget accommodations will be no more."

Plump and puckish, Baltzell was a man alone who seemed to treat many of his twenty-five employees like family. After he died in 1982, his modest motel carried on without him. But not forever. Today, it's gone, replaced by mid-rise apartments, with balcony views of the Beltway.

Route 1 motel operators aspiring to classier clientele derisively referred to Baltzell's Colonial Plaza as the "Beltsville Recreation Center." This had not bothered its owner. "I'm VP. I'm in charge of the vice," he greeted me, laughing at his own joke. "Like they say on Capitol Hill, I don't care what you say about me but say something," he said. He then handed me a letter he had received from an anonymous patron. It said, "I have just lost a very dear friend—someone who filled a need in my life and lifted my spirits physically, mentally, and emotionally. We met late in life, had good families, and wanted to hurt no one.... You were all the 'home' we had together—a place to be alone for the few hours we could take from the lives we were patterned into.... I thank you for providing the service you do. Look gently on those who come here. It may mean more to them than you ever realize."

Across Route 1, the Irwins's Del Haven White House Cottages required "positive identification of all local guests," to keep out prostitutes and "shack-ups," the desk clerk said. "We'll gladly rent to local people if they're man and wife," he explained. "It's not discrimination. It's a class rule."

Locals of all classes were welcomed at the College Park Motel, to the naked eye just an unpretentious collection of sixteen small cabins and a big house with four apartments. The main building was first a residence, built by a man named Beckwith in the 1920s. A second owner added a front and a rear porch and, finally, some cabins to cater to Washington-bound tourists.

"There was a huge tree there beside the road," recalled Beulah Keefauver, who with her husband Earl built their large brick home on the hill behind the hotel in 1924. "Someone hit that tree one night and it killed him," she said. "That tree is long gone." Tragedy seemed to plague the place over the years. I called it "Heartbreak Hotel."

Peggy Wangner, the woman in charge, had come to know "every cop in the county. It got to be where I'd walk in the courthouse door and they'd say, 'Hi, what's new this week?'" For years, she kept a diary, which read like a police blotter, detailing domestic disputes, dogfights, fires, suspected kidnapping of children, bounced checks, broken windows, death by natural causes and apparent suicide. Some entries from her spiral notebooks:

Jan. 20, 1976. 5:30 p.m. Mr. Mayhew called rescue squad for a lady in her room. Rescue squad took her from here at 5:30 p.m. She was drunk and out of her mind...

March 11, 1977. Found man dead. Truck driven eighteen hours on road. Wanted to sleep. Beltsville Rescue Squad said maybe alcohol and pot...and he fell and cracked head open... Autopsy: death from acute alcoholism...

April 7, 1977. No one answered in one cabin. TV on, curtains down. Man face up, lying on the bed with blood on his hands and shotgun standing on floor upright next to his bed... The sheets, bedspread, mattress, bed pad, blankets and pillows were ruined with blood.

A single day, December 19, 1975, alone filled several pages. It began around 8:30 a.m. when a man at the motel (on a weekend pass, it turned out, from a mental hospital) phoned his counselor to say he planned to kill himself. When the counselor arrived, Wangner noted, the man "was breaking windows, etc." Her husband "went to the room and the man slashed both his wrists and started throwing things." Police arrived at 11:40 a.m., the rescue squad ten minutes later. At 5 p.m., she listed the damage: bloody mattress pad, bedspread, pillow cases, blanket, towels, broken wall mirror. "No chance of recovering," she wrote. "He had no money."

Two hours later, her sixteen-year-old son "came running up to the office and asked me who was living on the porch...because some man is dumping about twenty-five dogs in crates in a room behind the wall." The tenant was a woman in her sixties who, Wangner wrote, "had put these twenty-five dogs in with different vets and never paid the bill, so this vet dumped them on her doorstep. I telephoned her immediately and told her the animals had to be out by morning."

When the animals were still there by noontime, uncaged, the motel manager called police, who arrived soon afterward. The woman then "proceeded to start taking two or three dogs at a time and walked up and down U.S. 1," Wangner recorded. "She also took a lot of them in a taxi. She again deposited them with different vets. Last I heard, the Hyattsville Animal Hospital finally had to put six of the dogs to sleep and she was suing them for this."

And so it went at the College Park Motel, home also to students and teachers at the nearby University of Maryland and at whose door the county welfare department regularly deposited the homeless and tempest-tossed in need of emergency housing at the taxpayer's expense. "Twenty-four hours a day, if we have the room, we take 'em," the resident manager said.

Months after my visit, the forty-four-year-old Wangner left the excitement of Route 1 for a staid apartment building in Washington's Foggy Bottom. And shortly after that there was a fire at the College Park Motel in which two small children died.

On my sentimental journey down old Route 1, I stopped also at the Skyline Motel, at the top of Buttermilk Hill in Elkridge. The wooden sign remained at the side of the road, but it was faded and the old motel above it looked abandoned. It wasn't. Daniel Duffy, seventy-six, and his wife, Dorothy, ten years younger, continued to live in the office section of the motel they bought in 1952 and closed in 1957. They closed it, they said, because the financial and psychic expense of modernizing a dying business was just not worth it. And besides, they added, they would have had to integrate. "We never did" accept blacks, Dorothy Duffy said. "When they passed that [public accommodations] law, we had to take everyone."

If most of the Route 1 motels had remained in business after integration, few of them had earlier bucked the Jim Crow tradition (not mandated by law) that permeated Maryland into the 1960s. Two that did were the Cedar Motel, built near "One Spot Flea Killer" in the early 1940s, and the Valencia Motel in Laurel.

"We didn't have that much to offer, so whoever came got a room here," said Morris Pet, the sixty-seven-year-old proprietor of the Cedar Motel. "Not too many white people came in because they always looked for the better places." When the Cedar was new, it offered a bed, a chair, and a coal stove for heat. When I saw it, it was still "not modernized" compared to the competition, the owner said. Its rates, which were three dollars a night in the 1940s, had risen only

Hillcrest Motor Court

Promotional material for two of Rt. 1's once-popular hotels—
Hillcrest Motor Court and Colonial Plaza in College Park.

to six dollars by the late 1970s, the cheapest motel on Route 1 between Washington and Baltimore.

Ida Fischer "always thought it was terrible that black people didn't have the right to stay everyplace," she said. "I was one of the first to be glad to accommodate them." When it opened in 1947, her Valencia Motel also offered more amenities than the Cedar Motel, including rubber-tiled floors, steel furniture, tiled showers, room radios, and, after a while, coin-operated television.

Whatever the owners' intentions, few blacks chanced humiliation by stopping at motels that weren't clearly identified as "Colored." Those that were went unlisted in the AAA guidebooks. While the auto association campaigned against billboards and for the Baltimore-Washington Parkway, staffers I consulted could find no mention in old issues of the club magazine of the racial barriers that were an integral part of life on U.S. 1.

The Jim Crow signs were gone now, of course, along with three of the black motels. A mile or less up the road from the Cedar Motel, I found Mary McClain sitting in the shade of a large sycamore tree on a hill overlooking the highway, her dog Duke resting under a picnic table. A dignified and self-possessed black woman approaching seventy, she was once the proprietor, with her late husband Luther B. McClain, Sr., of McClain's Motel and Restaurant.

The twelve units they built in 1949 were mostly unused after her husband died in 1968. But when McClain's was open, she said with pride, "the black people traveling, they found a place to stay." Now the restaurant was also closed, although upstairs rooms were rented to four tenants. It had been a good-sized restaurant, remembered by blacks familiar with Route 1's past just as Mrs. McClain described it: "The best place to eat." On a later visit, I found a Suisse Chalet, a chain motel, where McClain's had been. The only reminder of the past was a street sign. It said "McClains Avenue."

Gone, along with McClain's, were the Muirkirk Inn, its cabins razed and its soul food turned Mexican, and Bass's Motel, closed after the mysterious fatal shooting in 1976 of owner Lee Bass. Surviving were Hall's Motel in Elkridge ("Radio-Bath-TV"), always white-owned but always open to blacks and still serving a largely black clientele ("A lot of the older people just like it and come back," owner Charles H. Heber, Sr., told me), and, south of McClain's, the Log Cabin, a truck stop catering mostly to blacks with its menu of chitterlings, maw, and ribs. Log Cabin customers, drawn by word of mouth from the interstate, included a smattering of whites. I found the mood relaxed, as truckers and waitresses exchanged banter and smiles. "A lot of truckers come over here to eat and they tell others about us. We never really advertised," said Elizabeth Garrett, the owner with her husband, Melvin, the chef, since they bought the place in 1956. "Home-cooked meals, that's the attraction."

My trip southward along U.S. 1 had, almost incidentally, revealed how much Americans—and Marylanders—had changed, in their expectations and in their relationships with one another. The "obsolete" motor courts were no longer a match for the luxurious new motels, and racial segregation was also obsolete, at least in its rawest forms. Prejudices had subsided but not entirely disappeared when I rerouted myself down U.S. 1. Racial tension remained a subtle undercurrent of life. It was a tension born largely of white fear of crime, allegedly perpetrated by "locals," a code word for blacks from Baltimore and Washington. Several motel owners and merchants who complained about "locals" spoke of isolated incidents as though they amounted to a crime wave. But state police at the Waterloo Barracks on U.S. 1 said most of their calls were for minor things, like a Greyhound bus driver's request for help with a drunk who had missed his stop.

The shifting tides of traffic have taken a toll on whatever glamour was attached to the old highway. Not far from the police barracks, Pool's Evergreen Inn, built in 1936, and Motor Court, added a year later, was once a premiere place to stop on U.S. 1. It was now, the owner's son allowed, "a hole in the wall, just a local joint waiting for somebody to come along with some money" to tear it down and develop the twenty-six-acre site. "Ain't no bars on I-95," was a trucker's reason for being in Pool's one weekday afternoon.

But when the motor court was built, with real redwood from California, and, thereafter, when it was the first on the highway to provide room phones, the Evergreen was something special. It was said to have been a hangout for big-time gamblers and high-class prostitutes. In the roadhouse, big bands played upstairs (now a storage area), and affluent patrons dined below or occupied an outside beer garden. Such celebrities as Marilyn Monroe, Joe DiMaggio, Dorothy Lamour, Jane Russell, and Art Mooney, the band leader, were said to have been customers.

The place was owned, then, by "Mr. Guy" Constantino. A notorious numbers man, according to Pool and police, he also owned the land on which Laurel Racetrack was built. Tile mosaics of a racehorse and trotter on the second story exterior were part of Mr. Guy's legacy. In 1959 Norris (Pappy) Pool bought the Evergreen. He was no stranger to the highway, having acquired the Tip Top Motor Court in Elkridge eleven years earlier, at which time he was already a veteran of some seniority on U.S. 1.

"I made my living on Route 1 since 1932, one way or another," said Pappy Pool, who was born in 1915. "I towed cars, then was in the electric sign business.

I've enjoyed living on this road, seen a lot of changes."

In this sign business, he had lit up Baltimore's Block, that downtown tenderloin strip, and Gwynn Oak, an amusement park west of the city where the huge Social Security complex now stands, and he had done the same for the motels and restaurants of Route 1. "I sort of faded out when plastic came in and I couldn't climb ladders anymore," he said.

His Evergreen sign remained, although no longer lit up. It was designed to tell the motorist all there was to know: "Pool's Evergreen Inn / Cocktails / Bar / Pizza / Motor Court / Cut-Rate / Sandwiches / Hot Dogs / Carry-Out / Beer / Wines / Liquors / Miniatures."

To his utter amazement, Pappy Pool had won respect from a new generation that valued his life's work as art. The Evergreen Inn had become a highlight of Route 1 tours run by a group calling itself the Society for Commercial Archeology. And when Howard County wanted to enforce an anti-sign ordinance enacted during the days of "highway beautification," the sign aficionados succeeded in "grandfathering" Pappy Pool.

"At least once a month, somebody takes pictures," he said. "It amuses me because I have no education. I got into the sign business because nobody would hire me."

Signs of the times along U.S. Route 1 in Beltsville, Elkridge, and Laurel. Eugene L. Meyer

If the ghosts of the past continued to haunt the highway, there was, I discovered, life after death for yesterday's interstate. The tourist trade is gone, but Route 1 has survived as a born-again local artery. In addition to sixteen trailer parks and a few motels made into apartments, I counted a growing number of new industrial parks and truck terminals, seven or so between Laurel and Baltimore, including the Maryland Wholesale Food Center for the Baltimore-Washington region. By 1984 even the Baltimore Fish Market had moved to a site off old Route 1.

While the eighteen-wheelers were being loaded and unloaded, the truckers stayed at places like the Tip Top Motor Court, with hot tub and movies ("When all is said and done, our hot tub is tip top"), which was now owned by Pappy Pool's son, or the Ritz Motel (in-room movies) or the Terrace Motel ("satellite movies"). Foot-Long Hot Dog was nearby. The Elkridge Restaurant ("Truckers Welcome") was next to the Tip Top. The trucking terminals had given the old places on Route 1 in Elkridge a new lease on life.

South of Laurel there are no trucking terminals, and not even a five-dollar-a-night bed could lure the long-haul traffic from I-95 to the Transi-Truck Center at Contee. When it opened in 1950, there was no other major highway, of course, and J.W. Lyles's place did a booming business on both sides of Route 1. By 1977 the northbound truck stop had been replaced by a Ford dealership, and business on the southbound side had "dropped quite a bit" since the interstate had opened, the restaurant manager said.

The Transi-Truck Center owners were alarmed about reports of a new full-service truck stop going up above Laurel, near the Columbia-Jessup Holiday Inn, where the old road more closely parallels the interstate. "It would do a lot of damage to this place," predicted the bookkeeper at Contee.

When it finally opened in December of 1979, the Truckers Inn did not advertise its proximity to U.S. 1—who would care, even though the new place was closer to the old road than to the new one? Instead, the billboards and brochures all said, "Interstate 95 & Maryland Route 175."

How could the Transi-Truck Center ever compete against this thirteen-acre reservation with its five-story, 150-unit motel, swimming pool and whirlpool, its Eighteen Wheeler Lounge featuring live country music, its twelve service lanes and four attendants pumping 100,000 gallons of diesel fuel each week?

"We don't have diesel right now," Dorallen Davis, who bought the Contee center in 1980, told me. "But we have home cooking." So short-haul truckers from the nearby industrial parks in Laurel and Beltsville stopped for food and fuel, and independent long-haul drivers who couldn't afford to pay $32.00 a night for a room at the new place bunked in Contee, at the new low rate of $12.50. But it was not to be. Dorallen Davis went bankrupt in March 1982 and shut down a month later. "It was I-95 and Truckers Inn," she said. "We just couldn't hang on." Another owner lasted six months. After that, the old truck stop became a Pontiac / GMC dealership.

Before traffic so overwhelmed Route 1 that the case for a new highway became irresistible, there were repeated efforts to accommodate the increasing traffic on the old road itself. From the very beginning the highway, it seemed, was constantly being paved, widened, repaved, or straightened. Numerous bends known locally as "Dead Man's Curve" were eliminated. In one case, the name still appears on a highway map as a tiny road that now serves, in effect, as the driveway for Hall's Motel. Other vestiges of the old route remain, as Old Baltimore Pike, just east of Route 1 and the train tracks in Beltsville (north of Washington), and as Old Washington Road in Elkridge (south of Baltimore). Elsewhere, the new overpasses and cloverleafs have all but obliterated communities.

In Savage, the road work would continue years later. When I passed through in 1977, an expansive cloverleaf connecting Routes 1 and 32 had long been planned. But while the service station nearby was known as the "Cloverleaf Exxon," the enterprise hardly seemed imminent. There was, on the west side, a boat yard, far from any navigable water, where hobbyists were building half a dozen sailboats up to fifty-two feet long. Across Route 1 was a sliver of former highway, off to one side and below grade, overgrown with weeds and grass. It seemed to me, at the time, that this scene would endure forever. But nearly seven years after I first noticed these odd landmarks, the entire area was bulldozed and excavated. The expansive cloverleaf had finally arrived, and only the Exxon remained.

A few miles south, in Laurel, old-timers still refer to Route 1 northbound through town as "the bypass." Before Second Street was extended in 1952 to become the one-way "bypass," U.S. 1 was two-way, two-lane Washington Avenue through the town. The coming of the bypass left an island of trailer parks and businesses facing streams of traffic on both sides. It literally cut the Valencia Motel in half, making life especially tough on maids, who had to dash across the highway in order to clean all the rooms.

To drivers especially, the Baltimore-Washington Parkway promised everything that Route 1 did not: no traffic lights, no dangerous curves, no unsightly clutter. So, naturally, before the parkway was a sure thing, the Route 1 businesses formed the Baltimore-Washington Boulevard Association to try and stop it. "All they would talk about in the papers was how dangerous it was on Route 1," recalled Bessie Morell, who opened the Honeymoon Gift Shop in 1936 at the intersection of Routes 1 and 32, where she was still in business and still embittered nearly half a century later. "They never published the wrecks on the parkway."

After losing the battle of the parkway, the Route 1 merchants regrouped and tried, also without success, to have trucks allowed on the new highway in order to make the old one more attractive to cars. They even posted signs on U.S. 40 north of Baltimore that said "Follow Historic Route 1" and had the toll takers at the Baltimore Harbor Tunnel distribute Route 1 fliers.

The merchants successfully opposed official plans to designate the parkway "U.S. 1" and rename the old road "Alternate Route 1." It was only a symbolic victory. And just as things were beginning to pick up again on the old road due to heavy traffic on the new one, along came the interstate.

At both ends of the older highway, Route 1 has become Alternate 1; the newer, four-lane Southwestern Boulevard out of Baltimore and Rhode Island Avenue into Washington now bear the official U.S. 1 stamp. At the District line, when the parkway came, Baltimore Avenue became an extension of Bladensburg Road NE to the World War I Peace Cross erected at Bladensburg in 1926.

Traffic backed up from flash flooding at Peace Cross, where control of the Anacostia River became a political hot potato in the 1940s. There were also grade crossings to contend with, like the one in Hyattsville over the B&O Railroad tracks, before it was bridged in 1929. A steep, twisting bridge, the span a few miles outside of Washington was a widely hailed "grade separation" when it was built. But it was not hailed by everybody. "My father-in-law hated that bridge," declared Margaret Bowers Bright, from behind her desk at Anath J. Bright Realtors. "It ruined Hyattsville, divided it in half." The house where she worked had been her parents' home, converted, like many former houses built along old Route 1, into an office.

Across the B&O overpass, Gasch's Funeral Home is still at the corner of Baltimore Avenue and Emerson Street, where it has been since 1902. Gone, however, are the nine bars that had flourished before urban renewal came to Colmar Manor on Route 1's "Bladensburg strip" between the Fort Lincoln Cemetery and Berk Motley's Sirloin Room, whose owner continued to serve up large portions of old-fashioned vaudeville hoke and big band music along with prime rib and seafood well into the 1990s before this rustic-looking landmark shut down; on July 23, 1999, Berk also passed on.

"In those days," said Ernest (Mike) Mulligan, Colmar Manor's septuagenarian police chief of the once notorious Bladensburg strip, "the District bars stopped selling whiskey Saturdays at midnight, while the [Maryland] bars stayed open until 2 a.m. Around 11 p.m., people started coming over. During World War II, there was standing room only, and the usual number of fights."

A decade before the war, Mulligan told me, it was his unhappy lot to meet the Bonus Marchers at the D.C. line on their way out of Washington. While Maye Irwin's kindnesses had helped them on their way to Washington, his thankless job had been to keep them moving on the way out.

The old police chief remembered, too, Jimmy's Place, right on the District line in Maryland and just outside his jurisdiction. The club, owned by James A. LaFontaine before his death in 1949, was touted as the biggest gambling house between Sarasota, New York, and Miami, Florida. The place was eventually torched by the Cottage City Fire Department in 1955, as part of a drill. A gas station stands there today. There is no plaque.

The older people remember LaFontaine as sort of a benevolent rogue, the kind of person who, as Berk Motley put it, "if you couldn't afford milk for the kids, would hand you your money back and tell you not to gamble anymore."

"During the Depression, he did a lot for people in this community," Mike Mulligan said. "If people needed a ton of coal or groceries, he provided them, which you couldn't get from bankers in those days. You got to give the Devil his due."

The same could be said for old Route 1.

10

Harbor Tunnel Vision

*B*efore the tunnel, there was Baltimore. Not the sparkling, spanking new city of the Inner Harbor and Harborplace, of Charles Center, urban homesteading, and ethnic festivals—a national model for urban living—but grimy, old, rowhouse Baltimore. It was a negative image implanted in the minds of generations of interstate travelers who threaded their way through the city on U.S. 1 bound for Washington or Philadelphia or New York. Baltimore, to them, was simply "the bottleneck."

"In the thirties, travel bureaus were reportedly routing clients from Philadelphia through Gettysburg to Washington in order to avoid the bottleneck," according to a state roads commission history published in 1958. The administrator of the US. Bureau of Public Roads was said to have called Baltimore in 1944 "the worst city in the United States, as far as I know, on the matter of taking care of its through traffic."

And then came the tunnel, first authorized by Congress in 1938 and finally opened on November 29, 1957. "White marble steps are a thing of the past to travelers through Baltimore," gushed the state roads commission. Promotion literature promised the eighteen-mile system of approaches to and passage under the Patapsco River would "whisk north-south traffic through the metropolitan area at open country speed."

One brochure urged motorists to "Save Time / Avoid City Traffic / Use the New Baltimore Harbor Tunnel." On the cover, cars whizzed out of the tunnel's south portal. "For years," the brochure said, "Baltimore's crowded streets and many stoplights have formed a roadblock for through traffic from New York to Washington. With the opening of the New Tunnel-Expressway System, this bottleneck is forever broken."

But almost as soon as it opened, the 1.7-mile twin-tube tunnel itself became the bottleneck.

Each December, signs over the toll plaza wish travelers Merry Christmas and Happy New Year, and many needed all the good cheer they could muster to get through the tunnel in good spirits as traffic backed up for miles at both ends. Its five million gritty white tiles and sometimes pungent odor made it seem to some like the world's longest urinal.

To be cursed and maligned and avoided at all costs—including $750 million for a new tunnel to bypass the old—seems a sad fate for the tube touted as "this magnificent feat of engineering, utility, and convenience...one of the modern wonders of the world" by Baltimore Mayor Thomas D'Alesandro during the dedication ceremonies.

Within a year came calls for a second tunnel, and an option was acquired to buy 15.6 acres near Hawkins Point, just in case. After lengthy controversy, the Francis Scott Key Bridge, part of the Baltimore Beltway, was built there instead. Traffic in the Harbor Tunnel dipped, but not for long. Within a few years, work would begin elsewhere on a brand-new Fort McHenry Tunnel, to take the motorist under, over, and through the city on a completed I-95. Ironically, this was the route originally pushed for by "Baltimore city interests" seeking local as well as interstate service.

The once-wondrous Patapsco River Tunnel, as the original tube is still called in annual bond reports, cost $138 million to build. Twenty-one sections, each 300 feet long, were laid in a trench between the industrial city areas of Fairfield and Canton. The Norwegian-born engineer in charge delayed the laying of the first section nine times because he wasn't satisfied with the grade of sand spread along the trench's bottom.

"I am building you a tunnel to last one thousand years," said Ole Singstad, the master tunnel builder.

Henry Hopkins, later chief of maintenance, told me that on opening day a local undertaker provided the chairs, complete with funeral parlor fliers—Hopkins had to remove them—and employees were given brand-new blue coveralls they had to turn in after the ceremony. The first patron was a man remembered only as "Mr. First," whose mania took him to the front of every line leading to a new traffic facility. His prior conquest had been a new bridge in South America.

Early on, Hopkins said, a junk man with a horse and cart was denied entrance to the tunnel because his rig couldn't maintain the minimum speed. The minimum speed has doubled since then, from twenty to forty miles an hour, but the tunnel toll—used to maintain the approaches as well as the tunnel itself—changed little over the years, from forty cents for interstate travelers and twenty-five cents for commuters to seventy-five and thirty-five cents a quarter of a century later. The next increase, on July 1, 1985, brought the toll to one dollar and forty cents, respectively, where it remains today.

"We are definitely one of the lower-charging toll facilities," said Bernard (Bernie) W. Jedrowicz, the Harbor Tunnel director, in his office overlooking the toll plaza and commanding a view of the Baltimore skyline. "New York just upped its tolls. The Jersey Turnpike, you gotta get your checkbook out...."

The tunnel may be a bargain, but there are some drivers you couldn't pay to drive through it. These are the victims of tunnelphobia, a common ailment, I learned from Jerilyn Ross, director of the Phobia Program in Washington. "There is a feeling the tunnel is never going to end," she said. "There's a fear of being trapped, of losing control, a general feeling they can't get out. It's an overwhelming panic." The tunnel looms so large for such people that driving through it fear-free is often a goal for patients who enter the program.

A related tunnel terror stems from the notion that the tube leaks, even though it sits buried under twenty-five feet of muck. This fear is fed by icicles that form from condensation of hot exhaust gases in the air duct above the traffic portion of the tube. "I used to go around to schools, and the first question was, 'Has a ship ever hit the tunnel?'," Bernie Jedrowicz, guilty only of tunnel vision, sighed. "I had an idea we should send an employee dressed in a scuba suit with tanks on his back and a flashlight into the tunnel, as if he were looking for a leak, to speed drivers through. That idea was rejected."

Tunnelphobiacs beware—entrance/exit to the Baltimore Harbor Tunnel. Maryland Transportation Authority

For the worst cases of tunnelphobia, the authorities supply a driver or, on occasion, a police escort. Among those who dreaded the tunnel was Mary Jedrowicz, the director's wife. "Most of the time, I only drive through there if I really have to," she said. "If possible, I'll take the long way around, just go through the city to get away from the tunnel. I don't know. I guess I just get claustrophobia. It seems like the walls are coming toward you. So I just hope I don't have to slow down, and I look at the light at the end and get out as fast as I can."

If Mary Jedrowicz suffered from tunnelphobia, her husband's affliction was just the opposite. He couldn't get enough of the place. After moving to an administrative post at the Key Bridge a few years after we first met, he complained about missing the tunnel: "I'd be sitting at home, hearing about backups at the tunnel, and my wife would say, 'Aren't you glad you don't have to put up with that?' But I really miss the tunnel. If I had to make the choice over again, I'd think long and hard about leaving."

As Bernie Jedrowicz would happily testify, there's much more to the tunnel than meets the eye. Its catacombs contained thousands of boxes of civil defense stores, aged crackers and old water, and darkened rooms that were supposed to serve as shelters along with the tube itself for more than ten thousand persons during a nuclear attack.

The tunnel also offers a panorama of the passing scene. Changing times at the tunnel have revealed themselves in topless women drivers on hot summer days and breast-feeding mothers in any season, according to toll takers. The bills that must be changed have gotten larger with inflation, and exact-change machines were modified to gobble up the Susan B. Anthony dollar. On occasion, fireworks have been dropped down the chute.

On the toll plaza, on the southern approach to the tunnel, babies have been born, shoot-outs held, presidents whisked through, and criminals (including bank robbers) stopped cold. The head of the toll takers fondly recalled a convoy of Navy buses bound for the Army-Navy football game; they barreled through her lane. Other veterans could remember the day the touring Beatles came through.

The tunnel is daily drama: Flashers reveal themselves to toll takers before driving on. Fluorescent tubes are intentionally broken; there was a particularly bad rash of breaks during the summer of 1979, the suspected culprit a trucker with a sling shot. Gates are crashed—about ten a month— and crashers who are caught were dunned $9.75 each. On the northern approach to the tube, an airplane has landed and a herd of cattle roamed free.

One year, there was gunfire on the toll plaza that left two dead when four men from New York argued over their take from a drug sale. "They were coming up to pay the toll when one man got out of the car and took off, and then another man got out," said Jedrowicz. After the two men on foot were gunned down, the other two were apprehended.

There was also the time, tunnel officials recall, when a local oil company presented a perfect driving award to one of its own at Carson's Inn, just north of the tube. There were food and drinks, and the award winner left for home in good spirits and promptly hit the tunnel wall. He was charged with reckless and drunken driving. So far as is known, he got to keep his award.

Of those unable to pay the fare, the tunnel is tolerant, accepting signed pledges of payment in place of tolls. The tunnel even, over the years, sold small amounts of fuel to hapless travelers riding on empty—a service abused and abolished during the gasoline crunch of the early 1970s.

The tunnel's busiest day was July 2, 1982, when 90,950 vehicles went through. The lightest day was February 19, 1979, during a record-breaking blizzard, when 10,469 hardy (and probably tardy) drivers braved the tunnel trip. The first fatality, blamed on speeding, came on September 18, 1975. The tunnel was never closed on purpose until 1980, when it shut down one weekend for repairs.

The tunnel's first fire was intentional, part of a drill during the early days when traffic was light enough to close one tube. During the drill, the hoses would not hook up to the water pumps. The fire, fortunately, burned itself out. "We were a young outfit," maintenance man Hopkins recalled. "We learned the fitting for the fire valve didn't match the fittings for the fire hose. The next day, all the fittings were changed. Without the drill, who knows what would have happened?"

The most memorable fire was in 1976, when an oil truck hit from behind burst into flames at the northern end of the tube. It was a weekday afternoon, vividly remembered by Henry Hopkins. "Jedrowicz and I were in his office," he said. "We seen this big column of black smoke on the north side of the Patapsco River. Jedrowicz got out his field glasses. We had to close all our entrances and exits. We were shut down at least three hours."

With two hundred cars trapped inside, tunnel workers built an earthen bulkhead and desperately diverted the leaking oil from the road into the harbor, averting a possible catastrophe—to the vocal dismay of state environmental officials on the scene. "The Natural Resources people were there hollering at me," said Hopkins. "I was busy trying to fight the Natural Resources people and the fire."

The environment is, however, on the minds of tunnel authorities. There was even a greenhouse, hidden behind the maintenance building below the roadbed, to supply the Mexican roses (the only plant that seems to survive the fumes in truck lanes 1, 2, 3, 12, 13, and 14), pansies, and marigolds that sit in homemade concrete flower pots on the islands between toll booths. You may not have noticed them, but don't tell the gardener.

Jay Seltzer, the gardener and also a carpenter, was a beefy, bearded Eastern

Shoreman whose ancestors had plied both trades in this country since the 1600s. He proudly showed me the twenty-by-thirty-foot greenhouse motorists never see. Among other things, it housed an asparagus fern and a rubber-tree plant that were "wintering here," as he put it. But Seltzer was frustrated. "In the past, I could spend two full days a week," he said, but recently road work had kept him away from his beloved greenhouse. "The end of February or March, I'll be starting plants in here for the toll plaza. I'm operating this damn thing on a shoestring," he said.

Before Seltzer, there had been a period of years when no plants were grown for the tunnel. Prior to that, back in the 1960s, a German gardener reigned supreme over the greenhouse and landscaping. With thirty state prisoners working for him, the German was a force to reckon with. Legend had it he apprenticed as a gardener to Hitler.

"Every place he wanted to put a tree, I wanted to put a sign," recalled Hopkins, the maintenance man. "He wanted to put three oak trees at Exit 3. I said you can't read the sign. He said the sign is not pretty. I'd put up a sign, Christ, he'd come along and put up a tree in front of it. I said you gotta move the tree. He'd say, no, it's easier to move the sign. Nine times out of ten I had to move the damn sign."

Use of prisoners was discontinued after some of them allegedly got into the civil defense supplies and stole drugs from the medical kits. Also, Hopkins said, the prisoners complained that trash pickup, one of their assigned tasks, was too demeaning.

In one sense, some tunnel employees are prisoners in their jobs. They're the people who take your money. There is a secret passageway under the fourteen toll booths that is connected to the tunnel office building. It is locked at all times, an empty corridor that sounds busy with the constant clanking of coins dropping into huge metal vaults from four exact-change chutes above. Fourteen sets of stairs lead from the passageway to the booths, but toll takers may descend into the corridor only when a sergeant inside a control room pushes a button.

There were fifty-five toll-taker slots, and, invariably, vacancies. The hours are lousy, the pay abysmal, and the work tedious. Toll takers must make up the difference if they come up short, and they must turn in anything extra. Toll takers often take the rap for tie-ups over which they have no control, and sometimes the bills they change are greased with spit. Normally they work different shifts every week and rarely get their holidays when everyone else does. Little wonder that in any one year, half the toll takers quit.

The toll takers work under carefully prescribed rules. They may wear "no visible jewelry," according to the official "Toll Collector's Manual." They are also required "to control long hair styles by wearing hair nets or wigs." Toll takers are instructed what to say to drivers. "Thank you" is mandatory. "Expressions like 'Okay,' 'That's it,' 'That's right,' etc., will not be acceptable," according to rule 50 in the book.

When the tunnel opened, Maryland Bridges and Tolls Administrator Louis J. O'Donnell boasted, "Our toll collectors are all women. We were the first major facility in the country to go to an all-female collecting force. Women are best suited to the job: they are accurate, more courteous, and the work doesn't seem to be so monotonous to them." What sounds sexist now seemed to signify an occupational triumph of sorts for women in the 1950s.

One of the first female toll takers was Bea Hasenei, who wound up in charge of the entire force. "When I started, more of our employees were more dedicated," she said. "We required a high-school education then. Now we'll accept eighth grade. In the '60s they couldn't get enough with high school, so instead of raising salaries, they lowered the requirement."

The first male toll taker was hired in March 1968. He left eleven months later, to an unknown future. At last count, there were twelve men and thirty-six women in the toll-taker army.

The original uniform of Oxford shoes, Sam Brown belt, necktie, overseas cap, striped shirt and skirt has given way to a more unisex and comfortable covering. Toll takers got a $150 annual cleaning allowance and $50 a year for shoes—an amount that would be doubled by the year 2000. "Without sounding like chauvinists," said the employee newsletter, *Toll Topics*, "we would like to note that female collectors have been permitted to wear slacks as part of the uniform and to provide more relaxed and comfortable attire, especially during the cold weather months."

Tunnel toll takers were encouraged to aspire to the elite job of Toll Collector III, the highest-paying non-supervisory job (up to $13,607 in 1983; $34,073 in 1999), available to those able to conduct at least four hundred transactions an hour. "Rather than just a job," *Toll Topics* urged, "Toll Collectors should look upon their position as an opportunity for career growth."

"The first week I was ready to quit," confessed a female toll taker who had nonetheless been on the job for three years when I found her in her booth. "Especially if there are tie-ups in the tunnel, they think it's your fault and really get mad. Right after Thanksgiving, a man from New York or New Jersey said, 'Who's the brains behind this?' This has been going on for years."

"This is the worst place to be, outside of jail or the hospital," Lane 1 toll taker Charles Wallace told a truck driver passing through the same night. He wore earplugs, he explained, because "a couple of people who spent nine or ten years inside these booths have trouble hearing out their left ear. It's especially bad in Lane 2, where you have trucks on both sides. Still, they say the noise is safe for you."

The job can be far from boring, sometimes. Wallace was working Lane 12 one weeknight, he recalled, when a man "drops three dollars out the window and a girl jumps out of the car, grabs me, and says, 'He's gonna kill me, he's gonna kill me.' I'm trying to keep her out of the booth. He rolls down the window and says she has his money and she was robbing him.

"She says he picked her up on Howard Street [in Baltimore] and was forcing her to stay. She pressed charges. He's charged with battery and having a deadly weapon. I had to go to court, and you only get paid three dollars an hour for court time. I took five hours of my own time, and she wasn't there. I have to go again Wednesday."

Wallace, who was twenty-eight, said he had earned twice as much as a laborer and assembly-line worker for a copper company but had been laid off. "Times are hard now," he said. "You gotta have security nowadays." A toll taker's job offered that. But a career? Hardly.

Turnover among the 102 tunnel police, who also patrol the approaches, was almost as high: about one-quarter of the entire force left each year. Starting pay was lower for a tunnel cop than for a state trooper or a Baltimore City officer. The pay ceiling was also lower, and it took longer to get there.

"About thirty percent of our people come here intending to get training, then shove off for greener pastures," shrugged Major Walter Wallace, a former postal clerk who was about to retire as chief of toll police. Toll police often attend Law Enforcement Day ceremonies held by schools to gain new recruits, "but you're competing with the FBI, Secret Service, all these other agencies," Wallace said. "Well, you can understand...."

Ineligible applicants are weeded out with lie-detector tests that have shown more than half have experimented or are quite involved with narcotics. "It used to be at one time a large percentage were on soft drugs, now it's everything," said Wallace, bemoaning the fact that of 150 applicants on one recent list only 6 could be hired.

The first female officer was hired to work the tunnel on April 2, 1973. Having gained some seniority, she moved over to the Key Bridge. "Bridges are considered a more desirable job than the tunnel," the outgoing chief said. "All recruits start off here at the tunnel."

Boredom is the biggest problem for those patrolling the tunnel. "It takes a certain kind of person that can resign themselves," the night shift commander informed me at the police service building above the tunnel's southern portal. "If you have a proper frame of mind, you can overcome the discomforts and apply yourself in a manner where you'll survive."

To improve the survival odds, police work two hours in the tunnel, then two hours out. The tunnel police are also responsible for the approaches at both ends and may appear in the courts of the three counties and one city their road transects.

"It's a job. I'm not unemployed. Somebody's got to do it," was the best that tunnel policeman Mike Alban could say for it from inside one of the glass-enclosed booths in the northbound tube. "The reason we're down here is for traffic enforcement and if people break down, which happens quite often. If cars follow too close or cross the solid double lines, we notify the police station outside and we have the violator stopped."

At twenty-three, he was a two-year veteran. "I hope to climb the ladder somehow, become a corporal, maybe," he said.

The booth in which Alban stood helps to mute the whooshing sound of traffic, loud enough to constitute noise pollution by federal standards. The tunnel cops are required to wear earmuffs. Officer Alban phoned in a horn violation by an impatient motorist, and was later disappointed to learn the offender had only received a warning. His two hours up, he went to a small brick building by the toll plaza to inspect overweight trucks caught by hidden sensors that trip alarms as the vehicle approaches.

As it often did on Friday nights, the tube experienced what is known in tunnel talk as "a stoppage" in both directions. It was caused by a large truck with engine trouble in one direction and a car with a flat tire going the other way. This was the big excitement that occurred after Alban's shift.

Two of the tunnel's three emergency vehicles descended quickly into the tube. These trucks are tall and snub, like a compressed accordion, able to turn in narrow spaces. They can push, lift, or tow. They also carry fire-fighting equipment. Thanks to their efforts, the stoppage was short lived.

Above the south portal looms the nerve center of the tunnel, a one-story building where police broadcast warnings of tunnel backups over citizens' band channel 3 (the truckers' handle for the tunnel transmitter was "hole in the wall") and interrupt your AM radio reception inside the tunnel with public service messages. (To allow AM reception inside the tunnel, the state spent $50,000 for its own receiver and transmitter. Few other tunnels in the country could boast of such a feature; the new Fort McHenry tunnel would also have FM.)

Prisoners were kept here, in a converted shower stall known as "our little slammer." A few feet away, seven softball and pistol trophies attested to the athletic and shooting skills of the tunnel corps. It was here, too, that carbon monoxide levels inside the tunnel were closely monitored and sixteen huge fans located in ventilation buildings at both ends regulated. The fans sucked the bad air from one duct over the tunnel roadway as fresh air was pumped in from a second duct underneath.

"We get constant read-outs on CO," said the night shift commander, who had begun working the tunnel in 1958. The signs over the print-outs, however, said "Out of Service." He quickly explained, "After twenty-three years, these meters were just replaced. These things are still being calibrated."

The motors that drive the big fans have failed five times in twenty-three years, I was told, and it cost $13,000 each time to make repairs. "We're considering having all of them removed, two at a time, to clean, bake, and reshellac them," Hopkins, the maintenance man, said. "We want to get a few more years out of them because they're obsolete. No one makes them anymore."

Such fancy maintenance, however, awaited completion of the new I-95 tunnel under Fort McHenry, which opened in November 1985. The new, eight-lane tube was being touted as the world's widest and the largest in the history of the national interstate highway system. Such superlatives did not bother the old tunnel's guardians one bit. Their hope was that the new tube would ease the flow through the old one. "Then," said Hopkins, "maybe we can get in and keep ours nice and pretty."

Emerging from north-bound Fort McHenry Tunnel, travelers
stop at toll plaza before continuing on I-95.
Maryland Transportation Authority

The opening of the second tunnel created a new bottleneck even as it eliminated the old one. It also left the older tunnel largely unused, except by me. Well, okay, that's a slight exaggeration: On the average, 56,000 vehicles pass through the old tunnel each day, but that compares to 114,488 through the new one. As traffic backs up at the foot of the Fort McHenry Tunnel toll booth, the approaches to and from the old Baltimore Harbor Tunnel often appear to be virtually free of traffic, making I-895, as it was now called, one of the best kept secrets on the East Coast—until now.

11

Baltimore
Lost and Found...Again

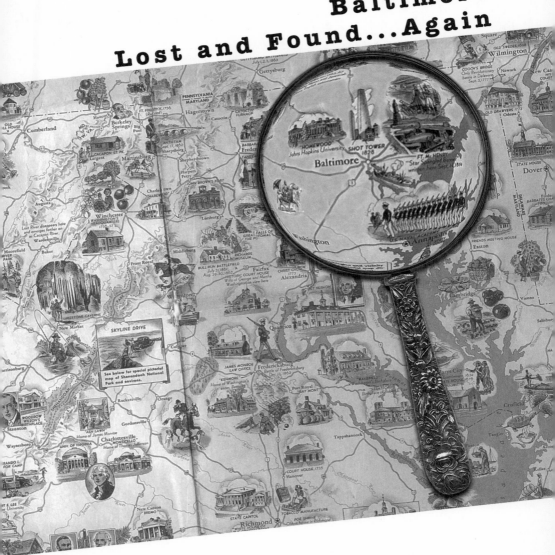

*B*altimore seems to have a remarkable ability to reinvent itself. A metropolis of the New South at the start of the twentieth century, its downtown was devastated by fire in 1904. But disaster begat opportunity, and a new skyline rose from the ashes. At the dawn of the twenty-first century, Baltimore is once again reinventing itself. Charm City, it seems, is two faced, losing some of its charm, for sure, but also finding in the industrial ruins of Rust Bowl America a rebirth of sorts. Thus the abandoned old fish market becomes Port Discovery, a wonderful children's museum a block from the Inner Harbor where kids "work" at a widget assembly line, to learn what Baltimore used to do—make things—before it became an Entertainment Zone. In many ways, Baltimore is the old and new urban America, formerly industrial, now a would-be theme park.

If these days the business of America is fun, then the latest American ethic is well-reflected in the newest Baltimore.

The old power plant becomes the new Power Plant, with a Barnes & Noble bookstore, a Hard Rock Café, and the ESPN Zone, upscale enterprises with floors of offices above them. Across the Inner Harbor, an old paint factory morphs into a funky art museum (with a parental advisory).

Promenade around Inner Harbor leading toward the Power Plant and National Aquarium. Eugene L. Meyer

A 29-story, 249-unit condominium tower, marina, and "yacht club" building are risen on the site of the old Bethlehem Steel shipyard on Key Highway. Rowhouse Baltimore seemingly declines—as demolition, not restoration, becomes the new mantra for the city's current crop of leaders—but formerly working-class Fells Point and Canton further east revive with new residents and businesses. In the latter neighborhood, a former can factory becomes Bibelot, another mega-bookstore.

The population has plummeted, old office buildings downtown stand virtually vacant, the public schools are in terrible shape. But still there is hope. Old department stores are being remade into apartments. The vitality of the popular Inner Harbor is spreading eastward, creating a new and exciting synergy. Downtown is again becoming a fashionable address, though perhaps not for families with children. Other, family neighborhoods, in the city's northern reaches, survive, even thrive.

Like many travelers, I discovered Baltimore by passing through. The year was 1952. Route 1 was the way to Washington, and the way then went through Baltimore. The image of rowhouse upon rowhouse, of marble steps as far as the eye could see, lingers. Though in hindsight one could see in this the virtue of uniformity, even beauty, there was a dreary sameness about this cityscape. It was not a pretty picture, then. Baltimore was a place to be avoided at all costs, and how wonderful the harbor tunnel seemed when it opened a speedier route to somewhere regarded as much more important in the scheme of things: Washington, D.C.

It was a time when Jack Lait and Lee Mortimer, two muckraking newspapermen, described Baltimore as "the slumming ground for thousands of escaping Washingtonians." In their tawdry book *Washington Confidential*, published in 1951, they referred to "our mythical refugee from Washington, who comes to Baltimore for only one purpose—and that's no good. You can be sure he finds what he wants in Baltimore. It's got everything that's no good."

Having myself arrived in the nation's capital to live, I revisited the old port city twenty years later. The place still ranked at the lower end of the Baltimore-Washington axis, geography notwithstanding, but something was stirring. It was a kind of quiet progress in urban affairs, on a human scale that contrasted sharply with what I'd seen in the District of Columbia. Neighborhoods were being renewed, seemingly for the people who already lived there, not abandoned or bulldozed as in the Capital City to the south. Downtown, the city of the future was starting to sprout, in the form of a high-rise cluster-cum-plaza known as Charles Center.

I was writing about urban renewal in the District, and the contrast between the two cities was striking. Those seeking to improve the quality of life in local Washington were all but powerless, so overshadowed were the neighborhoods of the capital city by the national capital. But Baltimore seemed to be in the midst of an exciting time, when all things only envisioned in Washington seemed eminently possible, even practical. The leaders I met on a trip I took with a reform-minded group of planners and citizens from Washington were both involved and inspired: Robert C. Embry, Jr., at thirty-four the Baltimore housing chief, and his deputy Menasha Jacob (M.J.) Brodie. Both of them had been raised there and were deeply committed to improving their hometown.

Baltimore had thirty urban renewal areas, compared to Washington's ten. It was fixing up 1,400 rowhouses for public housing, compared to 100 in the District. It was making greater use of loan and grant programs to enable homeowners to refurbish their own houses; its downtown urban renewal far surpassed the District's.

This was a time before novelist Anne Tyler, producer-director Barry Levinson, and the television series "Homicide" had enshrined the city in the national consciousness. It was a Baltimore little known beyond a small circle of progressive city planners. But soon enough the secret got out. "Baltimore is a city of unique assets that will soon be making the travel and convention hit parade," predicted Robert H. McNulty, president of a group called Partners for Livable Places, in a 1979 book titled *Learning from Baltimore.*

By the 1980s, Baltimore had seemingly arrived. No longer cursed and scorned, it had become fashionable, even trendy—so much so that the *Columbia Journalism Review* chided the press for catching a "hot city" virus over the place. Its redeveloped Inner Harbor and its colorful Mayor William Donald Schaefer made the covers of national magazines from *Time* to *Government Executive.* Cover stories also appeared in *New York* and the *Philadelphia Inquirer*'s "Today" magazine, which posed the skeptical question, "Is This Place for Real?"

The author of an article in *Bon Appetit* was downright gushy about the place. Whereas twenty years before she had seen only "grim urban sprawl" there, she had recently received "surprising" reports from "well-traveled friends of mine" who "began talking about—of all places—Baltimore. 'Have you seen Charles Center?' they would ask. 'Inner Harbor?...and the new Hyatt Regency is a crystal palace.'" Her bon appetite whetted, she paid the town a visit and observed, "From the rubble had risen a born-again beauty, a city as dazzling as anything Disney might design." Miraculously, it seemed, Baltimore had become the new symbol of "the city that works." Having lived down such names as "Nickel City," "Mobtown," and "Washington's Brooklyn," it adopted as its slogan the unabashed boast: "Baltimore Is Best."

The hoopla hit new heights with the opening in 1980 of Harborplace: twin, two-story, glass-enclosed pavilions, a veritable food fair and boutique bazaar plopped down by the water. This was the fabled Inner Harbor, formerly an area of rotting wharves and warehouses, an uncared-for collection of dilapidated nineteenth-century leftovers. Now, it had all changed. Instead of the merchant marine ships of yesteryear, sailboats anchored here. Ethnic festivals attracted sizeable crowds on summer weekends. Almost year-round, they came to feast, shop, sit, and stroll along the waterfront promenade or ply the water in rented paddle-boats.

Anchored nearby, the USS Constellation, an historic 1854 naval war sloop, provided a sharp contrast between the new and the old. A few hundred feet away, lines formed outside the National Aquarium in Baltimore. Widely praised for its modern architecture, it quickly became a chic after-hours setting for charity events, corporate feasts, and political fundraisers (so much so, in fact, that the fish suffered from fatigue and evening activities had to be curtailed). The celebrants congregated in the Harbor View Room, in the lobby, and by such exhibits as "Surviving by Adaptation," to eat buffet dinners, sip wine, and gaze at the four thousand overworked fish. "We try to tell people this is not a ballroom or a country club, but they insist," said a volunteer who worked on party arrangements at the Aquarium. "I guess we're the sexiest place in town."

But even as the Inner Harbor glittered, the old downtown north and west emptied. "For lease" signs sprouted on office buildings along Charles Street. "Single office or up to full floors available. Many downtown locations," said the signs on vacant buildings. Department stores on Howard Street closed down. Charles Center, the proud centerpiece of the city's earlier urban renewal, was reported to be in trouble. My wife's employer, the Maryland State Teachers Association, left its building at Charles and Mulberry for new quarters in Annapolis. The Peabody Book Shop, a long established fixture a few blocks north, closed for good.

Before the exodus had accelerated, I had lunched at another Baltimore tradition, the Woman's Industrial Exchange gift shop and tea room. Founded in 1880, "the ladies'," as my wife and her office mates called it, had its origins in a charitable impulse: to sell on consignment goods crafted by financially ailing young women. What distinguished the place in recent years was its cheap prices, its old-fashioned food, the venerability of its staff and its loyal clientele. The place seemed of another era with its octogenarian doorman and Old Baltimore atmosphere. It was a comfort zone of familiarity, and, after a depressing walk along the street of empty spaces, I returned there for lunch.

The place was celebrating its 119th birthday, but struggling. The other summer it had closed in July "because of our financial problems," explained my waitress, "but we got a lot of donations that got us on the go. We're not expecting to close up." A sign on the wall said, "Dollar By Dollar You Are Saving the

Exchange." Said the menu, "Today we welcome you to our gracious and historical setting where we are carrying on a Baltimore tradition with the help of your patronage." I was happy to support the cause, though luncheon platters for $5 and $6 seemed a modest price to pay to preserve this precious piece of Baltimore. Here you could feast on "Baltimore's Best Chicken Salad," with deviled egg and tomato aspic and a homemade hot roll.

"This is an oasis of civility," said the man seated at the next table, Guy Arceneaux, forty-five, an ad agency art director. "It's timeless. It gives you hope for the world." Here a twenty-four-year-old waitress is described as "the baby of the family." Waitress Charlotte Zimernock, seventy-one, had actually retired months before, but was temporarily back at work. "They're a little short, so I'm helping them out," said "Miss Charlotte." Said Bill Fortsch, the man bussing the tables, "This is the only place in the world that when you retire, they give you a license to be rehired." The cashier, Phyllis Sanders, who was seventy-seven, had come here to work in 1939 at the age of seventeen and never left.

As I paid my tab, I saw another sign that said "THANK YOU. THANK YOU," referring to over $125,000 raised for the Exchange. "We would be closed (forever!) without you." And that would be a shame.

Despite all the glitter and glamour, the hope and the hype, Baltimore remained the "city of violent contradictions" noted by New Deal guidebook writers. The week the city made the cover of *Time* was also the week an English tourist was slain as he pursued a thief who had snatched his companion's purse. "Harborplace and the National Aquarium are the real Baltimore, but so are endemic violence, poverty, despair, and hatred," editorialized *The Sun*. "The two Baltimores are the same."

It was the nitty-gritty renaissance city, still an ethnic blue collar town, though less and less so as the manufacturing jobs disappeared and those with European immigrant roots moved to the suburbs. It was, in fact, a city in transition. It had, for the first time in 1980, a black majority, 55%, which approached 60% a decade later. The demographers discovered a substantial cluster of black middle-class neighborhoods concentrated on the city's west side, but many of its residents were leaving too. Between 1970 and 1998, Baltimore lost an astounding 260,000 people, most of them middle-class taxpayers, black along with white. The city of 905,000 I had visited with the group from Washington was down to 645,000 by the late 1990s. The Inner Harbor was still gleaming, in fact expanding eastward, the city had new twin stadiums for the Baltimore Orioles and the NFL Ravens, a new "light rail" line from Baltimore-

Washington Airport and Glen Burnie on the south to Hunt Valley on the north. Yet Baltimore was hemorrhaging people.

"Obviously, the city's continuing to lose population," Bob Embry told me from his office near the Inner Harbor, where he now headed the private Abell Foundation. "That means houses are going to continue to become vacant. The city's faced with either fixing them up, leaving them, or tearing them down. Fixing them up for middle-class people, lending them financing has not been a high-priority for the city. The focus is on demolition. I think [rehab] was a good idea then; it's a good idea now."

Another fact about Baltimore emerged: As it got better for some, it got worse for others. In a city where home ownership was still widespread, change had come with minimal duress for families who opted to sell and move elsewhere. Renters have been more subject to the whims of the private marketplace. Despite public efforts to renew neighborhoods without removing the neighbors, "gentrification" had invaded at least some sections, replacing lower-income renters with higher-income professionals.

Of course, the newcomers tended to be singles, empty-nesters, or couples without kids. Still, their investment in the city was viewed by some as a plus. "We need more middle-class people," Jay Brodie, who succeeded Embry as the city's commissioner of housing and community development, told me in his office a few blocks from the redeveloped Inner Harbor back in 1982. "You can't avoid displacement one hundred percent, but we're trying a number of programs to reduce the effects."

Jay Brodie himself embodied the changing character of Baltimore. Born in the city, the son of immigrants and the first in his family to attend college, he had left for school and work "because I felt Baltimore was a hopeless place to practice contemporary architecture." He was lured back in 1960, from Houston, by a planning job at the city's redevelopment agency. One thing led to another, and he rose to the top spot in 1977. Soon, Baltimore was bursting with new buildings and had become a mecca for young architects from other cities seeking a challenge.

Amidst all the boosterism and self-congratulation over the "new Baltimore," which was good for architects, builders, and the like, and the contrasting despair of the shipyard workers, Brodie continued to exude pride in his city's much-touted "renaissance" while acknowledging the industrial trouble spots.

"That's the American economy changing," he said. "Those adaptable are survivors. Those not are losers." By bringing white-collar and service jobs to replace the factories, he asserted in 1982, the city was adapting. It was also reflecting new realities: From 1960 to 1980, the percentage of blue-collar workers had gone from 57.1% to 52.6% of employed, while the white collar percentage had risen from 43.9% to 47.4%. Metropolitan Baltimore's manufacturing work force shrunk in half from 1960 to 1997. In the new order, it was clear, not all of the beer-and-crab blue-collar ethnics would survive.

For nine years, from 1984 to 1993, Brodie directed the redevelopment of Pennsylvania Avenue in Washington. But he never moved, choosing to commute by train from Baltimore, where he has happily ensconced in Cold Spring, a utopian "new town" designed by Israeli architect Moshe Safdie.

In 1996, Brodie returned professionally to Baltimore to assume the leadership of the Baltimore Development Corp., which focuses on economic development. Brodie, too, was adapting.

"Our collective challenge is to reinvent ourselves," Brodie, still boyish-looking

A 1940s postcard view of Baltimore skyline from Federal Hill and photographed today. Eugene L. Meyer

at sixty-two, said in his office a few blocks from the Inner Harbor. "If we are going to have a city, we must reinvent our economic base." To him, that meant health and medicine, tourism, the Port, distribution warehouses, expansionist brokerage houses, and "niche" manufacturers, "not the old smokestack people." "There's a lot of life out there in business," Brodie asserted. "It [just] may not be the same business it was."

A quintessential city in crisis, Baltimore also mirrored the rise and fall of industrial America. Even as "Charm City" had risen phoenix-like, providing new service jobs in the Inner Harbor, the auto plants, the steel mills, and shipyards of this old port on the Patapsco River declined. (From 1985 to 1996, the number of manufacturing establishments in the city declined by 15.6%, while those in the neighboring suburban Baltimore and Anne Arundel counties rose by 20% and 24%, respectively.)

Beyond its gleaming Inner Harbor and its shrinking industrial core, Baltimore is a city of 277 neighborhoods. It is a city of points, parks, and hills from which the neighborhoods derive their names. They include Fells Point, Locust Point, and Wagner's Point, Forest Park, Roland Park, Moravia Park, and Graceland Park. There's Bolton Hill, Federal Hill, Reservoir Hill, Stone Hill, even Ten Hills. And there are "towns," like Oldtown, Highland-

Delivering mail to a rowhouse in Baltimore.
Joel Richardson, *Washington Post*

town, Sandtown, Greektown, and Pigtown. In these rowhouse neighborhoods the people of Baltimore live their lives far removed from the media glare. In the north and west are affluent neighborhoods of detached homes on large lots. Each city enclave has its own "feel" and flavor, but most Baltimoreans have at least one thing in common: Their homes are attached, and, in their family and neighborhood ties, so are their lives.

My Baltimore assignments, more often than not, took me to the neighborhoods where "Charm City" wasn't. I had walked their streets with the legendary Mimi de Pietro, the consummate ward politician, and an aspiring gubernatorial candidate with the unlikely name of American Joe Miedusiewski. There were neighborhoods worried about toxic waste dumps and chemical fumes; in one of them, Hawkins Point, Baltimore's version of New York's infamous Love Canal, African-American residents simply had to move for their own health and welfare, giving rise to charges of environmental racism. But the same happened too to the white neighborhood of Wagner's Point.

There were other working-class neighborhoods whose residents were newly unemployed, casualties of the recession. Still other neighborhoods faced a seemingly endless if unsurprising cycle of poverty and social ills. There was also the virtual end of the infamous "Block," a four-block stretch of strip joints with barkers beckoning to passersby, and the residential Baltimore-in-transition I found as I traced the northward march of Washingtonians out to make a buck— or to live—in the changing city.

The yawning gap between Baltimore and Washington real estate prices brought speculators large and small in appreciable numbers in the late 1970s. Things were getting rough for the property flippers in the District's overheated market, and low-cost, blue-collar Baltimore beckoned. "It's the frontier," John M. Novosel, a Washington real estate salesman, told me after he'd bought thirteen Baltimore properties in six months. "The market, compared to Washington, is like night and day." In Washington, explained a buyer for a Washington-based syndicate, "ten or twenty houses is a big holding. In Baltimore, you're talking about hundreds of units, thousands of units," and at a price per house often under $5,000. "The bricks alone are worth that," the man said. Added a University of Maryland official who had become an investor, "I'll tell you, it's like taking cake from a baby."

The migration of money was hastened by the different economic and political climates of the two cities. Local Washington's notoriously sluggish bureaucracy made evicting tenants for nonpayment of rent a long, painful process for landlords. Then again, Washington had a speculation tax and Baltimore didn't. It hadn't needed one. In Baltimore, landlords had traditionally accepted the long-term yields of rental property instead of going for the fast buck from speculation. But now the "old landlord clan" of Baltimore, for reasons of age and equity, was getting out of that city's real estate market. Coincidentally, major Washington investors appeared on the scene. Half a dozen began "inventorying" the city, buying big and then "piecing off" lots to groups from Washington.

Washington's small-time investors were focusing on neighborhoods like Reservoir Hill, in north central Baltimore. Often they paid high prices by Baltimore standards, naively thinking they were getting a steal. "This is the up-and-coming neighborhood," said one Washington speculator who owned five Baltimore properties. Before choosing Reservoir Hill, he had studied the city's master plan and the planned route of the Baltimore subway, which skirts the neighborhood's southern boundary.

Bisecting Reservoir Hill is a wide north-south street known as Eutaw Place. It is lined with three-story rowhouses of brick and stone, many with stained glass above doors and windows, attractive iron grillwork, Victorian turrets, fine interior woodwork, and marble fireplaces. Real estate agent Judy Morris had sold properties in the neighborhood to several buyers from Washington. A New Jersey native, Morris lived with her husband and young daughter in a Eutaw Place mansion built by a coal industrialist in 1895. She owned "twenty-two or so" other properties in the neighborhood.

"We have a lot of people in this neighborhood who commute to Washington," said Morris. "There are a couple of National Gallery people, some attorneys." She complained, however, about Washington investors who "buy and can't maintain the properties. One house on Eutaw Place is for sale for the third time. It's gone through three Washington buyers."

Reservoir Hill, like many of the newly discovered neighborhoods, had been largely low-income and black. Inevitably, the infusion of Washington money threatened to displace the longtime residents, or so it seemed, should renovation and resale proceed apace, as indeed it had in Washington itself.

At least these Washingtonians had hired a local firm, Inner City Management, to look after the properties. Tenants complained the company was unresponsive to their complaints, but other Washington investors hired no one in Baltimore to keep up their properties. Problems with absentee owners prompted a city law barring out-of-town ownership without an in-town manager: someone would be around, at least, to receive the code-violation citations.

"We've had some very good Washington investors," Jay Brodie said. "On the other hand, other people came up for a fast buck and discovered we have code enforcement." One such investor (who, with a partner, owned more than a hundred properties) had to be extradited from the District of Columbia. There, two Baltimore law enforcers had staked out his home in the middle of the night to serve the summons. Ultimately, the man pleaded guilty to ninety-five criminal charges and received a $10,000 fine for his transgressions. If there was money to be made in Baltimore, it seemed it would have to be made on the city's own terms.

Pretty quickly, what had looked like the Emerald City to Washington speculators had reverted to the Nickel City of yore. Those who had bought at the final flip of the coin had lost. Many Washingtonians had gotten out of the market. Still, the advertisements beckoned. "Buy Baltimore prices today—Get Washington prices tomorrow" said one in the April 11, 1983, *Washington Post*. It demonstrably wasn't so, at least not any more. The seller was a Washingtonian who wanted out after eighteen months, and he was just hoping to break even. "I thought when they built that Inner Harbor, Baltimore should be on the move," he said. It was, but at its own pace, which was not fast enough for fast-buck artists—at least until the 1990s, when the *Baltimore Sun* chronicled more rampant flipping, this time with local speculators in the mix and low-income buyers as the victims.

"The people living in Baltimore to begin with who commuted to Washington are continuing to commute to Washington," said Judy Morris. But she knew of no new arrivals from Washington to her neighborhood, except for Bill Bonner. Originally from Annapolis, Bonner had moved his publishing firm from Washington's Capitol Hill to Baltimore's Charles Village, near the Johns Hopkins University. He had moved himself to Reservoir Hill. The neighborhood, he said, was "dirty, disgusting, rat infested, probably crime ridden. I like it. There's a real sense of community among the renovators."

He had come, he said, to stay.

"I prefer Baltimore," said the then thirty-four-year-old publisher. "It doesn't have quite the glitter of Washington. There are not as many fancy restaurants, movie theaters, or young, trendy people on the streets, but there's a feeling more of community here. It's more like a real city. Here...changes occur much more slowly and are harder to predict."

"The city doesn't appreciate the flipper. The city does appreciate the producer," said one Washingtonian who had ventured north to become a producer. I knew the man first as a District of Columbia redevelopment official. A Bostonian by birth, Ron Russo had become increasingly frustrated by the bureaucracy and racial tensions afflicting Washington. In the 1970s, he, too, joined the northward migration, both professionally and personally. Twenty years later, he was still there.

"This city is vibrant," he beamed as he showed me around seven townhouses he was restoring on the northern edge of Federal Hill, near the Inner Harbor. "People are happy...I meet a lot of Washingtonians at Harborplace who say, 'Why couldn't we do something like this in Washington?' I love it here. At first, I felt like a stranger, a visitor, more like a Washingtonian than a Marylander. Then, I began to think like a Marylander, to think about the job and getting it done."

Russo and his wife divided their time between a house on two acres outside Upper Marlboro in Prince George's County, their condominium in Baltimore, and North Beach, where he was also involved in development. Russo's enthusiasm for Baltimore remained high. He had joined the Baltimore Athletic Club and the Club Nautilus at the Hyatt Regency. "You generate friendships where you do business," he said, happy to report, "I have a whole new circle of friends." Occasionally he would go to the Kennedy Center or the Capital Centre in the nearby suburbs of Washington—but he also attended Orioles games in Baltimore. "It's a lot of fun mixing it up," he said.

Fifteen years later, Russo's daughter lived in the Federal Hill rowhouse he'd restored, and Russo still owned some rental units there and on Seton Hill. Though his residential mailing address remained Upper Marlboro, Russo said, "Baltimore is really my home base." Indeed, he was heavily involved in a new urban frontier, on the city's near West Side, where he planned to restore ninety-five units of housing in century-old buildings. They would be sold as condominiums, and there would also be ground floor space for retail shops. "I like doing those kinds of things," he said.

Russo's rehabilitation plans—along with others for the restoration of the 2,500-seat Hippodrome Theater and the conversion of the old Hecht Co. department store into 173 apartments—were widely applauded. But much else about the proposed $350 million West End redevelopment was controversial. Harkening back to the earliest days of urban renewal, they called for demolition and clearance of entire blocks of buildings. There were still a few residents and merchants who would be displaced, and a few arguably historic buildings would have to go. Jay Brodie, who had emphasized rehabilitation years before, was at peace about all this, viewing the vast vacancies "as an opportunity," he said, "to assemble and clear some land without devastating relocation," a negative turned positive to make Baltimore better. In this swath of the inner city, it could hardly have been worse: block upon block of empty storefronts along the Howard Street right-of-way of the light rail line. Former residential neighborhoods a few blocks to the west presented, for now, an equally dismal picture.

The mass exodus from the city had left 40,000—"Can you imagine that?" Ron Russo said—units of housing vacant, and neighborhoods that had literally turned into ghost towns, just north and west of the sparkling Inner Harbor. Several of these abandoned blocks lay just west of Martin Luther King, Jr., Boulevard, in the neighborhoods of Union Square, Franklin Square, Sandtown, and Winchester.

Driving west on Baltimore Street, I passed boarded up shops and empty lots, then I turned north on Stricker, drove past vacant rowhouses, and west again onto Fayette Street. I stopped and parked my car in the 1800 block, where half of the two dozen rowhouses were vacant. Many of them bore the red cardboard sign signifying they had been condemned by the city. "Private Property - No Loitering - No Trespassing - If Animal Trapped Inside, call 896-6286," advised the words on one building whose windows were broken and boarded. It was election time, and these shells were also serving as billboards for the candidates, whose workers had plastered their campaign signs right alongside the advisories.

Up the block on this sunny summer morning, I met a man from New York who said he was visiting with a neighborhood woman. They were stoop-sitting in front of a vacant rowhouse, drinking beer. A twenty-eight year old, who identified herself only as Erica, had walked around the corner from Fulton Street, where she lived. "Would you like living around a bunch of vacant houses?" she said. "I been around here all my life, seen people go, leave, [buildings] close down. They can fix all that stuff for the Inner Harbor. They ought to do it here, tear them down. I'm getting the fuck out of Baltimore. Ain't nothing here."

But a few stoops up the street, a sixty-year-old woman named Pauline, who had moved to Baltimore from Montgomery County in the 1970s, said she had no intention of leaving. Of those who'd left, she shrugged, "I guess a lot of them bettered their conditions and lifestyle. Maybe some of them moved out to the suburbs." But not her. "No, no," she insisted. "I'm gonna stay here."

The Baltimore that attracted tourists to the Inner Harbor was a mere mile or so from here, but it could've been a thousand. "I don't go to the Inner Harbor," Paulene said. "I used to, but there are so many people. It's too crowded. Everything is so expensive. You gotta have a pocketful of money." In her neighborhood, she said, the politicians "need to make it safe for kids and the elderly."

The woman, who owned her rowhouse, could still look at the half-empty block and see that, in her eyes at least, it was half-full. The corner liquor store had shut down, and the cops had shooed away the alcoholics and drug dealers from the street. "I like Baltimore," she said. "It's not real bad. The city is noisy, but it's convenient. You get used to it." On the other corner was a mom-and-pop grocery store, still open, with an official sign from the police department: "No loitering within fifteen feet of this building." But things on the block were quiet now, Paulene said, since the police had cleaned up the corner. Clearly, she hadn't given up. On her block, abandoned by landlords, condemned by the city, hope was alive.

There were brighter parts of residential Baltimore. The old blue-collar milltown of Hampden, further north, was becoming fashionable with singles and artists. The communities of Homewood and Roland Park, near the Johns Hopkins University, were still solidly middle-class enclaves. Cold Spring, no longer a "new town," remained a place that appealed to '60s-style progressives like Brodie. And then there was Dickeyville, in the city's far western corner, forgotten but not gone.

In the 1970s, my former wife's professional interest in weaving had brought me to the old mill town of Dickeyville, which its boosters called "Baltimore's best-kept secret." In fact, Lee Smith, who with her husband, Keith, owned The Weaver's Place inside the old textile mill, had had trouble getting a permit from the city. "When I paid my license fee, the guy wasn't going to accept my money," she said. "He said, 'You're not in the city, you're in the county.' The city doesn't seem to know we exist."

It's little wonder, considering. Dickeyville sits at the city's western edge, hidden in a stream valley and virtually engulfed by hills and parks. It is a collection of 136 stone and frame buildings that could be a movie set for a nineteenth-century English drama. Dickeyville—formerly known as Wetherdsville and Hillsdale—was, I learned, one of Baltimore's first gentrified neighborhoods. It began to change in the 1930s, during the Depression, when its industry folded and the company town went on the auction block. Millworkers were offered the first chance to buy their homes, but only if they could afford to upgrade the properties. None could. Two-family houses rented to mill workers became single-family homes owned by professionals.

The bittersweet tale of Dickeyville—offering so many parallels to Baltimore today—was related to me in part by Charles Wagandt, a great-grandson of the Dickey who bought the place in 1867. When I met him, Wagandt was in his sixties, a pleasant and unpretentious man with thinning blond hair. As we sat on a stone fence alongside Gwynn's Falls and the old mill buildings now occupied by crafts people, the sound of the stream mingled with noise from men and machines laying new sewer pipes.

Decades before the Dickeys' arrival, a paper mill first brought settlers to the area in the eighteenth century. In 1829 the Wethered family bought the mill and converted it to the manufacture of wool fabric. They also built other mills nearby. The Wethereds built stone houses for their workers, and the family donated land for a church. The mills produced both blue and gray cloth during the Civil War, until Union forces closed them in 1863. After the war, William J.

Dickey paid $82,000 for the three hundred acres, three mills, and the houses that comprised the village.

The Dickeys bought another mill in Oella in Baltimore County in 1887, Wagandt said. They left Dickeyville in 1906, having sold their interests there to the first of a succession of luckless owners. Wagandt, a Dickey on his mother's side, bought back the remaining mill in 1954. When in 1972 all the Dickey mills—here, in Oella, and in the Carolinas—closed for good, Wagandt envisioned turning the Dickeyville buildings into an arts and crafts center with a restaurant. Then, thirty-six hours after Wagandt and a partner purchased the place from the family corporation, Hurricane Agnes swelled the stream and swept away the only bridge connecting the old factory building to anywhere. Two years later, another bridge was built. Eventually there were tenants, and in 1983 Wagandt and his partner sold the place. He still owned eight-and-a-half acres, "billy-goat land," he called the sharply rising tract above the stream, but mostly what he had were memories.

He remembered being driven as a small child through the village, when it was "very much down at the heels." The developer who bought the town and mills, for $42,000 at a foreclosure sale in 1934, was "something of a trail blazer," in Wagandt's view. Nowadays, with tax benefits for restoring historic properties, said Wagandt, who was also board chairman of the Maryland Historical Trust, "it's very fashionable.... You didn't hear about gentrification and displacement in those days. But nonetheless, the problem was there."

Indeed, Wagandt's concern was the imminent revitalization of Oella, which he still owned and which now had indoor plumbing, with his help and government aid. He hoped the old people of Oella, some of whom had moved there from Dickeyville, would not now be displaced again. He worried, in particular, about the older woman there who rented from him.

I found Mabel Moore, then seventy-four, and her husband, William, seventy-nine, at their home in Oella later the same day. She had been born in Dickeyville and, like most of the town's children, went to school only through eighth grade. The nearest high school was a three-mile walk each way, an expense in shoe leather most families couldn't afford. "Kids didn't go downtown until they were sixteen," she said. In fact, many worked in the mills starting at age fourteen. They worked for "Mr. Harry" Dickey or his son, "Mr. Bill," as the Moores still called them. "The old Dickeys were like God to these people," she said. Mabel's mother ironed shirts for the mill bosses. Her father was a foreman.

Mabel Moore had moved to Oella when she married in 1928, a few years before the rest of her family had to leave the village. "My mother picked up five kids and moved to the city," she said. In her mother's new neighborhood, only two miles from Dickeyville, "for one whole year, those people next door didn't even speak to her. My brothers wouldn't go to the city. They stayed with friends." When the residents of Dickeyville were forced to move, it was a sad day, Mabel Moore declared. "Everyone sat down and cried when they left because it was very close knit."

The developer's sales brochure called it

Quaint Dickeyville...a self-contained community boasting a long and honorable history. For many years now it has been vegetating complacently—basking idly in the sunshine and dreaming of its long-vanished days of glory. But now all this is changed. Things are happening again in placid Dickeyville. Hammers and saws are at work in the little white houses and the solid stone dwellings which sheltered the mill workers and their families in better times. Bathrooms are being built. Plumbing and electricity are being installed. Hot water systems are going in. Coats of paint are going on. The simple, lovely old homes are rapidly being transformed into exquisite, reasonably priced homes for people who love country life and take to simple village ways....

The new Dickeyville, in short, retains all of the character and charm of old-time Dickeyville to delight those who prefer the sedate beauty of a fine old American village at its best. At the same time, it offers people of taste and discrimination the home advantages which they have come to associate with the better type of suburban community today. When you see Dickeyville, pick a day when the realities of life are pressing heavily on your spirit. The serenity of this pioneer village will give you a strange new sense of peace.

The Dickeyville I found looked, at first glance, like a Currier and Ives scene. "Village" still seems an appropriate term for the place, even though it is, technically, a city neighborhood. The appearance is preserved by ordinance and

Dickeyville—a quaint American village amidst the concrete city. Eugene L. Meyer

by the civic association, which must approve all exterior changes to homes. This was no pastel "restoration," but neither does Dickeyville today resemble the grimy mill town it once was: The once dreary-looking mill-workers' homes of the 1930s are uniformly painted bright white with black shutters. "Let's all work together! Dickeyville is beautiful in the spring and the village sells itself if we all help," said a poster announcing a 1999 house and garden tour that attracted 500. "Everybody was so uplifted," said Susan Wiest, who'd grown up in Dickeyville and now sold real estate in the village. "It reinforced for people visiting that Dickeyville is a wonderful place to live."

Dickeyville, she declared, is "a very professional community and artsy." Or as Bob Huber, an electrical contractor with a workshop inside the old mill put it, "They're all weirdos." His brother Mike added that the "whole temper of this area is artsy-fartsy." There was even a man living over on Pickwick Road, Bob Huber noted, who made "nuclear-free" lightbulbs, whatever they were.

At the Forest Park Avenue entrance to Dickeyville, near the community sign erected by the Dickeyville Garden Club, I met David Cammack, a retired minister who'd lived here off and on since 1980. Answering my knock on his front door, he invited me inside and onto a back deck overlooking Gwynns Falls.

Dickeyville was, he said, repeating the village mantra, "One of the best residential secrets in the Baltimore area." People had been discovering it, driving down Weatheredsville Road, into the village, until villagers successfully lobbied to have the road closed just past the mill, thereby cutting it off from the rest of west Baltimore. Now, the entire enclave was for "local traffic" only

Residents included teachers, doctors, a writer, and the poet laureate of Baltimore City. There was a welcoming committee, a three-day Fourth of July festival, Christmas caroling each year, all traditions of the "new" Dickeyville. But there were other signs of the present encroaching on the past. They said "Beware of the Dog" and "No Trespassing," and they announced the presence of security alarms on individual homes. The community newsletter advised residents to install motion detector lights, put porch lights on timers, and use a club on all cars—precautions more befitting a big-city neighborhood. But then Dickeyville, I learned, was not immune to big-city crime. Break-ins especially were a problem, and the "close-knit" nature of the place was also changing. During a visit in May, 1999, I counted eleven homes for sale. Though Cammack and Wiese assured me they were "for the right reasons," a coincidence and not a symptom, the sudden cluster was startling.

"There are an awful lot of people here I don't know," said Dot Mowers, editor and founder of the *Dickeyville Town Crier* and a resident for twenty-seven years had told me during an earlier visit years before. "A lot of young people come and go. Whatever they're looking for, they don't find it."

One thing they are looking for, after they start their families, is good public schools. But as the neighborhoods around Dickeyville have changed, from integrated to black, so have the schools. Public education has declined, in the view of many of both races, and Dickeyville parents now send their children to private schools. Except for one family, David Cammack confided, who took an apartment in suburban Catonsville so their two boys could attend Catonsville High School. "They lived in both places," he said. "Now the boys are out of high school, they live here one hundred percent."

Located in the black belt of West Baltimore, Dickeyville remains virtually all white, and excluded Jews, it is said, until the 1960s. "Houses here are mostly sold by Dickeyville residents to their friends," explained Jeanne McGowan Smith, one of two resident real estate agents I had met. She herself had lived in three different Dickeyville homes. "This is not a snobbish neighborhood."

Yet, while the Inner Harbor is only six miles and, in rush hour, no more than thirty minutes away, Dickeyville remains amazingly isolated. Residents complain about the lack of shopping nearby. But by the same token, said Theo Lippman, Jr., an editorial writer for the *Baltimore Sun* and a Dickeyville resident off and on since 1965, "I can drive two miles without seeing more than one house" on the parkway heading downtown. "We're fairly close to everything, but not real close to anything."

There is this ambivalence about the place that makes it, like Baltimore despite the "renaissance" hype, more real. Dot Mowers, no starry-eyed booster, had expressed it best: "Especially in this era of frantic nostalgia, this plastic, throwaway age," she wrote in the village newsletter,

the poetic imperfections of our village with its irregular streets, its varied houses, its decaying dam, its winding stream, appeal to the sense of beauty that exists in varying degrees in the human heart. If sterile perfection and neighborhood one-ups-manship are your meat, then Dickeyville will annoy you more than its charms will enchant. What we have here is the genuine article which developers up and down the Atlantic Seaboard are frenetically imitating and mass-producing, simply because there is not enough of the real thing to meet the demand.

12

On the Metropolitan Frontier

Wilbur and Mary Ann Ford had always wanted to live in a place like Buckeystown, south of Frederick. The small village, settled around 1800, seemed like a good place for the rootless to sink roots. The same families had occupied the old frame houses along Main Street for generations. There was a comfortable familiarity about the place, a small-town ambience that appeared to offer what urban life often lacked and the Fords wanted: a sense of belonging, a sense of community, in a rural setting.

Indeed, when they moved into their antebellum home in 1966, the second new family in town, they found just that. Ford, a land surveyor raised in Frederick, and his wife from the Eastern Shore got to know their neighbors. But they learned, too, that the welcome mat wasn't always out for strangers.

"One old, retired farmer, every time I walked by, said, 'There goes that goddamn hippie,'" recalled Wilbur Ford, who, beefy and middle-aged seventeen years later, hardly looked the part. "I finally said, 'What's your problem, redneck?' He didn't really know. After that, we became very good friends."

But time and tide were running against the Buckeystown that had always been. One by one, the old people died off, their grand old homes went on the market, and new people moved in. The turnover was almost total. Within a few years following nearly two centuries during which very little had changed, almost everything had.

The newcomers were mainly from metropolitan Washington, and they continued to commute there to work. Their ties were outside Buckeystown, and although they, too, had come for the small-town life in the country, the community in the truest sense was gone.

The Fords no longer knew their neighbors. The town looked the same, but it felt different. It *was* different.

"The idea of an old house in a stable community that had what appeared to be an interesting mix of people was appealing to us," explained Mary Ann Ford. "We were looking for diversity, didn't want to be trapped where young professionals all lived. But as soon as the old folks died, the larger homes were bought primarily by professional people. So what you have in Buckeystown now is not a viable community anymore. There is no club or organization or church that attracts a majority or even fifty percent of the people living here. Their allegiances are in all different places."

From farmland to subdivisions, aerial views of Braddock Heights and the Middleton Valley near Frederick (early twentieth century postcard and late twentieth century photograph). Craig Herdon, *Washington Post*

Before the rapid change, Wilbur Ford had joined the nearest volunteer fire company he could find, as part of his entry into rural society. It happened to be Carroll Manor in Adamstown, a nearby hamlet roughly the size of Buckeystown. There Ford assumed a leadership role, and he learned other things about country life he did not like. He learned that the Adamstown company had no blacks and no women. (The Fords had adopted biracial children, and Mary Ann Ford had become president of the Frederick County League of Women Voters.) It had barred blacks from membership by charter until 1968. It still contained a written ban against women, who were relegated to a ladies' auxiliary.

"I have one of the finest groups of women in this county and in this state," said the Adamstown squad's leader of the auxiliary, whose members helped raise money for new equipment and a new building by running the largest food tent at the Frederick County Fair and sponsoring other fund-raising events.

Wilbur Ford, admittedly a headstrong individual, broke with his Adamstown neighbors and decided to try something different, something he hoped would break the racial and sexual barriers and at the same time re-create a community in Buckeystown. Along with two others from Carroll Manor, Ford founded the Buckeystown Volunteer Fire and Rescue Squad. They were quickly expelled from their old unit for starting what was viewed as competition.

But that was just the beginning. No sooner had the squad organized itself, rented an old service station, begun training, and acquired a few pieces of equipment, than the trouble began in earnest. The rules of the firefighters' association said no squad could operate within four miles of an existing company without its approval. Buckeystown and Adamstown were only 3.5 miles apart.

The Buckeystown Volunteer Fire and Rescue Squad nonetheless managed to sign up 203 members, 40% of them black (including its president) and more than 30% of them women. Instead of the traditional ladies' auxiliary, Buckeystown had a "people's auxiliary" that raised money by butchering hogs and sponsoring community events.

Ford maintained that the new subdivisions sprouting between Buckeystown and Frederick needed the new service. His community spirit did not win community approval, however. Some two hundred old-line area residents signed petitions opposing the new squad as unneeded. Among them were Lester D. Dudrow, a retired farmer in Limekiln, just above Buckeystown, and his wife, Dorothy, the president of the Buckeystown Homemakers' Club, who said, "By golly, we signed the petition right off the bat. People just weren't behind it. The man [Ford] is behind it. You take what he says for a grain of salt. He likes to be the big chief. You just can't walk into a new community and take over. You've got to prove yourself. People moving in lately, some of 'em come in and go, come in and go. A lot of young women have gone to work. I've been homemaker president eight years. People here don't want change. They like it the way it is. I think it's good."

No matter that thirty Buckeystowners took emergency medical training through the University of Maryland. They weren't allowed to respond to calls, and the very existence of their squad was in doubt. "As far as I'm concerned, they don't exist," the head of the county firefighters' association told me. Rejecting charges of racism and sexism, the established volunteer fire companies argued the area just didn't need another one, especially so close to Adamstown. Fund raising was hard enough as it was, without more competition from upstart fire and rescue squads.

The turf war escalated when county authorities took back the truck, sirens, and lights they had given the new squad, after Buckeystowners had spent hours refurbishing the old four-wheel-drive brush truck, overhauling its engine, painting the body olive green, and outfitting it with lights and signs. Wilbur Ford was ordered to drive the truck under sheriff's escort to the county garage in Frederick. He did so, under protest.

Early one Sunday morning a few weeks later, the Buckeystowners struck back. In a daring guerilla raid engineered by three of the squad's members, the Buckeystowners reclaimed the old 1954 brush truck, minus the rotor, using a tow truck. "We just did what we had to do, that was all," Ford said, proudly recalling the memorable event. In the wake of the dispute, the Adamstown squad admitted two blacks to its roster of 135 members and eliminated the men-only rule from its charter.

It did not end happily for the Buckeystown squad. The county fire and rescue association laid down a set of requirements the squad could never meet, including that it relocate the fire hall to a site that satisfied the four-mile limit. The new site was, necessarily, north of Buckeystown. The new squad would also be required to begin rescue and ambulance service simultaneously, although it had three ambulances but no fire trucks yet. A fire truck would cost $90,000, a new site as much as $100,000, Ford reckoned.

"The chances of our group raising $200,000 with no guarantees of ever being certified are nil," he told the county commissioners, who had final say. "If you approve the association's recommendations today, our organization is dead."

Nonetheless, the commissioners accepted the association's guidelines as binding. Since county approval was needed (along with it came a $12,500-a-year subsidy), Buckeystown was through. Two months later, the Buckeystown squad was evicted from its service-station quarters and the building was put up for sale.

"The people who did this [the Buckeystown squad] weren't politically savvy," said Mary Ann Ford, who did not exclude her husband from the critique. "They rubbed people's noses in it. They should have won the firemen's association to their view. Instead, there was a lot of brashness, a 'We're gonna fight 'em' spirit. But not enough to win the war. That was the weakness."

"It was worth every damn bit of it, to prove that racism and bigotry existed, every damn bit of it," insisted Wilbur.

Four years after it had begun, the Buckeystown fire company was history, but the controversy had helped open up other companies in the county to women and blacks. Even Adamstown had female rescue workers. Wilbur Ford took some consolation from that fact. But, his old firecoat and hat hanging forlornly in his garage office, he remained bitter about his own experience. And he and his wife still wondered how in the world the quaint old village where they lived would ever become a community again.

It was happening across Maryland's megalopolis, from the foothills of Appalachia to the Chesapeake shores, as commuters moved outward for reasons of aesthetics, lifestyle, and cost. Invariably, city and country cultures came into conflict as natives and newcomers clashed on the metropolitan frontier.

In the Mitchellville area of Prince George's County, I met native Walter Calvin Arnold, who had already lost the battle against suburbia in his own backyard. But he wasn't quite ready to admit it. He was too busy making hay.

Arnold was a man out of his time and place. His "new" tractor was vintage 1949. His old one was new in 1939. He was a Southern Marylander, not a Washington suburbanite. When he was growing up on the family farm, Prince George's County was country almost to the District line, and the bureaucracy was what they had downtown.

Then came the suburbs. The law of the land became the county code. But Walter Arnold didn't get the message. He thought it was still the country. So when the stables on his 32.4-acre farm near Route 50 and the Capital Beltway burned down, he hauled some old milk and laundry vans onto his land to store hay and thought nothing of it. That was in 1961. A dozen years later, as subdivisions marched closer and closer to his domain, law and order came to the hay and cattle farmer. His vans, he was told, had to go. He was told this repeatedly, as the county bureaucracy cranked out edicts demanding the vans' removal and citing various zoning ordinances it said Arnold, by now a grizzled grandfather in his sixties, was violating by "operating an automobile junk yard."

They fought it out in court. Arnold won the first round at the Upper Marlboro courthouse, then lost in Annapolis, when the county appealed. When I arrived on the scene some weeks later, three inspectors were on hand to tell him he was in contempt of court and could go to jail if the three remaining vans (one filled with fertilizer, the others with hay) weren't removed forthwith. "You're at the end of your string now," the county zoning enforcement officer said.

The official suggested Arnold show me around "the plantation." He turned to the farmer and said, "We'll see you, Mr. Arnold. Have a nice day." Then the three county people drove off in their official car, out the long gravel driveway, leaving Arnold and me to ponder his fate. "I don't know where in the hell to put my hay," he shrugged. "I'm debating whether to keep on bailing or go buy a shotgun...and use it." Arnold laughed. "They told us when we went to school the Constitution tells you you can do anything you want to so long as it doesn't interfere with the health and welfare of anyone else," he said, not laughing.

Arnold lived alone, in a trailer. County inspectors used to cite him for his septic system, too. But since his well had run dry the previous fall, he hadn't used it, anyway. Instead, he hauled his drinking water in jugs from a neighbor's house and used an old privy out back.

Arnold had attended school through seventh grade, which was in 1935. Then, "like every damn kid I knew," he went to work on the family farm "while my father laid underneath the shade tree. I knew how to farm, that's all I knew then," he said. Over near Central Avenue, they grew corn, tobacco, tomatoes, cantaloupes, and watermelons. Of his classmates, Harry Townsend, Jr., was the big success story. He sold insurance.

"I was brought up during the Depression. I don't know what good times are," he said. "When they were having good times, I was having wife trouble. I was still having hard times." He had seven siblings. "All that's got any sense left Prince George County," he said, pronouncing the county's name the way only old-timers did, without the apostrophe s. He also left, for World War II. He was in Africa, Italy, France, and Germany with the 6617th Engineering Mine Clearance Company. "Souvenir of Italy, 1944," said the white and yellow fabric hanging in his trailer.

He bought the farm in 1949, from an uncle. That was the same year zoning came to Prince George's County, although zoning inspectors then were few and far between. The tract he bought had a house, now used for storage, "partly for agricultural use." It had been condemned. "They're hollering at me for not tearing it down," farmer Arnold said. He got his first trailer in 1968. That, too, was used for storage. Located about his property were a dozen "VW" auto crates placed on cinder blocks and one stamped "Indonesian Embassy" he'd gotten from Fidelity Storage in Ardmore.

In 1973 someone had offered him nearly $10,000 an acre for his farm, subject to zoning approval for light industry. The homeowners down the road at Willow Grove protested and won. The sale fell through. Shortly after that, zoning officials acting on a complaint from a nearby civic association inspected his property. They sent their first violation notice on December 20, 1973. In 1977 they threatened him with ninety days in jail and a $500 fine for each day the vans remained on his property.

When the county finally took him to court, he told the judge that the mostly wheelless, engineless vans were perfect for hay. "The sheds are too air tight," he said. "The hay could mold."

The judge ruled the vans were, in fact, accessory farm buildings and therefore exempt from regulation. "Sheds of an odd configuration but buildings nonetheless under the ordinance," he said. The state's court of special appeals reversed the judge, and the state's highest appellate court declined to review the case. Arnold was dunned $179 for court costs and ordered within thirty days to remove "all inoperable and junk automobiles, trucks, and vans and to cease and desist and not in the future to use or permit the use of such land for a junkyard or automobile salvage yard."

The junkyard description bothered him most. "I haven't got my first damn penny out of it," he said, "and they're gonna throw the book at me." Except for two or three hours during a child support-custody dispute with his first wife, he told me, he'd never been to jail. Nor had he ever gone on welfare or gotten food stamps. He wanted to increase his herd of seven cows, cross-breeding dairy with beef. Meanwhile, he was scraping by on some savings and money he earned operating a backhoe and front-end loaders for builders one or two days a month. He'd had the equipment since 1968 to "push out a few trees now and then." Inspectors had told him, "It's illegal to have that on the farm."

As he spoke, the sound of trucks on Route 50 could be heard in the distance. Train noises from another direction competed with the rumble of bulldozers being used to build an industrial park across Lottsford Vista Road. In the other direction were winding suburban streets and split-level homes, barely visible through the trees. The development was called The Meadows, which better described Arnold's field leading to it. The homes adjoined his property across a stream called Folly Branch.

Under threat of imprisonment, Walter Arnold finally yielded to civilization. With his son's help, he gave the vans away. Then he called me. "It didn't cost me nothing but the aggravation," he said. The neighbors, he said, had derelict autos in the street near his hay farm. They were an eyesore, and the county hadn't done a thing about it, despite his complaints. That wasn't fair, he said, and who could argue with him on that?

Farm culture best endures away from the pressures of urban institutions and growth. Closer to the cities, it has withered from generation to generation as subdivisions have spread across the countryside. In a few short years, I watched the country disappear around Washington, west toward Frederick, north toward Baltimore, in almost every direction. And yet, rural patches persisted in unlikely places, but not forever.

Countless times, I had driven past the old house just beyond the Capital Beltway, noticing what appeared to be an adjoining plot of farmland virtually surrounded by suburb, and one day I stopped to find out why it was there.

It was, it turned out, the last 3.91-acre remnant of what had once been a 200-acre farm. Now, it was all but hidden by bushes from the view of motorists speeding by on six-lane Georgia Avenue. The old stone house was occupied by Frederick Simpson Getty. At seventy-three, Getty was, indeed, the last farmer of Forest Glen. In the short time I knew him, he lost his land and moved away, and it is not too much to say that the world in some small but significant way would never be quite the same.

In this last patch of farmland, Getty cultivated his own garden and rented out plots to friends and neighbors. He also rented out himself and his tractor, to plow private or public ground, wherever the need arose amidst the clusters and congestion of the close-in suburbs and the city, where farm machinery is as scarce as a Southern States store or a grain elevator.

And yet, before he retired, he had been a surveyor by trade, transforming the farms of the past into the subdivisions of the present. "I staked out all these subdivisions in Montgomery [County]," he told me, casually. "Viers Mill Village. Twinbrook. I laid out all that. This one, right beside my house now, too. I can't remember the name of the damn thing now. Forest something."

His last job, which had taken seven years to complete, was mapping out Metrorail, including its Georgia Avenue alignment just past the property from which he had watched the country disappear. It was still possible to pretend, from certain parts of the property planted in peas or lettuce or tomatoes, that this was the country. It was just a pretense, of course, masking the unmistakable roar of traffic rushing by at all hours, even late at night, when the ambulances blared their sirens and woke up Fred Getty's dogs, whose barking interrupted his sleep "every damn time."

When Getty was a boy, he would run to the roadside by his house and watch a single car approaching and stand in awe as it disappeared in the dust. "Very few people had cars and, hell, I knew everybody who came down the road," he said. "This road wasn't paved for a long time. It was a pile of stones, a mudhole. The farmers would take stones from the field, haul and dump 'em on the road to get rid of them. This was nothing but mud in wintertime. In summertime, if there was a drought, it could get dusty as the devil."

Then, it was two lanes of macadam, until it was widened into a dual highway with such ceremony in 1952 that the governor came to the dedication. And as the cars and the people came, the farms that filled the countryside became history along with the Gettys.

Fred Getty was the grandson of Brigadier General George Washington Getty, a graduate of West Point who fought for the Union in the Civil War (despite his wife's southern roots) and later served on the western frontier. Before the war, George Getty's family lived in Georgetown, and it was his task as a youth to pasture their cows at what is now Connecticut Avenue and M Street NW.

George Getty first passed the Forest Glen farm in 1862 while marching to Antietam. After the war, and service in Texas, New Mexico, South Carolina, and Virginia, he asked a relative to find him a home in Maryland. The Batchelor Farm, which sprawled all the way to Sligo Creek, was purchased for $8,000 at a tax sale. In 1883 the old soldier moved into the twenty-two-room house big enough to accommodate family visits from his six grown grandchildren. He prevailed on the youngest, George Graham Getty, to give up his own dream of attending the U.S. Naval Academy in Annapolis and manage the place instead. It was three miles from the District of Columbia on the Brookeville Road, a toll pike that was to become Georgia Avenue. The post office was Forest Glen.

When General Getty died in 1901, soldiers came to carry his coffin all the way to Arlington National Cemetery.

In turn-of-the-century Forest Glen, the rural setting seemed perfectly intact. As recalled by Mildred Newbold Getty, Fred's sister and a schoolteacher who lived to the age of eighty-five, life was a country frolic for the four children of G. Graham Getty. "We gathered chestnuts in the fall, or played in the apple orchard and ate red apples," she wrote to Fred's son in 1959.

> Often Graham [a brother] and I rode in the four-horse wagon out to the fields with the men to bring in the hay. Or we would have great fun bringing in the corn. As we rode, we could look out over the adjoining fields, and perhaps see the winter wheat being sown as the corn was harvested.
>
> In the winter, snow came and sleds were brought out. We slid down the hill in the pasture...or we'd go for a ride in the red basket sleigh. If there was no snow, but the weather was cold enough for freezing, we'd go with the farm hands to the ice pond in the far end of the pasture and watch while they cut great chunks of ice to carry up to the icehouse in the wagon.
>
> In the summer, we spent long, lazy hours wading in the little brook which came from a spring in the pasture. Or we would climb the fence, and follow the make-believe river to the spot where the watercress grew thick and dark-green, its roots a tangled, muddy mass in the water.... In July, we always went out to gather dewberries. Their vines ran along the ground in the uncultivated fields....We all loved the free, outdoor life on the farm.

But their father didn't. In 1911 he persuaded his mother to sell half the land. Fifty acres went to an insurance executive for $12,000. After another transaction, the house was deeded to a Catholic church, which burned it down to make room for a new place of worship that is still there. G. Graham Getty, meanwhile, built the stone house in 1912 still occupied years later by his son Fred. He also sold half the remaining one hundred acres.

On his shrunken farm, G. Graham Getty kept a dozen dairy cows, and Fred used to help deliver the milk around Silver Spring. "He didn't last long because the milk route didn't pay enough," Fred Getty said. "Then my older brother and sister took care of him and he gave up farming." Upon his death in 1945, his children sold all but 3.91 acres to the developers of Forest Estates.

Fred Getty took to farming as his father never did. And, while he made a living at surveying, he remained, he said, "still a country boy." He did not let the little land that was left lie fallow. On Georgia Avenue, he grew tomatoes, peas, onions, spinach, sugar beets, corn, lima beans, lettuce, cabbage, potatoes. For years he also raised vegetables "up-county" and delivered his produce to buyers in the Silver Spring area. He used to raise a few chickens, too. Then chicken feed got too expensive and impossible to find any closer than Gaithersburg, way out I-270.

When I met him, his gait was slowed by age and his vision clouded by cataracts. The government had just contracted to buy his property, for $600,000. A developer had offered him three times as much, but the county had other ideas. The park commission, with its powers of condemnation, made him an offer he couldn't refuse. It wanted the land for a park with tennis, basketball, and handball courts, a playground, and parking for a hundred people a day. It would be landscaped, of course, and be known as General Getty Park.

The money to buy the land was there, but development would have to wait. Meanwhile, the house Getty's father built would be occupied by a park employee, and the garden plots and one-hundred-year-old tenant house would continue to be used, as before. That suited Carolan Getty Armstrong, Fred's surviving sister, who lived nearby, well enough, but it was little comfort to Fred.

"I'd just like to stay here the rest of my days," Getty told me one morning on his front porch. "I have to get out. I gotta find some other place to hang my hat." A week or so later, he had found his new place in the sun, six acres of cleared ground and a "typical old farmhouse" far removed from urban development pressures, across the Potomac on Virginia's Northern Neck.

"It's rich ground, sandy soil, really good for growing stuff," he beamed. "It's got two wells and a little stream, so if I want to have a couple of cattle, they can water there. It has a barn and a shed to put all my machinery, tractors, and what not. The man said to bring the tractor on down. It's not too late to plant, so I'm going on down, do some planting right away. Potatoes. Cabbage. It's not too late."

In the middle of Maryland's shifting metropolitan frontier sits suddenly transformed Howard County, shaped like an arrowhead pointing westward between Baltimore and Washington. For centuries, it had been rural and southern. Then, almost overnight in the 1960s and 1970s, the conservative, old-line "countians" were overwhelmed politically, socially, and ideologically by newcomers with their own ideas of right and wrong who inhabited Columbia, the "new town" of developer James Rouse.

Secretly, the man from the Eastern Shore had assembled thousands of acres, using "straws" to hide the total transaction. This farmland between Baltimore and Washington would be developed anyway, he argued, and how much better it would be for the development to occur in a rational, orderly way. There would be no suburban sprawl or fast-food strips in the brave new world of James Rouse. Instead, there would be nine "villages" with homes and shops clustered together, a "town center" and five thousand acres of open space. Before the countians knew it, Columbia was a fait accompli. With a projected population of 110,000, the new town aborning became a mecca for visiting city planners. The influx of new arrivals made Howard the fastest-growing county in the state and forever changed its demographic and political landscape. Columbians were politically more liberal and racially more integrated than any group Howard County had ever known. Indeed, the new city's first newborn was of interracial parentage.

It was, Rouse boasted in a slide and sound show at the Columbia exhibit center, "a city that works, not a perfect city, but a better city." Voices of Columbians testified on behalf of this claim: "It's like a great big family...more humanitarian.... It has a kind of openness and searching quality more reflective of what this country needs...not a community, a way of life."

It seemed as if almost everything the Columbians were for, countians were against, and vice versa. The Columbians were for "farm preservation." The countians opposed it as a restriction on their agricultural property rights. Columbians had a Renaissance Festival. The countians held a county fair, an old-fashioned livestock show at the fairgrounds several miles west of the new town. Countians read the *Baltimore Sun*, Columbians increasingly received the *Washington Post*. Many Columbians commuted to work down Route 29 to Washington. Countians farmed where they lived or worked wherever the jobs were. In the Columbia Mall, many of the sales jobs were held by countians, who in effect serviced the new arrivals. But in one factory sportswear outlet, you needed Columbia identification to shop. It was as though the countians and the Columbians inhabited two different worlds. And, in fact, they did.

"I think the people in Columbia are lonely," Barbara Feaga told me on her dairy farm west of Ellicott City, the Howard County seat. "They have to look for things to entertain, to devote their spare time to. People out here don't have any spare time." Pausing from hanging the wash, she sat at a long picnic table while her husband baled hay. "There is just a difference in their style of life and our style of life," she reflected. "The countians had their families here, they had an established social life, they had their church suppers." Philosophically, she said, "they're liberal and we're conservative."

The dichotomy between the two groups was a simple fact of life to which leaders of the new town regretfully resigned themselves. Trying to see it from the countians' point of view, Columbian Gayle Saunier told me, "Here was this beautiful, placid agricultural county, and this big developer comes sneaking around buying up all the properties and puts this big city right in their county. Some of these people will never forgive the Rouse Company for doing this. However, it's brought a lot of conveniences to the county. Of course, some, if they had their druthers, would've left the amenities and kept the peaceful, agricultural county. We must work with these people. I think the worst is over, but a few people will never change their minds."

Saunier ran something called the "Columbia Forum," an annual meeting of the minds to which all residents of the new town were invited. In a series of workshops, the Columbians discussed their community's growing pains and the fact that it was so new it even lacked a cemetery to call its own. They dwelt on domestic policies. Only in passing did they address Columbia's foreign relations with the rest of the county.

The forum was under the auspices of the Columbia Association, a private, nonprofit corporation initially dominated by the developer's representatives that was evolving into a form of self-government for the new city. It was housed in an anonymous one-story building whose inconspicuous looks were part and parcel of the Columbia style. The association's president was a suave, silver-haired man named Padraic Kennedy. Like Saunier and most other Columbians, he was not from Howard County.

To Kennedy, a former Peace Corps official who had also played a major role in the 1960s' federal war on poverty, the greatest impact of Columbia over fifteen years had been what he described as a "demographic revolution" in the county. "In the late '50s, there were 'Whites Only' signs over the courthouse drinking fountains," he said, recalling what he'd been told by others who were around at the time. "Now, there's a black on the county council [who grew up on a Calvert County farm and now lived in Columbia]. And there isn't a village, a neighborhood, or a street in Columbia that's not racially integrated. To me, that is the one thing about Columbia that is astonishing."

It was astonishing, too, to countians like Charlie Amoss, who ran the last segregated bar in a tiny, ramshackle building near the county fairgrounds in, of all places, West Friendship. Times had changed all around the eighty-four-year-old man, whose tavern was open for business from dawn to dark every day except Tuesdays. New houses dotted the rolling countryside, nearby I-70 cut a wide swath across the land, and the new town of Columbia, eleven miles to the southeast, had come to dominate his native county. But Charlie Amoss's world remained in many respects rooted in the past.

At Charlie's tavern, whites entered through the front and blacks through the side, and they remained separated from each other by a thin wooden partition. In 1983, Amoss's fiftieth year in the bar business, the divider still stood and, by custom, according to the proprietor, so did the racial separation, an anachronism he and his patrons seemed to accept as the normal way of doing business.

Since the laws had changed, he stressed, he did not discriminate. "They pay the same damn price," he informed me, adding that whites sometimes go to the other side "if it gets crowded." But "very seldom" did it work the other way, he said. "All the old colored comes in that side," he noted, pointing to the partition. "You never have one in here. It's by habit, by habit, that's all. In a year, I don't have many colored strangers. They're all born and raised here."

On the day I visited Charlie's tavern, he had just two black customers. Both entered through the side door, one with a white co-worker. "I don't fool around here much," said one black man, a longtime customer who dashed in and out with a six-pack and cigarettes and said he was in a hurry to get to work. The rest of the patrons, numbering two dozen or so, all of them white and many of them elderly, ambled in the front door.

A year or two before, the Howard County NAACP had sent a team to test the racial barrier. Blacks and whites were served together in the "white" section, and the county human rights commission voted to drop the matter. "There have never been any complaints filed," the human rights office administrator, a black woman who lived in Columbia, informed me. "It is a very minor anachronism, in my opinion." But there it was, anyway.

The "black" side of the bar had a table, a bench, and the refrigerator where the beer was stored. The "white" side had five chairs Amoss had acquired at auction, a step-stool he occupied when customers came around, and several gritty aluminum ash trays that had once held TV dinners. Behind the bar were an outdated number (111585) for the Maryland lottery, a 1980 calendar, and a sign that said, "Enjoy the American Way," touting the American Beer label, a brand that no longer exists. Two ancient ceiling fans cooled and two single light bulbs illuminated opposite sides of the partition.

Although racial attitudes were deeply ingrained at the slightly sloping tavern, and new yellow vinyl siding out front only partly hid its age, Charlie Amoss's place was much more than a relic of Jim Crow days. For many, it was a tradition. Thus, the two black customers came and went without comment. The talk of the day centered, rather, on the economy, on the reported death of a local house painter "up to Sunshine," on raising cattle and the Baltimore Orioles and the apparently fruitless efforts of seventy-two-year-old George Rittenhouse to sell two sixteen-dollar tickets he had haplessly bought for the bull roast at the Howard County fairgrounds.

Despite the new industrial parks, offices, and mall in Columbia, the feeling was that Howard County offered little for the working man. "Goddamn if this county ain't going to hell for work," said Mike Bledson, who hauled wood. "Yep," agreed Nimrod Walker, "you have to go down the road."

Walker and Marie, his wife, looked after Amoss. On his way to work each morning, Walker brought Amoss coffee. "If I don't, he gets mad at me for two days," he said. "We're all family here," his wife explained. "This is the only bar I go to, this and the VFW and American Legion."

The wall that divided white and black was erected in 1930, the same year Amoss married his wife, Edna, who died in 1976. The partition's initial purpose was to separate the then-grocery from a sandwich counter, both run by the Amoss clan, which had lived here for as long as anyone could remember. Charlie Amoss was the last of the breed. He was born and raised in western Howard County, where his people were dairy farmers and his father operated the tollgate on what was then the privately owned Baltimore-to-Frederick road. As a youngster, he drove the horse-drawn dairy wagon to meet the 7 a.m. milk train in Sykesville. He could remember well the days before electricity and a time when, if you had indoor plumbing, "Ye God, you were somebody." Now, he had twenty acres, two geese, two roosters, a couple of cats, and a dog named Rebel. In summertime he lived in an old house down the road. From October into spring, he lived in the tavern, warmed by a wood stove.

Although he read two daily newspapers and hadn't "missed a vote" since his first in 1920, Charlie Amoss lived in an insular world. Amoss had seen his last picture show about the same time he'd gone into the bar business. That was April 7, 1933, the day beer came back and he sold brew at ten cents a bottle, or three for twenty-five. A half century later, he owned a seven-year-old car that had logged only eleven thousand miles. He had repeatedly refused to visit a sister in Florida, and he hadn't been to Baltimore in ten years. That trip was to buy a suit, his newest. He had last ventured into the District of Columbia in 1941 or 1942, to settle an estate. "Washington's mostly colored, isn't it?" he asked me, seeking to confirm relatively recent reports that the District had a black majority.

He had never been to the new city of Columbia, which he said had "ruined the county" but "there ain't much we can do about it. A fellow in here yesterday said he wouldn't vote for anybody from Columbia. About ninety percent on the ticket come out of Columbia."

Local blacks, he said, "flock to Columbia now." They also patronized a black bar in nearby Cooksville. "That way, they don't bother me too much." As closing time drew near, as many as thirty empty beer bottles graced the top of Charlie Amoss's bar on the "white" side of the partition. But the black side was quiet and empty. "I ain't bothered with 'em much, just a few of 'em," Amoss said, matter-of-factly. "I got rid of most of them."

Charlie Amoss operated his tavern the same way, while the world changed around him, for half a century. Then, as the winds of winter chilled the Howard County countryside, Charlie Amoss and his segregated bar both passed into history.

13

Maryland, C.S.A

*E*very year, in the not-too-distant past, they gathered at the old Monocacy Cemetery on a very special day in June. The women brought box lunches, the children marched, the politicians spoke. It was a proud gathering, a celebration of lives invested in a lost cause.

Now, nobody comes to lay wreaths or flowers on the stone tablet bearing the names of Marylanders who fought for a cause in which they believed. They fought for the Confederate States of America, and the day of remembrance was June third, the birthdate of the Confederate president, Jefferson Davis.

The names on the tablet are Chiswell, Pyles, White, Wootton, Butler, Hays, Jones, Veirs, Dade, and Dickerson, among others—sixteen separate surnames, thirty-two names in all.

But for a twist of geography, they would have been Virginians, plain and simple, their southern sympathies taken for granted and of little note. But they were Marylanders, a small segment of the twenty-two thousand who crossed the river to fight for Dixie in the Civil War. They had seceded, even if, officially, their state had not.

I had come here in search of a monument, a starting point from which to learn about a place and a people. My search ended—and began—in this obscure country cemetery that sits on a bluff above the tiny village of Beallsville, thirty-five miles northwest of Washington, in Montgomery County. What I found was a world that had slipped away, and a new perspective on the supposedly "northern" Maryland suburbs of Washington, D.C.

Through the story of these men and their descendants, I gained a different view of Maryland's Montgomery County. Its self-image and the image it likes to project to the outside world is one of affluent chic: a place populated by highly educated, upper-income, cosmopolitan citizens, a setting where northern liberals who move to the Washington suburbs feel at home. Yet, it is no longer comfortable for all concerned: Some of the natives no longer feel at home in their own county.

"If the Potomac River had bent in the opposite direction, we'd be in Loudon County [Virginia], and I might feel more at home," said Charles Elgin, the tall, lanky mayor of Poolesville and a descendant of Confederates Thomas Henry White and John Elgin. Elgin was also secretary-treasurer of the Monocacy

Cemetery association. His wife, Dorothy Jones Elgin, a direct descendant of Confederate Michael Thomas Pyles, kept the burial records.

Remembering the Confederacy in Monocacy Chapel, Montgomery County.
Gerald Martineau, *Washington Post*

The Confederate veterans buried in Monocacy had returned from the war dishonored by the government whose oath of allegiance they ultimately took but honored by their families, friends, and neighbors. For generations, their service was a badge of honor in their county, and their families dominated its politics and its commerce. With names like Allnut, Beall, Butler, Chiswell, Dade, Darby, Dickerson, and Elgin, on down through the alphabet, they were known as "the ABCs of Montgomery County." Then, ever so gradually, as memories of the past ebbed, so did their power. The county changed, and it all slipped away.

"We thought we were a cliche, had everything our own way," summed up Dorothy Butler Hopkins, granddaughter of Confederate Charles Martin Butler, "Then, everything opened up."

Through the generations, they farmed the land until it could no longer sustain them, and then some drifted away, finding jobs and homes in Washington and its growing suburbs. Others stayed and commuted or worked where they could. Some who had left returned in retirement. Their bloodlines intertwined to the point where area news was family news. "Maybe that's why we're not so smart or successful," said one self-effacing descendant.

They came, first, from Anne Arundel, Prince George's, and Charles counties in lower Maryland to upper Montgomery County in the 1700s. They brought with them their slaves and their southern way of life. Until the soil gave out, they raised tobacco. Then they filled the rolling countryside and the rich bottomland along the Potomac with grazing cattle and wheat, corn, and grass.

There were, by 1860, 5,421 slaves and 1,552 free blacks—comprising 38.1% of the population—along with 10,500 whites in Montgomery County.

White sentiment was mostly pro-South and overwhelmingly proslavery, except for a few seemingly quixotic Quakers over in Sandy Spring. Even Unionists owned slaves and opposed abolition.

In Medley's District, the election subdivision comprising the northwestern end of the county, Abraham Lincoln received not one vote in the 1860 presidential contest (and only fifty in all of Montgomery). Free blacks had established communities at Mt. Ephraim and Big Woods, but slaves were still deemed essential to the economy. An 1867 census of freed slaves disclosed how extensive were the slaveholdings of the families whose sons fought for the South: Mary E. Chiswell, whose brother-in-law led the Montgomery Confederates southward and whose son Edward Jones Chiswell joined them as a second lieutenant, owned fourteen slaves. George Walter Chiswell, her fighting brother-in-law, had eight. Eliza Hays, whose son Richard Poole Hays championed the lost cause to his dying day years later, had twenty-four. Joseph C. White, father of Confederate Thomas Henry White, had twenty-three. And so it went.

Phillip Johnson, a slave who later helped found the freedmen's town of Sugarland south of Poolesville, belonged to Dr. Stephen N.C. White, whose farm in the Edward's Ferry area near the Potomac had thirty-six slaves. In the 1930s he would tell New Deal interviewers that "we all liked the Missis," but the overseer was "so cruel...I promised him a killin' if I ever got big enough." But he enjoyed farm work, he said. "It was pretty to see four or five [wheat] cradlers in a field and others following them raking the wheat in bunches."

The down-county suburbs of Chevy Chase, Silver Spring, Wheaton, and Bethesda didn't yet exist. The county seat, then as now, was Rockville, a hub of activity far removed from Washington. Located 16.8 miles west of Rockville, Poolesville was the second largest community in the area. Its population of 350 would remain virtually unchanged for more than a century. Around Poolesville were satellite settlements: Dawsonville, Beallsville, Barnesville, Edward's Ferry, Conrad's Ferry, Dickerson.

When the war broke out, the cavalier tradition was well established here. Benjamin Stephen White, a leading Poolesville merchant, led cavalry practice Saturday afternoons on Thomas Gott's farm, now a housing development outside Poolesville. White, at age forty-three, would be among the first to cross the Potomac in the spring of 1861 and pledge his allegiance to the South.

Those who stayed home were non-cooperators, and some actively helped the Confederacy. Thomas Gott, among others, was held at Washington's Capitol Prison for erecting a cannon on his farm to shell the 8th Illinois Cavalry, and was eventually imprisoned at Point Lookout, in St. Mary's County. Joseph Hoyle piloted, by his count, between one and two thousand Confederate soldiers across the Potomac at night. The Hays family entertained and fed Confederate troops passing through Barnesville. The wife of Charles M. Butler hid Confederate soldiers at her farm near Poolesville. Her husband and brother-in-law had gone south, and their father followed to look after them.

Poolesville itself was under federal occupation and martial law during the war. As few as sixty and as many as twelve thousand Union troops were garrisoned there at different times. Beginning in 1861, the citizens filed claims against the U.S. government for damages they blamed on the federal troops. On October 31,1861, Charles M. Butler, who soon thereafter joined the Confederate army, and Mary E. Chiswell filed claims for $125.86 and $476.45 for fence rails, corn, and fodder commandeered by federal troops.

A Union regiment's postwar history described Poolesville as "a small insignificant place...everything had a tumbled down, decayed appearance...two poorly kept taverns, two stores and a church. Yet this village was surrounded by one of the richest agricultural districts in Maryland, whose broad fields, sloping hills and valleys yielded immense crops of wheat, corn, hay, etc. But the people lacked that thrift and ambition that Northerners possess to make the most of their resources."

The people, of course, had a different view. According to recollections half a century later of Richard P. Hays, the soldiers "seemed to realize that all of our best citizens were in full sympathy with the South; therefore, they showed their resentment by all manner of ill treatment."

On August 13, 1862, some forty men of Medley's District openly cast their lot with the South, cutting the telegraph wires below Poolesville and swimming the Chesapeake & Ohio Canal and fording the Potomac to fight for the Confederacy. A Union draft agent canvassing the Poolesville area for eligibles shortly thereafter scribbled next to the names of most if not all potential draftees, "Gone South."

Led by Captain George Walter Chiswell, they became known, unofficially, as "Chiswell's Exile Band" and formed the nucleus of Company E of the 35th Battalion Virginia Cavalry under Colonel Elijah (Lige) Veirs White, who had moved from Montgomery to Loudon County in 1857, with his bride, Mary Gott, of Dickerson. Joining his unit were three other Gott sons-in-law, Thomas Henry White, Benjamin John Jones, and Robert Lee Dade.

Lige White's battalion, nicknamed the Comanches for its fierce and unpredictable fighting style, crossed the river on more than one occasion. Once, in December 1862, White's soldiers surrounded a Poolesville Presbyterian church where forty Union troops were attending Sunday services, and as they emerged captured them, along with forty-three horses.

On an earlier visit, former slave Phillip Johnson recalled, Captain Samuel Chiswell White, a son of Dr. Stephen White, "come home from the Confederate Army and say he going to take me along back with him for to serve him. But the Yankees came and he left very sudden and leave me behind. I was glad."

During the fighting in Montgomery, Poolesville became a familiar dateline in dispatches that appeared in newspapers throughout the country. Confederates raided it six times. Barnesville, five miles north, changed hands five times in one day. And in Beallsville, two miles from Poolesville, the old chapel at the Monocacy Cemetery was destroyed by Union troops who used it to stable horses and burned the pews.

Across the Potomac, Chiswell's men chafed at regimental control. They were, they insisted, an "independent command" committed to serve along the border but otherwise unattached. When Company B, along with the rest of White's battalion, was placed under a larger brigade as "regular troops," its members were near mutiny. "Company B claimed that as Marylanders, they owed no allegiance to the Confederacy," Captain Frank M. Myers, the battalion historian, recalled in his 1871 book about White's troops. "They had come over voluntarily, because their sympathies were with the South, but being foreigners they had the right to select for themselves the manner in which they would serve her."

The rebellion within the Rebellion fizzled, and the men of Montgomery proceeded to fight in some of the bloodiest battles of the war, some distance from the Potomac border. "We have whipped them in every fight," George Chiswell wrote his wife in May 1863. "Truly they will find at this time that Richmond is a hard road to travel." However, Chiswell wrote, "A number have been wounded. [Overall, Company B's casualties amounted to two dead and twenty-eight wounded.] Frank Williams has a flesh wound in the thigh [his leg would have been amputated had not Battalion Surgeon Edward Wootton intervened], Alonzo Sellman in the hand slightly, Col. E.V. White slightly in the face." Alonzo, a sergeant with Company B, would live another fifteen years. His brother Wallace, who served with Company A, 1st Maryland Cavalry, C.S.A., died of typhoid fever in the Valley of Virginia on May 22, 1863.

Captain George Chiswell was himself injured on June 9, 1863. At the cavalry battle at Brandy Station, which cost the 35th Battalion ninety officers and enlisted men killed, wounded, or missing, Chiswell sustained a leg wound that took him out of action. Secretly, he returned home to be nursed back to health and, after returning to his unit in October 1864, wrote his wife, "I have thrown away my crutches or rather given them to Elijah Veirs [who was injured May 6, 1864, in the Wilderness]. I get along very well with the use of a cane." He had been, he wrote, "waiting for 'Old Abe' to take the pickets off the river so I could come over, but it seems he will not do it this season."

Private Elias Price had his leg amputated by a Union surgeon after being injured on November 29, 1863, in the Wilderness Campaign. He took the oath of allegiance rather than face life as a Confederate prisoner of war, and was allowed to go home. As a shoe merchant in Poolesville after the war, he would forever be known as Peg Leg Price, a familiar figure with a crutch.

Not all Montgomery men who were wounded wore the hero's mantle. Ben White, who had rushed to join J.E.B. Stuart's staff and rose to the rank of major, sought transfer to the cavalry. After suffering a neck wound at Brandy Station, he wound up far from the fighting, in charge of a horse hospital.

When Lee surrendered, Lige White's warriors withdrew to Lynchburg to await further orders. They never came, and the group disbanded, going in twos or threes to federal officers to be paroled. Chiswell's exile band returned from war defeated men, their slaves freed by Maryland's new state constitution, narrowly approved in 1864 (but soundly rejected in Montgomery, 1,367 to 422). A plan to compensate the former slaveowners was scrapped.

Emancipation had drastically changed the region's economy. Several of the farms sustained further losses from the presence of Union troops. Their owners again filed claims for forage and fences: Mary Elgin sought $1,194 for fence rail, timber, and fodder. Elizabeth White, widow of Dr. Stephen White, waited until 1874 to file her claim for $2,605 against various Union units that had camped on her farm. "Due to the pecuniary embarrassment of the period," St. Peter's Church in Poolesville decided to hold services every other Sunday and to reduce the rector's pay.

In this setting, the population of Medley's District stagnated during the 1870s and 1880s. Some people moved west to Missouri, joining relatives who had migrated before the war. Henry B. Veirs, for one, went in 1879 to Calloway County, Missouri, where he died in 1902.

Poolesville's boosters, however, saw the postwar period as one of opportunity. With hopes of overtaking Rockville, the town incorporated in 1867, giving it more municipal powers than would be allowed downcounty suburbs decades later. Anticipating growth, Poolesville was empowered to control its development and tax its citizens. The town also had its own bailiff to make arrests, while the mayor doubled as justice of the peace, a necessary expedient since the sheriff and courts were in Rockville, a good half-day trip by horse and buggy over primitive roads.

Optimism over Poolesville's future was founded on location: It was centrally situated a few miles in either direction from two main avenues of commerce. The C&O Canal was one, from the 1830s on carrying Montgomery wheat to the tidewater port of Georgetown. The other, beginning in 1873, was the Metropolitan Branch of the B&O Railroad, stopping at Boyd's, Sellman's Station, Barnesville, and Dickerson on its route to and from Washington and Frederick. Colonel Lige White and Dr. Edward Wootton, his battalion surgeon from Poolesville and a Georgetown College graduate, went into business together in 1878 with warehouses and mills along the canal. Conrad's Ferry became White's Ferry. It survives today as a seeming anachronism, the place from which the General Jubal Early—a ferryboat named after the Confederate officer who nearly captured Washington—carries cars across the Potomac River.

Lige White sold all his Montgomery County interests in 1886 to Wootton and moved to Leesburg, establishing a bank and running his feed business there. Wootton's name, meanwhile, was boosted for Congress as early as 1878, but he bided his time. In 1887, following in the footsteps of his father, also a doctor-politician, Wootton ran as an anti-machine Democrat for the House of Delegates and garnered the largest vote in a field of nine competing for three seats. In Annapolis, Delegate Wootton served on the internal improvements committee. In 1889 he won a seat in the state senate. Soon his house seat would be filled by Lieutenant Edward J. Chiswell, nephew of Captain George Chiswell.

Benjamin S. White, the old major, fared less well. Penniless after the war, White moved to Baltimore "to make an honest effort to support my family" as a merchant. But business did not go well, and he returned to Montgomery in 1883. He ran for clerk of the circuit court two years later. Word was his brother wouldn't even vote for him, and his residency qualifications were questioned. White responded in a newspaper notice peppered with Confederate code words designed to elicit support ("waver not in line, but stand like a stonewall"). He lost anyway. Two years later, White ran last in the nine-way race for the legislature, losing to the popular Dr. Wootton. During his campaign, he won no significant endorsements, but he himself endorsed a cure for rheumatism, indigestion, and dyspepsia manufactured by the Swift Specific Company of Atlanta, which in turn described him in print as a "Distinguished Soldier and Gentleman."

White died in March 1891 in Barnesville, a frustrated man. But he left a son by his second marriage who went on to serve as an army surgeon in the Canal Zone and eventually retired to Poolesville. (A granddaughter, Sarah Ellen White

Pyles, lived to the ripe old age of 101 before she died in 1981.)

Life around postwar Poolesville, meanwhile, could be genteel. There was the neighborhood trotting contest in Dickerson and, early each June, the ladies of St. Peter's Episcopal Church held their annual strawberry festival, a tradition that continues to this day. In January 1882 the Literary Society met at the home of Mrs. E. Poole for readings of selected works, and, afterward, the *Montgomery County Sentinel* reported, "a number of young ladies and gents repaired to the [Masonic] Hall and indulged in dancing for several hours to the harmonious music of 'Dr. Fectig,' a colored musician in our town." On another occasion, an Italian band played for the group.

But the rules were not the same for blacks and whites in postwar Poolesville. In January 1880 the town had one of a handful of lynchings in the county's history. George Peck, a twenty-two-year-old black man, was hanged for the attempted rape of a white woman he allegedly attacked while she was milking a cow. The unreconstructed *Sentinel* praised the summary execution: "This mode of meting out justice to such a miscreant when there is no doubt of his identity, will be commended by all law-abiding citizens."

Sugarland, Jerusalem, and Jonesville were among the black enclaves that sprung up around Poolesville after the war. They survive to this day. Unlike their counterparts in the Deep South, many of the newly freed blacks owned small tracts of land, enough to feed their families. On white-owned farms, black couples were sometimes quartered in a separate section of the house, blocked off from the family they served, he in the field, she in the kitchen.

By 1886 Poolesville was indeed the hub of a prosperous farming area. It was said by a visitor writing in a Baltimore newspaper to contain six stores, five churches, two hotels, a female seminary, a girls' private school and a public school, wheelwrights, blacksmiths, shoemakers, carpenters, tinners, a Masonic lodge, and "fine crops of wheat, corn, and grass raised in the contiguous countryside. There are milk and honey here...and those gifts enhanced and developed by marked progressiveness.... For hospitality as broad-sided as ever encircled you...in antebellum days...these Medley's district people stand pre-eminent; for charity. . . pure and unsullied."

In Dickerson, a railroad stop where they tended to look down on Poolesville, Confederate veteran William H. Dickerson was the postmaster. Brothers Lawrence and Edward Lee (Ned) Chiswell—both sons of Lieutenant Edward Chiswell—worked at the general store. Dairy farmers dropped off milk for the 7 a.m. train, then did business and swapped stories at the store. A trip to "the city" from the Medley district then meant to Frederick to shop, not to Washington.

Inevitably in this rural, close-knit society, the veterans' sons and daughters courted and married: two Chiswells married two Woottons; one Pyles married a Dade, another wed a White.

On June 3, 1906, the Confederate veterans were remembered at Monocacy Cemetery with the first of what would become an annual ritual. At this initial gathering, Richard Poole Hays proposed a statue of a Confederate soldier be built to honor their memory. As chaplain of the Ridgely Brown Camp, United Confederate Veterans, Rockville, Hays was instrumental the following year in establishing the Monocacy Memorial Association to raise funds for the monument he hoped would rise in the old cemetery. It was decided instead to erect the statue in Rockville.

One by one, the old soldiers died. George Butler in 1890, in a streetcar accident in Washington (his brother Charles M. Butler lived until 1918); Edward J. Chiswell ("a very gentle person," his granddaughter, Ruth Chiswell Brewer, assured me) in 1906; Michael Thomas Pyles and, over in Loudon, Colonel E.V. White himself, in 1907; Elijah E. Veirs (Colonel White's first cousin) in 1908; Benjamin John Jones, 1909; Edward Wootton and John Collinson White, 1910; William H. Dickerson in 1912.

Also in 1912, Richard Poole Hays "crossed over the river to rest under the shade of the trees," as the flowery obituary put it. "As he was a faithful soldier under the stars and bars, so also he was the same under the banner of the cross." Seven aged veterans escorted his casket, draped with a Confederate flag, to its final resting place in Monocacy Cemetery.

The year before his death, Hays had reflected on the Civil War. "I have often thought," he wrote then, "if the old vessel called the Mayflower had sunk with all on board in mid-ocean how much better it would have been for our country."

The E.V. White Chapter of the United Daughters of the Confederacy had come into being in Poolesville in July 1911 with thirty-five members. At Hays's suggestion, it was named after the colonel under whom most of Medley's men had served. The first president was Hays's daughter, Nana Poole Hays. The daughter-in-law of Captain George Chiswell was vice-president. The wife of Dr. Edward Wootton was treasurer. The first formal meeting was held at the Poolesville National Bank, now the town hall, where they sang "Marse Robert Is Asleep," described in the *Sentinel* as "one number most touching to the Southern heart."

"With simple but appropriate ceremonies," the chapter historian would recall, the cemetery tablet was erected in November 1911. Little Alta Jones, granddaughter of Benjamin John Jones, unveiled the marker "in loving memory of the valor and self-sacrifice of the Maryland soldiers in the Confederate Army." Her grandmother had helped raise money for the memorial, and until her death in 1922, she faithfully planted flowers around it each year. The marble slab, brought from England in the eighteenth century, had been the gift of John Collinson White, on whose family farm it had been used for sitting in the front yard. The tablet contained thirty-one names (one would be added later). Twenty-three of those named served with Lige White's cavalry, the rest with other units.

The following June, the E.V. White Chapter "most strongly" condemned the erection of a monument in Frederick to Barbara Fritchie, allegedly fired upon as she waved a Union flag in the face of invading Confederates. The E.V. White ladies said Stonewall Jackson's soldiers would never have warred on women. "We of the South do not object to the truth," the ladies wrote the Frederick County commissioners. Meanwhile, the chapter also contributed funds for Confederate monuments at Shiloh and Arlington and to the White House of the Confederacy in Richmond and the Confederate Women's Home in Baltimore.

They were still living in the past, of course, but it was a past only two generations old and within the memories of many. Two world wars, the Depression, and the growth of the suburbs would shape a world they could hardly envision, a world in which their allegiances would appear quaint if not downright outrageous. But that world was yet to come.

The United Daughters of the Confederacy, Southern mores, and Civil War re-enactments remain a part of Maryland culture. Eugene L. Meyer

In August 1912 the local ladies of the U.D.C. decided to build a new stone chapel in Monocacy to replace the eighteenth-century brick building destroyed by Union troops (an act that had triggered several unrewarded claims after the war). After the cornerstone ceremony in 1915, the sister of Richard Poole Hays noted, "History had given them their rightful place, no longer rebels or traitors but soldiers under the immortal Lee, and from the ashes of old Monocacy Chapel will rise a new one." By 1921 the chapel was done, the surviving sister wrote, "a labor of love to those who fought under the banner of the Stars and Bars."

It was a bright and balmy day in Rockville on June 3, 1913, when the granite monument Richard Poole Hays had promoted was dedicated before three thousand cheering citizens in front of the Montgomery County courthouse. Fifty veterans were present. Among those of the youngest generation participating in the ceremonies were Edward Chiswell Wootton, Eloise Wootton Chiswell, and Hunton Dade Sellman, who helped release the Confederate and Maryland flags that had been covering the stone cavalryman, his arms folded, his sabre sheathed. "To our heroes of Montgomery County, Maryland," said the legend at the base, "that we through life may not forget to love the thin gray line." With the statue facing the courthouse, a witness hoped it would "ever be an inspiration to the youths of our land to hold principle, honor, and a firm trust in God above all else." During the redevelopment of Rockville half a century later, there would be pressures to do away with the statue entirely. Instead, it was unceremoniously moved to the rear of the old courthouse, where it now stands, its figure still gazing resolutely southward. It is, to the silent chagrin of the old families, all but hidden by trees. It is nonetheless the only Civil War statue in the county, and there is no Union counterpart.

But even as the past lingered, subtle shifts were occurring in how and where the people lived. After Joseph Thomas Chiswell—one of the captain's five children—died in 1912, his widow and five children moved to Washington, where one, ninety-one-year-old Marguerite Chiswell, still lived in 1983. Only one would move back to Poolesville, Carroll Chiswell, in 1918, to help his two old-maid aunts (Miss Lizzy and Miss Prudy) run the captain's farm outside town on Cattail Road.

Carroll returned to Washington for a few years to work for the B&O Railroad in Union Station and, for a while, with his brother Isaac in an auto repair business at 14th and U streets. He returned to Poolesville to marry a schoolteacher in 1936. They lived not on the farm but in town, where I met them forty-five years later. Carroll's grandfather's Civil War lance and sword hung in the couple's living room. After Carroll's death in 1982, the only

"Chiswell" left in Poolesville proper would be his widow, Mary.

With the United States' entry into World War I, the E.V. White Chapter endowed a hospital bed in Neuilly, France, and several descendants of the Confederate soldiers enlisted.

Back home, Lawrence A. Chiswell, another of Edward's six children, became a county commissioner in 1920. Brother Roland moved to Washington. Brother Thomas Chiswell worked at Hunter Hardware in the downcounty suburb of Silver Spring. Sister Edith also moved to Silver Spring, where her husband, Norman Wootton, operated a trash collection business. Their son Norman Douglas Wootton would become president of the Silver Spring Rotary and work in the post office for forty-one years, presiding over the automated sorting of mail and retiring as assistant postmaster in 1966.

Upcounty, the age of innocence merged with the age of jazz. Mail and newspapers (*The Sun* from Baltimore) came by train to Sellman's Station and thence to the outlying farms by horse and buggy. The sidewalks of Poolesville had been paved since 1911. A new high school, built in 1908 on two acres acquired from Dr. Edward Wootton for $410, expanded with a gymnasium-auditorium in 1925. But the new movie theater closed after one year, and some students still traveled by horse and buggy to school, where there were stables to accommodate the animals.

Then came the fires, three of them in thirty years. The first, in 1923, destroyed Albert Wootton's general store, the largest of its kind in the county. Albert, one of the doctor's six children, moved to Rockville a year later to live and work in the county treasurer's office until his retirement in 1943.

Who owned Poolesville's first automobile is lost to history, but in 1926, Joseph Newton Darby won an open Ford touring car at the annual Rockville fire department "he-night" raffle. Since he already had a 1925 Buick, he gave the prize to his son, who used it for school. "At fourteen, I was one of the younger drivers," T. Gordon Darby, a grandson of Lieutenant Edward Chiswell, informed me at his home near Poolesville.

The arrival of the automobile made Rockville and Frederick more accessible, and the people of Poolesville lobbied for state maintenance of roads, which would widen their horizons. But the world beyond both beckoned and threatened the town that once had sought to surpass Rockville as a center of culture and commerce.

"There are many ways in which we can co-operate to make Poolesville a more progressive town," noted the high school newspaper, "but the chief way is by patronizing our home stores. Now if we were to spend that same money in some nearby city, we would be the only one getting the benefit of the money and the whole town would be losing."

Beginning in the 1920s, accelerating in the 1930s, newcomers came from Tazwell County in southwestern Virginia, by car if they owned one, by mule if not, adding a dozen new family names to the area. Compared to their mountainous homeland, the rolling upper Montgomery County countryside was a virtual plain. So they came, according to Hubert Neal, who arrived in 1934, because "back there farmland is nothing but rocks and hills...I got hungry."

They were carpenters and painters, these newcomers. Some bought farms. Others became tenant farmers. Dr. Lige White (a nephew of Colonel Lige White) asked how the migration began. A Virginian replied, "One fool started it and the rest followed."

At first, especially in hard times when the new arrivals couldn't find work, there was a stigma. But eventually the sons and daughters of the Virginians intermarried with those of the old families. Mary Butler Neal, for example, would marry Hubert's son Larry, her class of 1959 high school sweetheart. "We were country. They were country," explained William Chiswell Hilton, Poolesville class of 1956. "Both of us kind of fit right in."

The Depression deeply affected the old families along with the new, all of them participants in small human dramas played out against a national economic stage. Edward Lee (Uncle Ned) Chiswell lost his job at the Poolesville Bank when it went bust in 1930. "Just about everyone got wiped out locally," remembered Charles Elgin, the 1931 senior class president who went to New York for schooling and work. He didn't stay away long, and he came home to be Poolesville's postmaster, for thirty-four years.

"I wanted so bad to go to Cornell University to take up interior decorating, but my father didn't have the money," said Dorothy Butler Hopkins, a 1934 Poolesville High graduate. On her back porch near the Potomac River, she sighed, "I always felt cheated in a way." Along with many of her contemporaries, she went to Washington. Several attended Strayer's College secretarial school, which advertised in the Poolesville school paper. She went to Temple Business School and then to beauty school. She found work in a beauty shop at 49th and Massachusetts Avenue NW, in the fashionable Spring Valley section. There she met her husband, who worked at a nearby gas station.

The Depression was hastening the end of an era, as large family farms were sold one by one, some willingly, others not. Dorothy Hopkins's father lost his dairy farm in Poolesville; there are houses there now. Bankrupt, he managed to acquire another in White's Ferry, under his brother's name. In 1937 his daughter and son-in-law would move there, to stay.

Others were less fortunate. Joseph Gorman Butler lost his farm in a sheriff's sale. "It was kind of rough going," recalled his son, Gorman Lee (named after General Robert E.), who went on to become a Montgomery County cop, a job from which he would retire in 1969. But not back to the family farm; that was gone, forever.

Another White's Ferry farm would remain in a different branch of the Butler family until 1970, when George R. Butler, brokenhearted and in ill health, was forced to sell. The Pyles place on Route 28 between Dawsonville and Beallsville was sold in the 1930s; it became Spring Valley Hereford Farms. The White family farm on Westerly Road, Colonel Lige White's birthplace, went in 1940, to a Belgian baron. Carroll Chiswell held on to his grandfather's farm as long as he could. He sold it, finally, in 1964. "Heaven's alive, the last time we made hay, he only had a twelve year old to help him," Mary Chiswell said. "You couldn't get help for love or money."

Framing the decade of the 1930s were the deaths of two old veterans. Thomas Henry White, a courier and scout for Robert E. Lee, died in his ninety-ninth year in 1930, at the Glenolden, Pennsylvania, home of daughter Mary Estelle White Elgin. In 1941 John B. Munger, a ninety-nine-year-old Virginian who had moved to Poolesville after the war, was the last to go. His name would be etched on the Monocacy memorial tablet, the thirty-second and final one to be placed there.

In February 1930 they commemorated Lincoln's birthday at Poolesville High, all singing "The Battle Hymn of the Republic," the freshman girls intoning "Battle Cry for Freedom." The southern story of Poolesville wasn't part of the school curriculum. "They never taught the Civil War history of Poolesville," recollected Retired Army Major E. R. Luhn, Jr., a descendant of E.V. White whose family moved from Poolesville to Rockville in 1941, when he was thirteen. "Some of the families cared, but never in public. It was almost as if they didn't want to be embarrassed or criticized for continuing to fight the war," Luhn said. "They always worshipped at this altar in private. Except on June 3, that was the big thing with my grandmothers, mother, and aunts."

"That was Confederate Memorial Day," remembered Dorothy Butler Hopkins, when people gathered at Monocacy Cemetery to hear southern congressmen extol Dixie, to enjoy a picnic lunch, and to honor the dead. "You didn't dare go the thirty-first of May," Dorothy Hopkins said. "You know, my father wouldn't wear a pair of blue jeans or anything else blue, no siree, you couldn't bring anything blue in his house. He wore khaki, gray, anything but blue." This son of a Confederate soldier died in 1951.

When World War II came to the Poolesville area, the E.V. White Chapter's "honor role" of volunteers included forty-two direct and collateral descendants of Confederates. Two would not return alive. The list of those serving included Chiswells, Joneses, Woottons, and Pyleses. Gorman Lee Butler joined the infantry and fought in the Battle of the Bulge. He would later become vice-commander of a small American Legion post comprised of World War II vets in the Poolesville area.

By the late 1940s, the E.V. White Chapter of the United Daughters of the Confederacy had dwindled to eleven old ladies. "Being a few has drawn us closer to each other for it has been a struggle to keep life and interest when our members have been so widely scattered. But our loyalty has brought us to 1947," wrote Florence Pyles White, the wife of Dr. Lige White and the granddaughter of Confederate Michael Thomas Pyles.

With the death of its president (eulogized for her "love for the Confederacy"), the E.V. White Chapter disbanded. Noted Florence White, "It looks as though the E.V. White Chapter life has been well-lived." It ended the week before Thanksgiving.

"Our Chapel will represent our work for many years and it is a great asset to our beautiful cemetery," wrote Florence Pyles White. In time, the chapel would fall into disuse and disrepair, and the memorial tablet itself would crumble, but in the glow of remembrance, who could have predicted it?

Yet, even as the curtain fell on the E.V. White Chapter and its memories of the Civil War, it rose on another postwar era: a time of more unsettling, accelerating change for the old families whose lives for generations had revolved around their farms and their community of Poolesville and vicinity. The change would envelop what was once their county. Northerners with liberal ideas who had come to Washington in the New Deal and Fair Deal days of Franklin Roosevelt and Harry Truman were moving to the suburbs, changing the philosophical climate and political cast of the county.

At mid-century, the old families of Montgomery were gradually losing their clout. But, for the time being at least, they continued to reign over Poolesville and vicinity. Life around Poolesville was still insular and incestuous. "It was safe in calling them all cousins," said Dorothy Elgin, a 1937 Poolesville High School graduate who married Charles Elgin, then the postmaster, both of them descendants of Confederate soldiers on the Monocacy tablet.

The dawning of the atomic age briefly brought a new worldliness: For one year, 1948, the high-school yearbook was called "The Atom." In the postwar period, the "local" fire department was still in Rockville—a fire truck overturned on the way to the 1953 fire, making matters worse; Frederick (eighteen miles in another direction) was still the place to go for a movie; and the faraway Bethesda Hot Shoppes was the destination of adventurous teenagers.

In Poolesville proper, Butler's Lunch, operated by Lucille and Gorman Lee Butler, was the teenage hangout. It featured a soda fountain and penny candy. After the 1953 fire, which destroyed Elgin's Drug along with three other commercial buildings, county policeman Gorman Butler (who also served a term as mayor) took prescriptions with him to Rockville, where he worked. The prescription run was "a service," he said. "I didn't charge anything for it."

If life remained relatively relaxed for the people of Poolesville, there was still the underlying fact of race. The Monocacy Lions Club held its annual minstrel show, with its retinue of black stereotypes. It was commonly performed, too, on the Eastern Shore. "You can't have that anymore," remarked Poolesville Mayor Charles Elgin, still active in the Lions Club (which met in his former family home, converted into a restaurant) and sensitive to any discussion of race relations. "I can't help the fact that my ancestors were slaveowners. It's time to get past race."

For years, the small black enclaves had existed around Poolesville, populated by descendants of freed slaves who, under the state's segregated system, were forced to send their children to separate, small, dilapidated schools. For a time in the early 1950s, Poolesville area whites also faced the prospect of a long bus ride to high schools in Rockville and Gaithersburg. The proposal to close the Poolesville school reflected the area's diminished voice in the county. Parents and the PTA loudly fought to keep it open, however, and won.

Saved from extinction, Poolesville High School uneasily faced integration in 1956. That September, Poolesville and two towns on the Eastern Shore were the only localities in Maryland where integration did not go smoothly. Confronted with the presence of fourteen black junior high schoolers, some white parents picketed and some kept their children home from school. There were mass meetings and talk of setting up a segregated private school.

According to a former school official, newspaper clippings, and other sources, the anti-integrationists were largely "newcomers" from southwestern Virginia who had migrated north two and three decades before. The old families whose ancestors had "gone South" to fight for the Confederacy didn't like it either, but they were more willing to accept the inevitable. "That was the law, there wasn't nothing they could do about it," said Gorman Lee Butler who, when I met him, was driving a school bus part time in retirement.

Poolesville High had its first black graduate in 1959. By 1978, it had a black principal, a man widely respected by parents of both races for his traditional, conservative values and approach to education. The combined junior-senior high, with fewer than 800 students, was the county's smallest secondary school, although it covered the largest area, following the boundaries of the old Medley's District. The seventy-fifth anniversary class of 1981 had 102 members, the largest yet. About two dozen white and ten of the fifteen graduating black students were the sons and daughters of families deeply rooted in the Poolesville area.

In 1959 the entire population of Poolesville—298 persons—had posed in the town's main street for an aerial illustration to a National Geographic article about the upcoming census. For comparison purposes the magazine noted that the country grew by the size of Poolesville every 54.6 minutes. The people were, a local woman wrote in 1961, "a cohesive group with the same economic background and problems who go to school together, marry each other, attend a neighborhood church, shop at a neighborhood store and are buried side by side in Monocacy Cemetery....The people of Poolesville have reason to be proud that their main characteristic is stability rather than mushroom growth."

In the ensuing decade, prospects for large-scale growth divided Poolesville. It was then that a Washington supermarket-chain executive who, starting in 1943, had quietly bought 3,175 acres between the town and the Potomac, unveiled his grand design for development. Bernard N. Siegal, a sometimes emotional man of vision, wanted to build a "Potomac Valley Planned City" for 35,000 people. But he encountered opposition, first from the county and then, when he sought to annex his land to Poolesville, from the town. With all but 11 eligibles voting, Poolesville decided 101 to 74 against his scheme. The county then granted limited approval, but Siegal couldn't get the necessary water and sewer permits and, in October of 1966, committed suicide. The Potomac Valley Country Club he started—by 1980 the scene of twenty-five years of Poolesville High School reunions—was his legacy.

Development came anyway, in the 1970s, as townhouses and tract homes sprouted on new streets named after old families: Wootton Avenue, Chiswell Road, Gott Street. The 1970 population of 349 was up only slightly from the count in the last census, but by 1980 the number of residents had multiplied nearly tenfold, to 3,400 (in 1996, the number stood at 4,100). The old families this time welcomed the growth as a sign of progress and a way to expand the tax base to pay for new water and sewage facilities required of the town by distant bureaucracies. Politically, however, the influx further diluted the power of the Poolesville old-timers in their own backyard. For a few years, they lost control to antigrowth newcomers who had themselves benefited from growth but wanted no more.

Many of the newcomers were as transient as the old families were planted. Working for the government or research firms that line the I-270 corridor, they turned over at the rate of one hundred households a year. One result was three special town elections in one year, as officeholders moved on. With so much flux among the new, the old returned to power, with the election of Charles Elgin as mayor in 1978 and the adoption of a new master plan that allowed for much more growth in the years to come.

For the time being, at least, the new developments on the outskirts of Poolesville look out of place. It is still country, offering on a clear day a majestic view of the Blue Ridge across the Potomac and of nearby Sugarloaf Mountain on the Maryland side. And, although, as the farms were sold and the jobs went elsewhere, some sons and daughters moved, many remain, or have returned in retirement, providing continuity with the past.

"I guess it's home," said Gorman Lee Butler, picking peas outside the stone rambler to which he'd moved after living for nine years in Rockville. His family had never recovered the farm his father lost in the Depression, but he had a small peach and apple orchard behind his house, which was right down the road from his daughter's place.

T. Gordon Darby, grandson of Lieutenant Edward J. Chiswell, C.S.A., had returned, too. He lived in a house overlooking the Blue Ridge where he kept his grandfather's tattered copy of Frank Myers's book, *The Comanches*, which was all about Lige White's battalion, and other family memorabilia. Darby had retired after a long career in the Silver Spring post office, where he had worked alongside his first cousin, Norman Wootton. "So many of our friends, city people, go to Florida or move away to retire. We put it in reverse," he said. "We had the [family] land available. Where else would you want to go?"

Charles Elgin's son moved away for a while, to work for IBM in Pennsylvania, but he, too, returned, still in his thirties, to work for the county fire department and live in a newly built home next to his parents. The Elgins' daughter, meanwhile, moved into one of the new townhouses across town.

"None of us strayed too far," said Mary Butler Neal, the mayor's secretary, who lived on the road to White's Ferry. "I never wanted to travel. I really never thought about going anywhere else. Our family's ties are so strong."

Her daughter Cathleen had just graduated from Poolesville High. Mary

A Confederate grave marker at a Southern Maryland cemetery. Eugene L. Meyer

Neal's siblings were all around, too: One sister lived in Beallsville, two miles north; three sisters lived in the Poolesville townhouses, as did her brother George, a landscaping foreman who commuted to and from posh Potomac, an exclusive Maryland suburb that still retained a rural flavor. "He's working with the earth," his sister said. "You can't afford to farm these days, so he took the next best thing." Explained Carol Butler Lawson, George's twin, "The family has kept us together. We all married people from Poolesville, and we all stayed here."

When Dorothy Butler Hopkins warmly welcomed me into her house on the family's farm, she had recently taken her two young grandchildren to the Monocacy Cemetery in Beallsville to show them the monument to their Confederate ancestors. They had asked, "Grandma, did you know them?" Such is the perspective of the young. And the not so young.

"I don't know much about that at all," said Carol Butler Lawson. "You know more than I do. I don't know a whole lot. That's terrible. I know we should."

Billy Hilton, a fourth-generation Barnesville undertaker and a Chiswell on his mother's side, had buried many people at Monocacy Cemetery. But he was unaware that his ancestors not only had fought for the South, but also that one had led the men of Montgomery into battle on behalf of the Confederacy. Never thought about it, he told me. Hilton had been born a generation too late to partake in the commemoration celebrated each June 3rd at the cemetery, and the memorial tablet with its family names—including his—had somehow eluded him.

A toppling tree in the winter of 1974 shattered the old marble slab. The following year, the ladies' auxiliary of the cemetery replaced it with the current stone tablet. The only living member of the E.V. White Chapter of the United Daughters of the Confederacy could not attend the dedication ceremony: Sarah Ellen White Pyles, Dorothy Elgin's aunt, who was then in her nineties, was confined to the Washington Home for Incurables.

One balmy spring day, I asked caretaker Tom Ahalt, Jr., to open the door of the old chapel adjoining the tablet. Inside, water-stained framed portraits of Stonewall Jackson and Robert E. Lee, misidentified by Ahalt as "General Grant," adorned the wall. "I guess Lee wouldn't like that," the caretaker said of his error. Tattered Stars and Bars and Stars and Stripes flanked a wooden pulpit. The pews were connected by cobwebs.

Above it all hung a crescent-shaped sign with the simple message, "Lest We Forget."

But forgotten they were, these Montgomery men on the tablet who lost their war, their county, their land. Buried in the records of the E.V. White Chapter kept by Dorothy Elgin, I found an epitaph for the names inscribed on the Monocacy memorial:

Bugler, sound boots and saddles
They answer not? Well, let them rest
Their warfare over, they are sleeping
And perhaps, 'tis for the best.

14

Channels

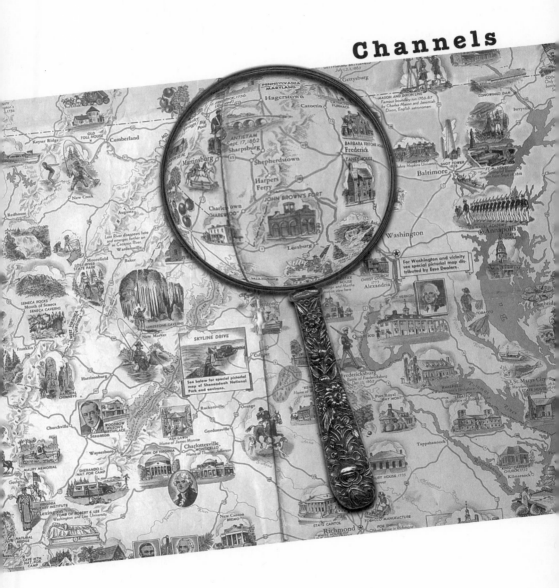

*U*nder the highway bridge that carries Maryland Route 79 over the train tracks and the Potomac at Brunswick is a handpainted mural. It depicts a man and a woman in nineteenth-century dress, a horseless carriage, a two-story building, and a locomotive spewing a cloud of smoke that contains the legend, "The Future of Brunswick is Rooted Deeply in Our Past."

Fifty-five miles upriver from Washington, Brunswick's past, present, and future have been tied to the ups and downs of the railroad for almost a century.

Here, above Tidewater, river commerce meant forging a link along the banks of the narrow valley to the west. The push to open up the hinterlands to trade brought the National Road (the nation's first interstate highway), the Chesapeake & Ohio Canal, and the Baltimore & Ohio Railroad—channels of commerce through Maryland.

The highway, which followed a northerly route later designated U.S. 40, had a short-lived heyday. The canal never lived up to the promises of promoters but lingered into the 1920s, linking towns and generations to its quiet course along the Maryland riverbank. In nineteenth-century America, the railroad succeeded beyond all other schemes.

From Point of Rocks to Harpers Ferry, the railroad shared twelve miles of narrow riverbank with the canal. Then, it continued due westward while the C&O meandered with the river to Cumberland, from whence it carried coal to the District of Columbia. Far more rapidly, the B&O also brought coal eastward from Western Maryland and West Virginia, to the port of Baltimore. Along its way, it brought prosperity—and pain—to towns like Brunswick.

Development of the area began in 1787, before rail or canal came along, on land belonging then to Leonard Smith, a Southern Maryland transplant who subdivided and sold part of his 280 acres. Since many townspeople came from Berlin, Germany, it is said, Smith named his town Berlin. Yet the post office that opened in 1832 bore the name Barry. Barry-Berlin became Brunswick in 1890, when the railroad came to dominate the town, many of whose citizens had immigrated from the town of the same name in Germany.

Although the railroad and the canal both reached the town in 1834, the "ditch" was the town's lifeblood through most of the nineteenth century. Lock no. 30 was right there, and many of the townsfolk were "canalies" who worked on or serviced the boats that passed through. The railroad was of little local importance until the B&O chose the town as the site of a major freight yard and repair shop.

Secretly, the railroad began buying lots in the 1880s. Part of the yard opened in May 1890. When finished, it spanned more than four miles along the river and could accommodate four thousand cars. Almost overnight, the town's population grew more than tenfold, from 200 to 2,471 by 1900. The railroad built homes for its workers, donated the town's first street light, gave land for public buildings, parks, and churches, and erected a YMCA, which housed train crews from 1907 until it burned down in 1980.

Looking north across the Potomac River from Loudoun County, Virginia, toward Brunswick, Maryland (postcard dated 1909).

Brunswick sits at the base of the Catoctin range of the Blue Ridge Mountains. Most of the homes are crowded together along numerical and alphabetical streets set in a grid on the steep slopes leading down to Potomac Street, where the stores are, and the freight yard below. The town has never become chic or trendy. City sophisticates riding through the countryside have seldom succumbed to its charms. Its buildings retain a drab (some would say dreary) look that testifies to its authenticity.

This is no ersatz restoration of a railroad town. This is the real thing, gritty and grimy as ever. A siding salesman must've made a fortune here in the 1890s, so many buildings are covered with aging, asbestos shingles.

Once a year, however, the town takes on a special holiday look. Crowds line both sides of Potomac Street, from end to end. Brunswick's is the largest Veterans Day parade in the state, if not on the entire East Coast. And it is no coincidence that the parade marshal is often the train yardmaster, possibly the most prestigious position in this old railroad town.

My first Veterans Day parade in Brunswick was the town's forty-ninth. The parade is a tradition that began in 1932, three years after the founding of the Steadman-Keenan American Legion Post 96 (named after two sons of Brunswick who died in France during World War I). The town had failed to hold its parade only once, during the gas-rationing days of World War II.

In a sense, Brunswick looks like America's small-town vision of itself harkening back to seemingly simpler times, a Norman Rockwell painting of brick storefronts (some now vacant, others filled with antiques) and old houses. In this setting, the American Legion hall, as well as the fire company, is a center of social activity and community spirit. So before and after the parade, they meet at the Legion building by the train tracks, movers and shakers and just plain folks.

"It's a plain German town, being proud of what they are," the mayor pro tem exulted in the dingy Legion basement. "All in all, it's a town where people stick together," remarked his companion, Mayor Jess D. Orndorff, a retired railroad cop who had spent most of his career patrolling Washington's Union Station and commuting to work by train from Brunswick. The mayor handed me one of his calling cards, displaying the Brunswick seal. It contained an old steam locomotive and a modern diesel engine and the town's proud description of itself as the "Home of the Iron Horse."

Over the years, Brunswick's parade had grown in size and spirit. In election years, politicians seeking state office flocked to this tiny town on the Potomac to be introduced and seen on the reviewing stand.

Between the speeches and the processions, at approximately 1:45 p.m., air force jets zoomed overhead, a scheduled show of strength which stirred patriotic hearts. "That always makes it nice, doesn't it?" said Mildred Robey, wife of Jim Robey, the Legion officer coordinating the parade. "They couldn't come over last year because of the weather."

From its beginnings, Veterans Day in Brunswick had changed from a strictly local affair to a regional event and more. From across the state and beyond came veterans, families, friends, and supporters to march and compete for cash prizes totaling, this forty-ninth year, $2,200.

They marched from one end of Potomac Street to the other, a dazzling display of baton twirlers, honor guards, marching bands, fire companies, drummers and buglers, and assorted theme floats—eighty-two units in all—a pageant of patriotism. Hometown marchers included Brunswick's Midget Football Team ("With Teamwork We Will Not Fail"), Brunswick's Cub Scout

Pack 27 ("Cub Scouting...an American Tradition"), and the Brunswick High School ("Railroader") Band.

The judging came later, at the Legion hall. While revelers danced to Sonny Purdham and the Good Ole Boys, the professional judges imported from Pennsylvania completed their work. "I don't know how you do it," one told the parade coordinator. "The big thing is you have the cooperation of the people. Nobody gives you a bad time. You don't have any of those smart-ass city people."

Among the winning floats, one featured "The Roundhouse Eight," a group of local square dancers who had promenaded to "God Bless America" in their seventeenth year in the parade. The Brunswick Future Farmers of America also won a prize, for their cornucopia float with the message, "America—The Land of Plenty. It Was Worth the Fight."

But Veterans Day in Brunswick is more than a holiday commemorating war heroes. It is also a homecoming weekend for former residents who return to visit friends and family, to watch the parade, and to quaff a few brews in and out of the bars along Potomac Street.

"Every year I can, I come back for the parade," explained one of the beer-sipping revelers standing in front of the Metropolitan Tavern along the parade route. Jeanette Cataldi had left in 1945 for Harrisburg, Pennsylvania, where she'd married and raised a family. Coming home for Veterans Day was like "reliving my childhood," she said. "I marched in this parade when I was in junior high school, I guess about 1940."

David Moss, a thirty-seven-year-old Brunswick native standing nearby, had come home from Hagerstown, where he managed a paint store. "I never miss it," he told me. "This is bigger even than the homecoming at the high school. You'll never find a smaller town with a bigger heart."

Also among those watching the parade were twenty descendants of Leonard Smith, the pre-iron-horse, eighteenth-century surveyor responsible for the town's existence. They came from as far away as New York State and as close as Frederick. Among them were two great-great-great-great-great-grandchildren, young Karl and Alexis Smith, who each held an American flag. Seated nearby, opposite the reviewing stand, was Helen Muse, Smith's great-great-great-great-granddaughter, who lived in Baltimore. It was her first Brunswick parade, and she loved it. "Next year, I think we'll attend even if we don't get an invitation," she said.

Muse did not attend the fiftieth annual parade (her husband was having surgery). Nor did the politicians who had fought to be seen the year before. For

Brunswick, the half-century mark may have been a milestone, but it also fell in an off-election year.

The rhetoric was different, too. "Veterans, like everyone else, feel the staggering unemployment," the state Legion commander said. The words had a special meaning in Brunswick, as I learned on a return visit a few weeks later.

The railroad brought boom times to Brunswick, but it also gave the town a one-industry economy. It was, one merchant informed me, "our blessed curse." When times were good for the railroad, they were good for Brunswick. But the reverse was also true. Railroad employment peaked in 1929 with 1,325 employees. It plummeted to a Depression low of 583 four years later.

Old-timers could still recall the bread lines at the American Legion, the fire company, and the churches. Richard P. Mullen, in charge of the freight-car repair yard, remembered when, as a youngster, he watched fifty or sixty citizens surreptitiously shoveling coal from loaded cars for use in their own home furnaces. He also recalled one boyhood Depression Thanksgiving.

"My daddy gave some food to a bunch of hoboes," he said from behind his desk at the repair yard. "Three or four of 'em had come up through the yard. I opened the back door. He cut a whole breast of turkey, also gave them a loaf of bread and a quart of milk. My mother gave him hell. The priest came for dinner, and he had to eat dark meat. I was six years old."

Although World War II boosted the work force a bit, the change from steam to diesel and the loss of locomotive repair work in the 1950s were further blows to Brunswick's prosperity. In 1967, when more than 43% of Brunswick's workers were with the railroad and local unemployment was way down, a planning consultant observed, "The painful economic recessions experienced locally reflected conditions of the railroad industry.... In regard to the future, Brunswick should continue its efforts to attract other industries; for a recession...could inflict the same economic pain so often experienced in the past."

When the deep recession of the 1980s hit, Brunswick was still a one-industry town; only the railroad's name had changed, from B&O to Chessie System. The repair-shop work force Mullen commanded shrunk to only 8 men from a regular roster of 251, and there were layoffs in other parts of the yard, as well. The Chessie credit union issued a layoff advisory to customers, urging them to work out payment plans if necessary. The city clerks began receiving requests from regular, paying customers to defer payments on water bills.

The coal cars that had regularly rumbled through Brunswick from the West Virginia mountains to the port of Baltimore were virtually gone. A year before, the yard had been jammed full of them, waiting to be hauled to the sea. "Now,

The Baltimore & Ohio Railroad became Chessie System, but Brunswick remained a one-industry town. Eugene L. Meyer

all I got is empty hoppers," terminal master Paul D. Brohawn told me as we drove the length of the yard that still extends for miles.

Generations of Brunswickers had been through the cycle before, but that did not help much.

Workers like Rick Campbell had staked their futures on the coal coming through. He had even sold his grocery business to work as a railroad repair-yard welder. "The coal miners had settled on a three-year contract," he said. "We were all told it looked pretty good for three years. It hasn't been the end of the world, but I've sat up nights worrying myself sick about it, too," said the heavy-set, twenty-nine-year-old father of three.

Campbell had been laid off for almost a year when we met. He could still laugh. When his twin daughters came home from their first week of kindergarten, he reported with relish, they knew their school days were Monday through Friday. "Guess what?" they said, full of wide-eyed wonder. "We get laid off Saturday."

The pain was eased just a bit by Brunswick's relative proximity to the federal employment centers expanding outward from Washington along the I-270 corridor, in adjoining Montgomery County. Thus, Campbell's wife had gone back to work as a secretary for the Department of Energy in Germantown. The nearness of the federal government was a new development in Brunswick's history. So were the commuters.

On the hills above the town, new subdivisions had popped up in the 1970s, 470 new homes resulting in a 28% population increase, to 4,572 (followed by nearly 1,500 more new residents by 1996). The newcomers, most of whom commuted to Washington-area jobs, made their presence felt in some of the local churches and at My Sister's Place, which did a booming coffee-and-donuts trade a block from the train station every weekday morning. But by and large they did their shopping elsewhere, the merchants complained, and they mostly shied away from local politics and institutions like the volunteer fire company. Nor did they participate to any significant degree in the town's biggest annual event, its Veterans Day parade.

As in many small towns, the fire company was a central part of community life. It thrived through volunteer efforts and pluck, paying a hundred dollars on one occasion to acquire a surplus Washington, D.C., hook-and-ladder truck and raising money over the local country music station of "Firemen's Day." The fire company's economic mainstay was Friday-night bingo, which was also a major social event in Brunswick. Except in hard times. Then the crowds shriveled and so did the take. Somehow, the fire company survived.

An 1896 handbill boasted that Brunswick had "no saloons." Indeed, Brunswick still had its own chapter of the Women's Christian Temperance Union half a century after Repeal, but by then it had plenty of bars, too. "They've got more liquor joints in Brunswick than churches," complained Elva Rollins, the treasurer of the Maryland WCTU and a Brunswick resident.

Richard P. Mullen, the freight-car repair-yard boss, agreed with her description without sharing her outrage, "It's a family town full of beer joints, whiskey stores, and churches," said Mullen. "You can't buy a necktie or a pair of socks, but if you want to go to a beer joint, a whiskey store, or a church, they're all within two blocks. It's full of 'em because it's a railroad town. All they ever did was go to church and drink whiskey."

No Veterans Day floats portrayed the canal days in Brunswick, so completely had the railroad come to overshadow the town's earlier era. For canal history, I traveled fifty miles upriver to the next sizeable Maryland town on the Potomac. I went to Williamsport, home in 1996 to 1,998 souls in the Great Valley, six miles south of Hagerstown, the seat of Washington County, Maryland.

In their working-class traditions, blue-collar taverns, and individualistic outlooks, the citizens of Williamsport and Brunswick are a lot alike. Williamsport's future may or may not have been, as the saying went downriver, rooted in its past, but signs of its canal days lingered. Even McDonald's, just off I-81, sports a local motif, its walls appropriately adorned with paintings of locks, locktenders, and canal boats.

Early twentieth century postcard illustrating the canal, Potomac River, and bridge from Doubleday Hill, Williamsport.

Like Brunswick, Williamsport has an annual heritage fling. T-shirts and posters showing a canal boat pulled by mules are sold. In the basement of the town library, visitors watch old-timers on videotape talk about canal life. Outside, there are booths and door prizes and exhibits.

As Mayor Walter (Muggs) Teach put it one summer evening, "There's nothing like C&O Canal Days here in Williamsport." With those remarks, the "Second Annual Miss Williamsport C&O Canal Days Beauty Pageant" was underway.

The contestants competed in traditional sportswear, swimwear, and evening-gown categories for the top title and vied also for Miss Congeniality and Miss Photogenic. Asked what issue she would run on to become the first woman president, Miss Congeniality shrugged, "I don't know." The master of ceremonies said, "You're doing as well as [the president]. Don't worry about it."

Miss Photogenic said if she could be someone famous, she would be Racquel Welch because "I just like to be in the movies a lot, have a nice time."

The outgoing queen said winning the contest had been "the most exciting moment of my life" and sang an off-key version of "Second Hand Rose." When it was time for someone to escort her successor to the "throne," no one did, but the show went on. "I'll tell you what, she's gonna make it herself," proclaimed the master of ceremonies. "This is the age of the liberated woman."

Williamsport, like Brunswick, began with the birth of the republic. In 1786 General Ortho Holland Williams, a Revolutionary War hero, laid out its wide streets and left the town his name. Long before the canal came along, the town at the confluence of Conococheague Creek and the Potomac petitioned to become the national capital. George Washington inspected the site in 1791. Ultimately, Williamsport was deemed too far upriver to become the federal city, and, as they say, the rest is history. While Georgetown in D.C. was a canal town destined to become fashionable, Williamsport was just a canal town.

When the flood of 1924 closed the waterway for good, an era in the town's history ended. The people stayed on to work at Cushwa's brickworks or the tannery. They also went to work making trucks and aircraft at the Mack and Fairchild plants in Hagerstown, a few miles north on U.S. 11. For years, the trolleys linked the old town to the larger city, and when the streetcars went the way of the canal boats, buses continued to shuttle people back and forth between work and home.

They gathered often at the main corner of Potomac and Conococheague Street in a place called Jeanne's Confectionery. On Sunday mornings they called themselves "the Knights of the Round Table" but townspeople with opinions could be found there most any day of the week. The establishment operated by Jeanne House featured home-cooked food and a wall mural of canal life. Jeanne herself was on the town's historic commission, comprised entirely of "newcomers" to Williamsport. Her mother had been born there, but she grew up in Hagerstown, and even forty years in Williamsport, including thirty-four in business at the same location, did not make her a native.

Nonetheless, Jeanne House had won the respect and affection of the townsfolk. She felt at home in Williamsport and, even though born elsewhere, had become something of a local institution. In recent years, though, newcomers of a different breed had arrived on the scene. Educated and affluent, they had little in common with most Williamsporters. As such, they were not unlike those who had recently moved to Brunswick. But the Brunswick newcomers commuted long hours to and from distant jobs, leaving little time for civic involvement. Fifty miles west, the newer residents of Williamsport traveled no farther than Hagerstown for employment. Opportunities for community activism were limited only by inclination, or so it seemed.

The newcomers, many of them inclined to restoration, were especially interested in preserving Williamsport's past. Proud of their heritage, the natives didn't dwell on it. But the new arrivals looked at the modest working-class homes and shops and saw historic chic. Strict restoration of existing structures seemed to hold out hope that things would not take a turn for the worse.

Their fears were founded on Williamsport's strategic location near the intersection of I-70 and I-81. The town benefited, or suffered, depending on one's point of view, from a locale a state study said gave it "a competitive advantage in penetrating the highway traveler market." Given the right attraction, the study projected half a million visitors a year would come to town. Williamsport would become another Gettysburg, full of ticky-tacky commercialism. The small town that attracted the newcomers in the first place would never be the same.

The obvious lure was Williamsport's still largely preserved past, about which the National Park Service, keepers of the C&O Canal, waxed ecstatic. "I think it's the most exciting area in the Park," Richard J. Rambur, an NPS official, told me at the C&O Canal Park headquarters over in Sharpsburg. "It has every feature of the C&O Canal: a turning basin, an aqueduct, a lock, a lock house. And it's an easy drive from Baltimore, Washington, and Harrisburg. Some people look forward to plates and spoons that say 'Williamsport.' I guess I'm a little naive, but I think it can be dealt with." (Rambur's last post had been the Little Big Horn in Montana, where he had clashed with the keepers of Custer's flame.)

For the time being, at least, the modern view of Williamsport remained almost identical to that displayed on the picturesque turn-of-the-century picture postcards still for sale at Eakles Drug Store on Conococheague Street. To preserve the "architectural integrity" of the buildings, the mayor and the town council created the Williamsport Historic Commission, innocently enough, it seemed. Because no one else volunteered, the commissioners were all resident "outsiders."

Any homeowner wanting to make exterior improvements was bound by law to gain their approval. Without any fuss, the commissioners approved eight applications and rejected one. Then, along came William (Bodie) Turner. A retired bartender bearing a striking resemblance to Santa Claus, Turner, seventy-one, had worked at the tannery and tended bar part time "ever since beer and whiskey came back." From 1945 on, he had been a full-time bartender. After retiring, Turner managed to win $50,000 in the state lottery, more than enough after taxes to fix up his house on South Vermont Street.

The commission said the German siding on Turner's house was historic millwork unique to the Williamsport area. But Bodie Turner didn't think it was historic. He thought it was old and ugly and made his home expensive to maintain and heat, what with the peeling paint and the cold penetrating the walls. He wanted vinyl siding instead, and nothing the commission could say—that it wasn't really energy efficient or good for old houses—could change his mind. "I was born here and we didn't need their help this many years," he scoffed. "They waited twenty years too late. Most people already have siding."

"You know what?" asked Warren (Bus) Seymour, going about his business as usual at the Town Hall despite his recent retirement as town administrator. "I can stand here in Williamsport and give somebody hell, but don't you try it, if you're an outsider. Then, everyone's against you." The commission, Bus Seymour added, had "tried to change night into day, that's what they tried to do, and you run into trouble when you do that. In Williamsport, you can't cram things down people's throat. You got to go along gradual or you ain't gonna get anywhere."

The commission deadlocked two to two on Turner's request. The chairman, a five-year resident who worked in his family's insurance business in Hagerstown, cast the deciding vote against Turner. "I told them the night before, if they turned it down, they might as well kiss the commission goodbye," said Jeanne House, who voted to let Turner go ahead. "I don't want to see Williamsport become Tin Pan Alley," she said, "but you can't fight the whole town, and there's no point in trying."

The Bodie Turner decision evoked a storm of protest. The townsfolk were proud of their heritage but fiercely opposed to government controls. Property rights over preservation was their platform, "A man's home is his castle" their battle cry. The manager of the town's all-country-music radio station editorialized over the air against the commission. Petitions were passed around. In a few weeks, 831 residents signed, in a town where 400 votes will get you elected mayor.

Leading the petition drive was Janie Rupp, the fifty-four-year-old daughter and granddaughter of canal workers. She lived in an old house on Conococheague Street, a former log cabin that had been added onto and covered four or five years before with vinyl siding. "We set our own sauerkraut, can our own tomatoes, and cure our own hams," she said proudly. "I think I'm kind of historic."

On the canal, her family had owned both a boat and the mules to pull it. "My daddy drove the mules," she said. "All my aunts worked on the boat, cooked, saw that the stables were kept clean on the boat. The boat went from Cumberland to Georgetown, and the family went right along.

"My daddy run a still," she continued.

> I helped to run that still. We still got the coil to it down in the shed. We always kept a boat at the crick. If we heard someone coming at night, my father would always say "Head for the crick." We also made home brew. If we'd all lived, there'd been twelve of us.
>
> When I was a kid growing up, we lived on Snot Hill. It was really Hospital Hill, but they said every kid there had a runny nose. We were from the wrong side of the tracks. My mother and grandmother washed and ironed for [others] on a scrub board. Back then, nobody had anything. You only had what you worked hard for. You got one pair of slippers a year, and your daddy would half sole and heel 'em.

Janie Rupp had finished one year of high school, cleaned the homes of the wealthy as the women of her family had done before her, and raised two children.

Her husband, Harry Rupp, Jr., had worked for the railroad and for the aircraft plant in Hagerstown, where she had also worked for a while.

"We like the town the way it is, really we do," Janie Rupp said. "None of your older people would sell their houses. I wouldn't sell mine, because I wouldn't be happy anywhere else. The whole nut in a shell is pressuring people, telling them what they can and can't do, that's not gonna work in this town. What people are up in arms about, they don't want this communist.... How do I want to word this? They feel like they're living in a constitutional country.... Why, if we pay our taxes, is someone gonna dictate to me what I'm gonna do with my property?"

Among the commissioners accused of being "communistic" was a Republican stockbroker. "The thing we cannot get across to the town is the tremendous outside interest in Williamsport," said Bradford Downey, the accused capitalist.

"It kept me awake nights," said Howard Weaver, another commissioner and an architect who had moved to Williamsport because he wanted to live in a small town. "Everyone sees [the threat] except the town. It's gonna take some shock to wake the people up. If we don't do something, the town as it is won't exist in five or ten years. This town is still largely in its original state. That's why I moved here. I really don't know the answer."

Faced with unyielding hostility, the historic commissioners found one answer. They resigned. All of them at once.

The mayor and town council members appointed themselves to fill the vacancies. Muggs Teach, a salesman for Cushwa Bricks who had given twenty years to the elected local government, vowed, "After all these years, I'm not going to run anymore and be subject to all this abuse." And he didn't. The commission itself became dormant. So, for a while at least, did Park Service plans to build a major "interpretive center" for the canal at Williamsport. Funds, following the example of the canal itself, had dried up—though in 1996 the river would twice flood the area, causing further damage and delays. In 1999, Jeanne's Confectionery would close, after fifty-three years a corner fixture no more. Nonetheless, Williamsport continues pretty much as before, an old canal town dressed up just a bit with a coat of vinyl siding.

15

Appalachian Springs

*B*loomington Dam is seven miles upriver from Bloomington, Maryland, an old mining town clinging to a steep mountain and overlooking the Potomac. The town was where the dam was supposed to be. But the mountains were found to be honeycombed with abandoned mine shafts, which would have caused the impoundment to leak into the hillsides, so they kept the name but changed the site of the $173.4 million edifice two hundred miles upriver from the nation's capital. It was the only one of sixteen dams once planned for the Potomac River basin that actually got built.

The earthen dam's completion was marked with a banquet lunch at the Potomac Motel in Keyser, West Virginia, on September 20, 1981. Luminaries from nearby Maryland and West Virginia joined in the celebration. The banquet was in a location as accessible as any in the mountains could be, but the dam and 5.5-mile-long reservoir nicknamed "the Blue Dragon" were in a spot so remote that dignitaries had to be flown in by helicopter for the dedication.

On a chilly, overcast day, the Maryland Army National Guard carried the colors; Oakland's Southern High School band played the national anthem; and a preacher from nearby Kitzmiller, Maryland, led everyone in prayer. U.S. senators were there. So was an official from the Chinese embassy who had come to marvel at an engineering feat to rival the Great Wall.

They were deep in the heart of Appalachia, where the river was no good for drinking and no good for recreation and hardly suitable for navigation. It was impossibly polluted with acid from the mines. Bloomington Dam and reservoir—twenty-seven hundred acres of Maryland and eighteen hundred of West Virginia—had been built to help the downriver water supply by controlling the Potomac's flow. It was not for use in a severe water shortage, or for swimming or fishing, either.

Under the direction of the Army Corps of Engineers, hundreds of men had moved earth and mountain. They moved two cemeteries, three miles of power lines, twelve miles of railroad, and thirty-nine families from Shaw, West Virginia, a coal and lumber town leveled and flooded in the process. Four new railroad bridges were built for the Western Maryland Railway, a section of which was relocated from the West Virginia riverbank below to three hundred feet up the mountain on the Maryland side.

For a decade, the men who built the dam and reservoir had been part of the local scene. Many had lived in Allegheny and Garrett counties, raising their children, participating in community life. With the job done, they, along with the heavy equipment, would be moving on to other places, other jobs, leaving behind only a crew of seven to run the dam. It had always been thus along the far reaches of the North Branch of the Potomac. People came to work, the work ended, the people left. The land remained, for better or worse, masking evidence of another time.

So it was at Bloomington Dam, and on up the line, in the grimy old Potomac River mining towns that once had prospered and now languished, their glory days a part of the past.

The town nearest the dam on the Maryland side is such a place. Kitzmiller had become a shell of its former self, its shopping district mostly shut down, its population largely depleted. When I first visited the once-booming coal community, it had been all but left to the miners' widows.

One of every three houses in this town of 387 in 1980 (12.6% fewer than in the last census, and just 275 in 1996, an even steeper decline) was inhabited by a widow. On East Main alone, widows occupied eleven of seventeen adjoining houses. By official count, forty-seven widows and three old maids were on the town tax rolls—including the tax collector, who earned $27.50 a year and whose husband had died in a mine accident back in 1948, when she was just twenty-two.

"This is the most unique town in the world," said Ross Sowers, who owned the only gas station in town. "Per capita, I expect there are more rooms and less people here than just about anywhere else. There are so many widows here."

They were women like Leanna Davis, sixty-five, who lived around the corner. Her husband, disabled in a 1942 mining accident, had died a decade

Sign at the Kitzmiller town line, 1979. Lucian Perkins, *Washington Post*

before my visit, but, like many Kitzmiller widows, she listed herself in the phone book by his name: Mrs. Charles W. Davis. Since her husband's death in 1969, she and her sixty-one-year-old sister had occupied four of the fifteen rooms in the weathered frame building she called "my tumble-down shack, such as it is."

The back porch was sagging, and the front steps needed repair, but inside, her living room presented a picture of warmth, anchored by a coal-burning heater and a 1945 Silvertone floor-model radio. On top of the radio were an American flag, a bronzed baby shoe, a small photograph of her minister and his wife, and an aphorism: "Love is the only treasure that grows more beautiful with time." In the kitchen was a sign that said, "SMILE. God Loves You."

"It's as cheap as anyplace else, and I don't like it as well in the city," the widow explained. "There's not too much up here, anymore. Just a settlement for retired people, I guess."

Like all the widows here, Leanna Davis hauled her drinking water from Short Run, which was past the school and the nearby town of Shallmar and up a country road. There, she and her sister filled twelve or fourteen plastic gallon containers with water enough to last a month. "Some of the good guys from Kitzmiller went up there and piped it in from the spring so people could get water from the road," Davis explained. Kitzmiller would get its own water system, finally, but not until the summer of 1985. Well water was only fit for bathing and just barely for that. "It makes your bathtub and sink and everything brown," she said. "In summer, it don't smell too good."

In addition to Social Security, she received her husband's black-lung pension, granted posthumously. The retroactive lump-sum payments and monthly stipends had eased the twilight years for many of the miners' widows, providing money for home improvements and even, for the first time in their lives, some savings.

"People around here have been through so many hard times, now is the best time of their lives," said David A. Burdock, the town's thirty-five-year-old undertaker. "There are so many widows in this community, women in their eighties and nineties, you wouldn't believe it. An old bachelor would have a field day here." But the future looked bleak, even for the bachelors, in this town of the aging. "I keep thinking," Burdock said, "one of these days, we're gonna be so busy, we won't know what to do."

The storefronts at the once-bustling corner of Union and Main were vacant. Next-door to Leanna Davis, trees grew in a vacant lot where at one time a business had been. Across the street, raw sewage flushed into a stream coursing to the Potomac. Nearly one of every four homes lacked indoor plumbing. Nonetheless, the old people stayed on, ritually congregating at Wilson's Barber

Shop in the evenings and, three days a week, taking their lunches in a federally subsidized hot meals program at the town hall.

The first settler had arrived in 1801, to build and operate a grist mill. One of his fifteen children married Ebenezer Kitzmiller, who built a woolen mill in 1853. The arrival of the railroad in 1882 sparked a lumber boom, and coal mining became the town's economic mainstay around the turn of the century. At its peak, Kitzmiller boasted 1,800 people, a movie theater, its own bank, three barber shops, a dentist, two doctors, three groceries, two dry goods stores, a beauty parlor, and a pharmacy. There were never any bars, however. A covenant in all deeds banned the sale or manufacture of alcoholic beverages.

Kitzmiller's miners found drink across the river in Blaine, West Virginia, and work in the mountains above the town, at the Hamill Coal and Coke Company in Blaine, and in the nearby Maryland towns of Shallmar and Vindex, where Leanna Davis's husband broke his back. When the mines closed after World War II, there was nothing else to fuel the economy.

"Now, it's completely in the slumps," said Gerald Chadderton, a man in his fifties, from the driver's seat of a rusting station wagon. A former miner, Chadderton told me he hadn't worked at any job in twenty years.

His nephew drove up the narrow side street, so that his car was facing Chadderton's. "He don't work, either," Chadderton said, playfully pointing a loaded .22-caliber pistol at his nephew.

"He's been trying to get a groundhog for five years," chuckled Chadderton's companion, a man named Buck. "He ain't got one yet."

For years before the mines closed, only the rising waters of the Potomac River threatened the town's existence. A devastating flood on March 29, 1924, nearly destroyed Kitzmiller, but the town bounced back to mark the installation of its first electric lights and the paving of its streets with a parade the following year. To end the flooding, the Army Corps of Engineers widened the river and built levees. In the process, a whole block of homes and the town's movie emporium, the Maryland Theater, were torn down. The theater was destined to close anyway. The business just wasn't there, the man who ran it said.

Route 38 winds down the mountain into Kitzmiller and crosses the Potomac over what was still called "the new bridge" a quarter of a century after its completion. The span replaced an 1870 structure, thereby moving the town center from Union Street one block west. Ross Sowers's service station, the only place in town that sold alcoholic beverages—and then only to take out—and a branch bank stood together on one side of Route 38 in town.

Across the street, almost hidden below the road, was a large white building divided in thirds. Bill and Carma White and their teenage son lived in the middle. On one side were rooms rented to deer hunters for two dollars a night until a few years back; two of the rooms were still occupied by boarders who paid thirty dollars a month, which included some meals. "I've known a time when I've even had people sleeping on sofas," said Carma White. But that time was long past.

On the river side of the building was White's Barber Shop. The shop provided full-time work for White when he opened it in 1957, but business had declined with the town. Now, he drove a school bus under contract to the county and barbered only at night, charging $1.50 for haircuts and nothing for conversation. The old men regularly came to sit in Bill White's chair, to reminisce, to talk about their children, who have moved away, and about how they themselves have not.

"You get your feet down in this valley, you can't get away," explained Orville Chapman, a retired miner.

Lawrence Elihu Murphy, who was eighty-three, said he'd thought about leaving a couple of times, but his roots were just too deep. "I can remember when everything around here was mud and nothing else," he said. "I bought a car in 1916, and if you got in a rut, you were out of luck. I remember the first auto came around here, you climbed up this mountain in second gear."

"My little Datsun don't do much better than that now," said White. "Nelson, how are you tonight?" he asked a customer.

"I could stand a lot of improvement, I guess, physically, financially, spiritually, and morally," said the customer, who did not look his seventy-eight years.

"I got too many irons in the fire and I'm gonna get some of 'em out," confided Elihu Murphy. He raised two hundred bushels of potatoes and had a cow, he said. It was getting to be too much.

White consoled his aging customers with a story about an eighty-four-year-old man from these parts "who got along fine, chased women, drank whiskey, until they got him to a doctor who told him he was sick, and he died two weeks later."

White, not yet fifty, was one of four town council members. His wife was the town clerk and secretary to the Garrett County Board of Education. Kitzmiller had once had its own high school. Built in 1922, it closed in the early 1950s, when Garrett County replaced several smaller secondary schools with two regional ones. For years, however, Kitzmiller parents continued to send their teenagers to nearby Elk Garden, West Virginia, and the government paid their out-of-state tuition.

Now, Kitzmiller's kids attended Southern High School in the Garrett County seat of Oakland, twenty miles away, and the old high school had been transformed into an elementary school, with all but 19 of its 129 students coming from outside the town. But old loyalties died hard, and the Elk Garden Stags football schedule still hung in Ross Sowers's Texaco.

Some local institutions survived, however. Among them were the volunteer fire company and the Lions Club, each with about twenty active members. For entertainment, there was cable television and a community library, open thirteen hours a week, which displayed a sign warning "No Loafing and No Smoking." There were four churches, including one that held a "Rally for Revival" every Saturday night. Another gathering spot, the "new" post office, dated to 1974.

On Tuesdays, the county took a busload of widows to the shopping centers of Oakland. On Wednesdays, Thursdays, and Fridays, hot meals were served to them upstairs in the Kitzmiller town hall which doubled as a community building, Mamie Shanks, a seventy-four-year-old railroad worker's widow, presiding. Forty cents bought lunch, following grace. On a typical day, the menu consisted of home-cooked ham, beans, cole slaw, potatoes, cornbread, and cake. Leftovers were taken, free of charge, to persons unable to walk over to or climb the stairs of the building.

"Last winter, it was so icy, they brought my meal over thirty-five times," said Catharine Barrick, eighty-one, a former grammar school teacher who lived alone in eight rooms above the grocery store her husband's family had owned for years. "I'd rather come over, because I get so tired of eating by myself."

Another local institution was Dr. Ralph Calandrella, affectionately known to all as Doc Cal. At age seventy-four, he was settled into semi-retirement, seeing only a dozen patients a day instead of a hundred, as before. Calandrella "doctors some in his home," as Leanna Davis put it. He had helped her, and many others, qualify for the black-lung pension. "People couldn't give him up around here," the widow said of the old doctor.

He had come to Kitzmiller in 1935, from New Haven, Connecticut, where, he said, there were two dozen doctors within two miles and nobody had any money. Kitzmiller was also the home town of his wife, Mary, a nurse he had met while attending medical school in Washington, D.C. The mines were operating when he arrived, and he signed on as doctor for several of the coal companies.

The first winter was rough, he told me. He reached his patients by walking or by riding a mule or a horse. "When I came here, there were very few phones and the roads were bad," said the gentle, white-haired man. "I did everything I was capable of and some things I'm not sure I was capable of."

He had an office right in town and built a modest brick house in 1947 in a flat riverside area known as "the bottom." He and his wife reared two sons, and Doc Cal was the town's mayor for a dozen years and served on the county's board of education for a while in the 1950s.

In the beginning, when people couldn't pay him, his patients would bring him chickens, beef, a bag of potatoes. Later, he charged them little or nothing for treatment they could not afford. While doctors elsewhere were raising prices, investing in motels, and forgoing house calls, Doc Cal continued as before. He held office hours six days and several nights a week, and trudged through the snow if necessary to care for homebound patients at all hours. He dedicated his practice to the people in and around his adopted hometown, eschewing membership in the county medical society and staff privileges at the county hospital.

Time-consuming paperwork required by government-supported medical programs had prompted his retirement, he said. He preferred providing free patient care to dealing with red tape.

"For a little while [after retiring], I didn't do too much," he said. "But we had a couple of bad winters, and the old people wanted me to do stuff. I don't charge 'em. I've treated some for three generations."

The career that made him a beloved figure—almost god-like, people said— ended in a Cumberland courtroom three years after I first met him in Kitzmiller. The short, slight man with a Lions Club pin in his lapel was fined $5,000 for illegally selling barbiturates and other drugs to undercover police. The Allegany County state's attorney said he had become a major supplier of controlled dangerous substances in Western Maryland.

The doctor's status was so special that the case had been moved to Allegany, the county immediately east of Garrett, where neither the chief prosecutor nor the circuit judge would have anything to do with it. "I was both amazed and saddened," said Jim Sherbin, the Garrett state's attorney. "It doesn't make sense."

Indeed, if Doc Cal had ever sought riches from his practice, he'd kept it a well-hidden secret. Apart from his house along the Potomac, he owned 130 acres, willed to him by a patient for "doctoring" the man and paying his taxes before he died, and a 1969 two-door Chevrolet. His only income, he testified, was his monthly Social Security check for $480.

"There is not even one Lincoln Continental," the prosecutor himself acknowledged. "There is no palatial estate, no holdings in Puerto Rico. He does not own IBM or Exxon stock."

"It was very isolated," Doc Cal said at his sentencing, explaining why he had his own office pharmacy. "At different times, when there was enough snow, we couldn't get to town for a week at a time. There were no drug stores closer than twenty miles away, so I began dispensing my own drugs. I guess I got in the habit of dispensing more than you usually do. But a lot [of patients] came from a great distance. You couldn't give them [just enough for] a day or two, so I gave them a couple weeks' medication."

The practice had apparently carried over to the present. Records seized by state police showed he had dispensed 120,000 more pills than he had prescribed one year. Many of the drugs had ended up in the hands of criminals who stole, burgled, and forged to support their habit, the prosecutor said. The drugs included potentially addictive sedatives, depressants, and hypnotics.

On his behalf, Wilbur H. Myers, a longtime friend, recalled the doctor's annual lectures at the local high school and his insistence that the children be inoculated against diphtheria and scarlet fever. "He was the instigator of that," Myers said, adding, "See, Kitzmiller was to Garrett County like Siberia is to Russia." Myers noted that Doc Cal was a charter member of the Kitzmiller Lions and hadn't missed a meeting in thirty-five years until the week of the sentencing.

"This is the man walking through the snow carrying a little black bag you saw on Christmas cards," said Ralph A. Burnett, his Garrett County lawyer who had once been a prosecutor, too. "He gave medicine when it was needed, and because of that the people of Kitzmiller are healthier today. What he's done for them ought to be bronzed. I'll continue to call him 'Doctor' the rest of my life."

"I admit maybe I didn't use the right judgment," the doctor told the judge. He had, the prosecutor said, sold an undercover officer more than twenty-seven hundred tablets on three different occasions, for a total of $510, or about 5¢ per tablet. Doc Cal pleaded guilty to five of ten counts, and the others were dropped. He promised never to practice medicine again.

"It's just one of those things," he shrugged, after the sentencing. "What can you say? My license expired yesterday. I didn't try to renew it."

The Doc Cal affair was about the worst news to hit the town of Kitzmiller since the mines closed. His arrest and brief incarceration (until he could arrange to post his bond) outraged past and present residents. Angry letters from his supporters filled columns in Garrett County's weekly newspaper. One former resident wrote that he was "one of the most compassionate and caring men who walks on the face of the earth." Kitzmillerites' anger intensified when the doctor suffered a heart attack after his arrest and did not have his medication because authorities had seized it along with his other pharmaceuticals.

"The community sure needs him," said Ross Sowers, the service station man. "It's a pretty rugged trip from here over the mountain in the wintertime, and you can't get a doctor to come down here if a person's confined to home. These old-timers won't go to someone else. But he shouldn't have given that many pills."

And from Lois Mosser, a Kitzmiller widow and the town's mayor, came this considered view: "I think that he's been a good guy in the town for a long time, and I think we all owe him a debt of gratitude. For the most part, people are upset about it. He's been one of us for forty years."

The triumphs and tragedies of the Doc Cals of the community were etched only in the memories of the living, for there was no written history of Kitzmiller to speak of. There were just the recollections and keepsakes of the people. Foremost keeper of the past was a grizzled old construction worker named Les Wilhelm, who raised rows of raspberries on a hillside in West Virginia overlooking the town.

His collection included the 1926 Kitzmiller High School yearbook, which contained a sober message from salutatorian Margaret Poole. The town, she wrote, should build a sewer system and purify its water supply. But even more important, Kitzmiller's businessmen should "help us get some other industry besides mining.... Why is it that all high school pupils leave the town as soon as they finish? Because the only thing left for girls to do is get married, and the boys' only means of making money is mining."

Margaret Poole never did get married, and she left Kitzmiller to become a physical therapist. She worked with crippled children until she retired. "Wasn't I a smart little character?" the seventy-one-year-old former Kitzmillerite said from her home near Orlando, Florida. "They didn't pay any attention to me."

The evidence was all over, but one shred seemed especially poignant. The Wilson-Fidler American Legion Post 113, which needed ten members to keep its charter, was barely clinging to life. Once it had sixty members and a meeting place in the old grammar school, whose windows were now boarded. Now, its rolls numbered seventeen, of whom nine lived elsewhere, in places as far away as Seattle.

"This is a sorry community," said Legion Post Commander Ross Sowers, "but it could be a lot sorrier. Don't paint it all black. Put some flowers in it. I hope things get better. They have only one way to go, haven't they?"

But there would be no help from the Free State of Maryland. Of that much he was sure. "The rest of the state thinks Maryland ended down in Frederick somewhere," Sowers said with conviction. "They don't know we're up here. They could care less."

The feeling extended all the way west, to the outer reaches of Maryland. Usually,

Once thriving, downtown Kitzmiller is a boarded up ghost town.
Eugene L. Meyer

it was resignation mixed with bitterness, but in at least one place I found indifference matched by indifference. That place was Kempton, a virtual ghost town at the southwesternmost corner of the state. There, two miles from the Fairfax Stone marking the wellspring of the river just across the line in West Virginia, the Potomac was a mere trickle.

Kempton owed its existence to coal and the railroad. It came into being in

1914, when the Western Maryland Railway spur arrived. A mine explosion two years later, which trapped seventy-two and killed sixteen, failed to dim its glow. By 1918 there were said to be 850 residents and 106 homes. It was a company town, and the company was Davis Coal and Coke. There were two 450-foot mine shafts. The main street was paved, and so were the sidewalks. The foremen lived on Front Street, the workers—many of them immigrants—on the back streets that rose along the mountainside. Kempton had a school, a playground, electric lights, a movie theater, a car dealership, and a company store. During the 1920s, it had a surfeit of moonshine—twelve stills were smashed in one raid by revenuers—and it had the Ku Klux Klan, which once burned a cross.

The Depression and the Western Maryland Railway's conversion to diesel power killed the coal business in Kempton. In 1950 the mine closed for good. With it went 260 jobs. The company houses were sold, and some of them were hauled away. The town of Kempton was left to the ghosts and just a handful of the living.

What's left of the town sits at the base of 3,360-foot Backbone Mountain, Maryland's tallest. It's a good twenty miles or more from Oakland, and it's in a setting that seems more in keeping with the Rocky Mountain West. Paved Route 219 passes three miles west of the town, in West Virginia. But there's an all-Maryland backway there. Table Rock Road is miles of gravel as it descends toward Kempton, past Mettiki Coal, the only large deep mine left in Western Maryland.

The first sight that confronted me in Kempton was the old coal tipple, along with piles of black slag. The train tracks had been torn up the previous summer, but there were the crumbling foundation of the old school, remnants of sidewalks overgrown with weeds, and half a dozen homes.

In one of them lived Elmer Clark, a retired miner, his wife, Martha, their daughter, who worked in a mine in nearby Henry, West Virginia, and their three-year-old granddaughter. Clark had gone into the Kempton mines at the age of seventeen in 1928 and worked there for twenty-one years before it closed. "I used to load nine three-ton coal cars a day," he said, remembering the good years.

He had left Kempton, like most of the miners, to find work elsewhere, and had returned in retirement in 1973, after spending fifteen years in Cleveland, where his other nine children lived. "I couldn't afford to stay out there and live on a [black-lung] miner's pension," he told me. In Kempton, at least, he had all the coal he needed to heat his house for practically nothing.

"This used to be a beautiful place," he said as he showed me where the school had been. "It looks like a wilderness now."

The Clarks got their mail from Thomas, West Virginia. A newspaper from

Parsons, West Virginia, and a single snowy television picture from Clarksburg were their other links to the outside world. "I wish they'd get the cable through here," Martha Clark said, "but they say the families are too few and far between."

And if this corner of Maryland went unnoticed by the rest of the state, well, the feeling was mutual. Of the rest of the state, Martha Clark said simply, "We never give it any thought."

16

No Free Lunch

In the mountains of Western Maryland, winter is a time of extremes. The people prepare for it and live with it, and, sometimes, they die from it.

One bone-chilling cold January, when temperatures dropped to ten below and the winds whipped over the snowscape, Austin (Audie) Urban Tasker froze to death in his drafty ramshackle house, a half-empty bottle tucked between his legs and a tub of unused coal sitting behind his stove. The seventy-year-old former miner, farmer, moonshiner, and drifter was the state's first weather fatality of 1981. He died in Garrett County, the coldest, highest, and least densely populated in the state, a starkly beautiful county that, in winter, often resembles a Currier and Ives print—with four-wheel drive jeeps and snowmobiles instead of horses and carriages. The winter beauty can be deceptive, however. Survival is not always easy and help not always close by.

The drafty house in Garrett County where
Austin Tasker froze to death in 1981. Steve Bittner, Cumberland

"Yes, sir, she's a rough life out here," said Paul Sharpless, a twenty-eight-year-old friend of Tasker who found his lifeless body next to a cold coal stove with a pot of frozen water on top.

Within days, several inches of fresh snow driven by squalls of up to twenty-five miles an hour caused drifts to pile up. Before the new snow could bury their memories, Audie Tasker's few friends and relatives who still cared pondered his life and mourned his death. He was survived by six grandchildren he didn't know he had, five children he hadn't seen in years, four sisters he saw only rarely, and at least two good drinking companions who visited him often.

An army veteran, Tasker had wanted to be buried at Arlington National Cemetery. Instead, he was buried in Garrett County, in a plain, cloth-covered wooden casket, "not a welfare casket, by any means," the funeral director told one of his friends. But far from the top of the line.

The mourners wanted to believe he had died from a heart attack. The medical examiner's verdict was death by hypothermia, where the body temperature drops so low a person can't live.

"Freezing to death," said Paul Sharpless, "that's the bad part of it."

Alcohol, which makes a person feel deceptively warm and comfortable, had numbed his mind as well as his body. The biggest mystery, however, was not the cause of death but what had become of the more than $200 in bills, from his freshly cashed government checks, which he had on Saturday, the day before his corpse was found. The rented, red-shingled house on Old Hotel Road outside the former resort of Deer Park offered no clues. It was, as usual, a shambles, with empty whiskey and beer bottles scattered about and dishes piled high in the sink. A frozen quart of buttermilk was in the refrigerator.

His eyeglasses were on the floor of the front room where he mostly lived, and died. There was a black-and-white television. One bare light bulb protruded from the ceiling. In the drawer of a small end table were a deck of cards, some envelopes, a few nails. "No, he won't have to worry about no one fighting over his estate," Sharpless said as we inspected the place.

Tacked to the wall was a holiday card from his sister Adeleane Stewart, of Glassport, Pennsylvania. "Merry Christmas, Brother," said the outside. "Hope you are well and you have a Merry Christmas and a Happy New Year," she had written inside.

"He joked about dying," said his other friend, thirty-one-year-old Ron Tasker, a miner who had left him on Saturday with a warm coal fire and half a gallon of whiskey, two quarts of buttermilk, and six coconut candy bars. "Before Thanksgiving or Christmas, he would say, 'I'll never see another turkey day,'" said Ron Tasker, who thought they were related but wasn't sure.

He spent little on groceries, and, said Sharpless, "if nobody fixed food for him, he wouldn't eat." Five feet, six inches tall, he weighed a mere hundred pounds when he died. He lived without a telephone or indoor plumbing. Water came from a spring when someone brought it to him. Mostly, he just drank. Even when he went to the hospital for cataracts, they gave him beer to get fluids into him.

He had grown up on a one-hundred-acre farm near Vindex, a company-owned coal town not far from where he died. There had been no tractor, only horses and hand plows, and his schooling had ended in fourth grade. His steadiest employment—lasting eight years, he told friends—was as a moonshiner for a notorious local distributor of bootleg whiskey.

"Way back yonder when you couldn't get no beer, no whiskey," said Effie Comp, at eighty-three his oldest surviving sister, "he made the best moonshine you'd ever drink."

When Repeal came along, Audie Tasker joined the army. He was stationed in Hawaii for a while, then left the service after four years in 1937. Back in Garrett County, he mined coal, married and divorced and remarried, to a woman twenty-two years his junior. She left him after seven years, on account of his drinking, she said, and she took the children with her.

Tasker worked for a time in Pennsylvania for a glass factory and a copper salvage yard. He also lived near Annapolis and in Washington, D.C., and did construction work in Southern Maryland. In 1972 he returned to Garrett County, where he joined the ranks of the unemployed and then enjoyed a retirement of sorts, visited by his drinking buddies.

Because of severe weather and his own infirmities, Tasker hadn't been out of his house since summer, when he visited a friend in Kitzmiller. Another friend kept him supplied with coal. A few weeks before Audie died, Ron Tasker had installed an oil stove in Audie's kitchen and helped him apply for free fuel under the county's emergency aid program for the needy.

On a small table a few feet from where he died, Sharpless and I found a letter saying his application had been accepted. It was dated December 30. "You will receive notification on the exact amount within fifteen days," the letter said. But neither notification nor delivery had come in time.

Of this cold, distant place at the westernmost edge of Maryland, Gladys Anderson, manager of the state unemployment office in Oakland, had said, "It's a rugged place to live and it takes people who are individuals to survive, because there really is no free lunch here in Garrett County."

It's a sentiment I heard expressed time and again during my visits to this mountainous country, the "tableland" of the Allegheny plateau. They measure time in winters here, as in "the freeway opened two winters ago." The winters are long and harsh, heightening the sense of isolation and boosting unemployment levels to as high as 20% during normal times here "on the mountaintop" many ridges removed from the rest of Maryland.

From Oakland, the county seat some 2,000 feet above sea level, Washington and Baltimore are about 180 miles east, Pittsburgh 125 miles north. Annapolis seems to exist only to infringe on the rights of the county's 29,238 citizens (as of 1996) with bureaucratic rules and confiscatory actions. Even Cumberland, fifty miles northeast of Oakland, is in another world of climate, altitude, and attitude.

It is reasonable, therefore, that Garrett Countians care nothing for the Washington Redskins or Baltimore Orioles or Ravens. They root for the Pittsburgh Pirates and Steelers and the West Virginia Mountaineers. Their view of the world comes by cable from television stations in Pennsylvania and West Virginia and Steubenville, Ohio, and, more recently, from Hagerstown, one hundred miles to the east. Crabcakes are almost a foreign delicacy and sauerbraten practically a native dish in this county peopled largely by what the 1940 Maryland Writers' Project guidebook called "citizens of conservative, Pennsylvania German stock who show little concern for the outside world." And vice versa, natives assert.

As Willis T. Shaffer, owner of the Ford dealership in Oakland, told me one fall day, "We're kind of the forgotten end out here. I used to be in the Maryland Auto Trade Association. I threatened to come to the meetings in cowboy boots. Several dealers in the state used to say, 'Where is Oakland?' and I had to tell them where it was. It's different from the rest of the state, and the people are different."

This is a land of great distances, where one may drive thirty miles for a movie theater, but with a grapevine that often transcends time and space. It is also a land of splendid scenery, of Appalachian ridges and high meadows, known as glades, laced with miles of macadam, dirt, and gravel roads. The mountains are aflame in autumn and serene in summer, when outlanders come to vacation at Deep Creek Lake, an artificial body of water created in the 1920s by a Pennsylvania utility company. In wintertime, skiers fill the cross-country trails and the downhill slopes of Wisp, overlooking the lake. Blinding snowstorms swirl over the high country, and Muddy Creek Falls, Maryland's highest, freezes into a dazzling display of icicles.

The county is named for John Garrett, a nineteenth-century president of the B&O who brought the trains and built resorts to lure outsiders onto his railroad line. It was an attempt to link the east and west, but west has always remained a world apart. Garrett is the only county in Maryland, for example, with a majority of registered Republicans, although members of both parties are, by and large, conservatives. Citizens tend to divide along "moderate conservative" and "ultra-conservative" lines.

"God has everything under control," says one bumper sticker seen in these parts. It appears to reflect majority sentiment in a county that has steadfastly refused to allow Sunday liquor sales. Another sentiment, scrawled in restroom graffiti at the county courthouse, perhaps by an outsider: "Fuck this faraway place."

In a sense, Garrett is to Maryland what Alaska is to the "lower forty-eight" states, a last frontier far from the population and political centers. It is a place peopled by individualists where resentment of outside government runs deep and where rules and regulations are tolerated but seldom welcomed.

The enforcers of such laws are also unwelcomed. That is why unknown persons are said to enter at their own risk a section called Bear Hill, a place known for its stills and seclusion. A few years ago, a truant officer was killed there. At the trial in Oakland, the defense rested on the belief of the accused that the victim was a game warden. Elsewhere in the county, bootleg ginseng competes with bootleg whiskey for the illegal dollar. The plant root, used for tea and valued in Asia as an aphrodisiac, is plucked by "sangers," as they are known, and usually sold without benefit of state license and weighing laws.

If Garrett County is a world apart, it is within itself two worlds, north and south. Some say the rivalry began with the routing of the National Road through the north in the early 1800s and was heightened by the coming of the B&O Railroad through the south decades later. The division was underscored in 1872, as soon as the county came into being—itself the result of a split from Allegany, whose seat of government, Cumberland, was just too far away. The north and south competed for the new county seat. The selection of Oakland in the south over Grantsville up north, by fifty-three votes, triggered demands that the new county be split in two. The hard feelings have survived into modern times.

"Grantsville is farther from Oakland in some ways than New York is from Los Angeles," explained Gary Yoder, whose Amish and Mennonite kinfolk are northerners. "They're still bitter about the county seat in Grantsville. They pass that on, from generation to generation, like granddad's old coat, with a handful of bitterness."

Northerners have also complained about what they regard as inadequate crime protection in their end of the county; they claim the south is better policed. Consolidation of the county's six high schools into two—Northern and Southern—in the 1950s added an annual football classic to the sectional rivalry, which has also extended to commerce and even, at times, politics.

When Oakland's DeCorsey E. Bolden, for instance, narrowly beat George Edwards of Grantsville for state delegate, the vote was largely along sectional lines. Northerners were envious when Bausch & Lomb, an optical company, located in Oakland in 1971, bringing 435 jobs to the county's southern end until it closed in the recession a decade later. Northerners rejoiced, however, over the

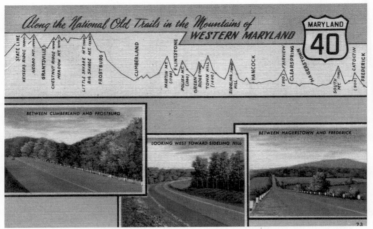

Postcard depicting Route 40, gateway to Western Maryland.

opening of U.S. 48, the National Freeway paralleling U.S. 40, the old National Road. In its wake a new Holiday Inn appeared, and the Casselman Hotel in Grantsville, built for drovers in 1824, added forty motel units. The road has since taken on interstate status, and a new number, I-68.

The sectional feud, some say, is subsiding, but the bridge over Deep Creek Lake is still called "the border" dividing the county in half. "It used to be," said George Edwards, who eventually won Bolden's General Assembly seat with countywide support, "when you crossed that bridge, it was like going into another country." Just north of the border, however, are two unifying factors: the county fairgrounds and Garrett Community College, where academic credit is given for "leisure studies" such as angling and backpacking, and an associate degree is offered in "Adventuresports."

Such pursuits are foreign to the plain people of Garrett's Amish communities, whose members farm the fertile land near Grantsville and south of Oakland. The south county Amish, about seventy-five families, use electricity and drive tractors and even black automobiles. But many in the Grantsville group still walk behind horse-drawn plows. Thus, the north-south split exists even among the Amish, who are deeply rooted here, unlike those in Southern Maryland, who arrived from Pennsylvania only in 1940.

The new order Amish have their own public school, a small brick building in an area south of Oakland known as Pleasant Valley. The Grantsville area Amish, on the other hand, send their children to a parochial school across the border in Pennsylvania, while the children of Mennonites attend the public school outside town. Begun late in the nineteenth century as a "subscription" academy for Amish and Mennonites, the Yoder School adjoined farms belonging to Elmer Yoder, Noah Yoder, Rufus Yoder, Norman Yoder, Alva Yoder, Lloyd Yoder, Raymond Yoder, and Pete Yoder. "You're either a Yoder or married to one around here, or so it seems," said Esther Yoder, the Mennonite principal, whose husband, Henry, a former old order Amishman, handled the school lunch program.

Opinions on the National Freeway, controversial in Allegany County, were also divided in Garrett. "That road was the beginning of the end," was how the county's chief prosecutor put it. The part-time state's attorney then recounted how two felons from Morgantown, West Virginia, had swooped down on helpless Oakland to commit a burglary and then kill the sheriff's deputy who answered the alarm. Without the road, State's Attorney Jim Sherbin assured me, "those fellas would never have been here. Last year, we had one of our first bank robberies. The criminals were from Baltimore. With easy access, we've opened it up—good and bad—to progress. But when we want something done, we cannot call West Virginia. We have to call Baltimore and Annapolis because the fact of the matter is, we're in the state of Maryland."

When a sensational murder happened elsewhere in the state, often as not the case was sent to Garrett County to be tried. The assumption was that nobody in these parts knew or cared what was going on in the rest of the state, making Garrett fertile ground for selection of an impartial jury. For their part, the citizens of Garrett in general—and the county seat of Oakland in particular—were happy to have the hordes of outside prosecutors, lawyers, and witnesses who filled the local motels and kept the economy humming in slack times.

For some, Garrett County was a place to flee to, a rural refuge for ideological metropolitan misfits. Bob Watkins owned a conservative newspaper in Howard County, where he also ran unsuccessfully for county executive. When the new town of Columbia, with its liberal ideas and voters, came to dominate the county, he fled to Garrett, where he practiced law and dabbled in local politics. "Garrett County is a lot like Howard was" before liberal newcomers arrived, he told me. "It's a beautiful place. There's a lot of rugged individualism here, with an opportunity for a person like me to do his thing."

Most of the county's lawyers, including State's Attorney Sherbin and his two assistants, were also outsiders, a word that encompasses just about anyone born elsewhere. As Gary Yoder put it, with only a slight touch of hyperbole, "Even if conception occurs in Garrett County and on the day of birth you happen to be across the Allegany County line and on the day of birth you come right back, that's too bad. Partum is what counts." By his own definition, Yoder was slightly suspect, having been born in Cumberland. His parents had moved there from

The Cove   The Oakland Road near Keyser Ridge, Md.
Elev. 2800-3100 ft.   C.E.G.

Vintage photo-postcard of the Oakland Road (Rt. 219)
in Maryland's northwest corner near Pennsylvania.

Grantsville to find work during the Great Depression.

Newcomers say there is no welcome wagon in Garrett County. "We have cold winters and cold people, until you get to know them," said Tom Butscher, a non-native whose five-hundred-watt radio station beamed Bible Belt gospel hours, country music, and birth and anniversary announcements from a small studio outside Oakland. The station and the *Republican*, a weekly newspaper published in Oakland, comprise the county's "mass media." The paper's letters, often, more than its news columns, mirrored the latest community controversy. Its editorials tended to be, by Garrett County standards, moderate. Butscher's radio commentaries were more consistently conservative.

"The conservatives here have ranted and raved about the new people," explained Don Sincell, the editor of the *Republican*, which his family had been publishing since 1877. Its office was above Proudfoot's Pharmacy, "Serving Oakland since 1893," according to the sign. Of the newcomers, some of whom had filled most of the county's top administrative posts, Sincell said, "They are very competent, and there weren't people here to fill the jobs." A member of the town's volunteer fire company, he abruptly ended our conversation to respond to an alarm that could be heard for blocks.

The widespread wariness of newcomers is especially acute in the case of those whose values and lifestyles place them at odds with the conservative traditions of Garrett County.

"They think they're up here on the mountain and it's God's acres and they're the only ones allowed up here," explained Dan Ledden, the twenty-six-year-old son of a minister, after eleven years' experience in the county. In at least one way,

Ledden had become part of the Garrett tradition of paying homage to tradition: He collected and restored old sleighs, of which he had sixteen stored in various locations.

"I have Amish do the wheelwork for me," he said. "I have done some buying from them but not vice versa because my vehicles are too worldly, too flashy for them. They're good if I have a question on a harness. Every piece I restore I drive. In winter, I drive a lot more. Very few people are actually restoring these, and if someone doesn't, our children and their children will never know what a sleigh is."

Bucking tradition, however, Ledden had long hair, which branded him as a nonconformist in the high country. He worked for the Garrett County Playhouse on Deep Creek Lake, as stage manager and lighting director. "Working with the playhouse to locals is evil," he said. "To them, it's sex and drugs and we don't do any work." Most of the theater workers, he said, are "lake people."

"It's an entirely different sociology," explained Gary Yoder, whose job was to manage the lake and its shores for the state. "It's an entity unto itself. Building lots cost between fifty and sixty thousand dollars, which is economically beyond Garrett Countians' means. Ironically, Garrett Countians use Deep Creek the least." (In fact, nearly one-quarter of the county's property tax base came from second homes, while one-quarter of Garrett houses were "substandard" by federal government standards.)

Famed outsiders, from Albert Einstein the scientist to Ted Koppel the television network newsman, had vacationed on the shores of the serpentine-shaped, twelve-mile-long lake, Yoder told me at the Red Run Inn, a restaurant and bar catering to lesser aliens on Deep Creek. As usual, much of the bar-stool conversation revolved around a perceived government effrontery, a tax increase that had been challenged as technically defective. The result, for the moment, was a legal standoff, with funds for snow plowing the following winter in doubt.

"You better pray to God we have a soft winter," Yoder admonished his beer-drinking companion.

"We drove thirty-five years without salt on the roads," said the other man. "The bureaucracy has gotten so goddamn big, somebody got to put a stop to it."

The problem was that the "bureaucracy" (meaning county, state, and federal government) accounted for twenty percent of all the jobs in Garrett County. Without it, normally high unemployment figures would most likely soar and many more countians suffer. The sad fact was that, as much as they railed against it, Garrett Countians needed the big, bad government.

Yoder recalled another local political upheaval, a few years before, when Garrett voters replaced three Republican with three Democratic commissioners and chaos in the form of a labor dispute ensued. "There was a county road strike and bridges were blown up. You couldn't buy an ax handle in town. Garrett is Maryland's answer to M.A.S.H. It's a little bit of an anachronism."

The lake culture, however, was something else, a second-home link to the modern metropolitan mainstream, especially to Pittsburgh. Fran McBride, who worked at the Red Run Inn, was one of five of nine children born in Pittsburgh who had moved here. Her grandfather had built a vacation home here in the 1920s, and her parents had met at Deep Creek, which made McBride a third-generation lake person. As a full-time resident, she was a relative newcomer, having arrived "permanently" only four weeks before.

"I just love it here," she said. "I came up here with three teenage kids, two dogs, two cats, an old Ford Torino, and forty dollars." Having left a newly furnished fancy home, a Cadillac, and her husband, she was staying at her father's place off Lake Shore Drive. "This is no longer fantasyland for weekends. This is reality."

The reality of Deep Creek Lake exists because of the Youghiogheny, a strangely northward-flowing river from whose tributaries the man-made lake was designed to harness power. Pennelec (the Pennsylvania Electric Corporation) acquired eight thousand acres of Youghiogheny River watershed to create the largest lake in Maryland, a state with no natural bodies of fresh water. Forty-five hundred acres were flooded to form Deep Creek Lake.

The Youghiogheny River flows through Garrett County from West Virginia to Pennsylvania, where it joins the Monongahela, emptying into the Ohio, the Mississippi, and the Gulf of Mexico. In local parlance, it is known simply as "the Yock."

The Yock was officially designated a "wild and scenic" river by the state over opposition from the riverbank landowners, whose families had been there for hundreds of years and had kept the river the way it was all the while, without what they regarded as government's heavy hand. But with land values and vacationers on the rise, state officials jumped into the fray.

As the natives saw it, the Maryland Department of Natural Resources, the largest landowner in the county, accorded them no respect. Their favorite target was DNR Secretary James B. Coulter, back in Annapolis, who had by administrative fiat, later ratified by the legislature, slapped controls on the twenty-two-mile "scenic corridor" on both sides of the river in 1974. "I used what some people said were questionable powers to stop coal mining and curtail logging on the Yock," he told me. It was regulation without compensation, no doubt about it.

Many of the landowners swallowed hard and unhappily accepted the government rules and regulations allegedly needed to protect the river "corridor" from outside intrusions. Thus, when the Yock was discovered by whitewater rafting companies and the state said the companies could not be banned from using the river itself, the anger resurfaced. Phrases like "benign neglect" and "double standard" were invoked to describe the state's attitude toward the Youghiogheny. The landowners prepared to fight, some of them with guns, if necessary.

"People here do care and have given a whole lot of thought to issues raised by [persons] out there who get more fun out of raising issues than seeking solutions," said an angry Secretary Coulter. He recalled with chagrin state efforts to bring better sewage systems to the Garrett towns of Oakland, Loch Lynn, and Mountain Lake Park, with the costs covered by government. The only price to the locals, Coulter said, was a pinch of autonomy. "After a while, it became clear not one of those communities would give up any of its prerogatives," he said, and the proposal died aborning. "There are things that just don't change very quickly. The Youghiogheny and the landowners are symptomatic of that."

"I don't know if I'd want to raft the river because of the hostility. You wouldn't want to go out in a savage land, where nobody likes you, would you?" said Bob Proudfoot, the pharmacist, who resigned as chairman of the state-sponsored Youghiogheny River Citizens Advisory Board out of frustration with both sides. "I'm not a politician. I'm a pharmacist and a family man. I'm basically a man who enjoys keeping our county the way it is."

For centuries the Upper Yock—the part that flows through Garrett—had gone unnoticed by the outside world. Then, around 1970, the first whitewater

From rafting to skiing, 1960s-era brochure promotes Deep Creek Lake's resort area.

kayakers and rafters began to test its treacherous waters. On these voyages of discovery, the steep waterfalls and swirling rapids were baptized. The river runs over Gap Falls and Bastard Falls, over rapids known as Snaggle Tooth, Triple Drop, Zinger, Meat Cleaver, Lost 'n' Found, and Double Pencil Sharpener, plunging precipitously for 3 miles at 115 feet per mile, perhaps the premiere whitewater experience east of the Mississippi.

One of the first to run the river was Imre Szilagyi, a native of Budapest with a master's degree in mathematics from Ohio State. I met Szilagyi at his office in Kingwood, West Virginia, fourteen miles west of Oakland. Over pizza at a local restaurant, he recalled that first trip. "It was raining when we started," he said. "Toward the end, with the really big stuff behind us, the rain stopped and the sun shone. The rain released the odors of the forest. You felt absolutely alive, like everything inside you is alive. It is one of the really high points of one's experiential history."

For years, veterans of the Upper Yock were a small fraternity of fifty or so adventurers. "If you paddled the Upper Yock, you wore that as a badge," Szilagyi said.

Now, as president of Appalachian Wildwaters, he was promoting the Upper Yock as "the ultimate challenge...where the action's at," and he had purchased a ninety-eight-acre farm and two acres of riverfront land from which to launch his commercial expeditions.

Rafters spoke with awe of the Upper Yock as the last frontier of whitewatering in the East. The lower part of the river, in Pennsylvania, paled by comparison, they said, and West Virginia's Cheat, New, and Gauley rivers had become but steppingstones to Maryland's mighty Yock. "On the Cheat, the big word is the Yock, just like the Gauley was a couple of years ago," said a guide with the Upper Yough Whitewater Expeditions, located in an old storefront in Friendsville. "Right now the Yock is in the spotlight," added the head of the company, which was geared up for twenty-five-hundred customers in its first commercial year on the river.

The lure of the Upper Yock had been boosted by population explosions of rafters on other rivers: 115,000 a year on the Lower Yock in Pennsylvania and, on West Virginia's trio of tributaries, as many as 10,000 each weekend in the whitewater season. The specter of so many rafters cast a dark shadow over the longtime landowners along the Upper Yock.

"Can you imagine what it would be like living here with thousands of people coming here?" asked John Hinebaugh, who had returned home to Garrett County after living and working in the Washington area, mostly for the U.S.

Army Corps of Engineers, for thirty-seven years. "A lot of people are afraid of being overwhelmed."

Hinebaugh was the great-great-great-grandson of John Friend, said to have been the first white settler in the area back in 1765. "Friend's Delight" was the name of the ancestral farm where Hinebaugh lived within thirty feet of the river in an area known as Sang Run. Inevitably, Hinebaugh said, rafters would go ashore to eat lunch, to scout ahead, to litter the land.

"A lot of these boaters come in and say, 'You don't own the land; you're only the stewards of it,'" Hinebaugh said, standing by the river. "Well, you want to make someone mad? They're ready to take up arms" over such talk.

"As I told one guy," said Hinebaugh's neighbor, Colonel Richard C. Browning, a square-jawed retired marine whose ancestor Meshach Browning was a frontier hunter here in the eighteenth century, "if you want the river, buy it. These rafters say they meticulously carry out more stuff than they carry in, but I question that. From what I hear, they're a weird group of people forming up at Friendsville. Hippie-like folks."

Under the law of navigable waters, the property owners held title to the river bottom but not to the surface. The legal distinction was understood but unappreciated by Browning, who was president of the Youghiogheny River Association, a group he organized "to promote and preserve the lawful constitutional rights of the property owners along the Yock. The regulations initially promulgated by the state and rescinded after his strong protest, he pointed out, would have kept him from flying the flag. "My approach to things is to be nonviolent, to work within the law," said Browning, a veteran of three "shooting wars."

Anger over state regulations imposed on riverside property owners had spawned several incidents three or four years before I first reported the Youghiogheny controversy. One rafter, charged with trespassing at Sang Run, was fined one dollar, which outraged the property owners but made him a legendary figure among fellow whitewater enthusiasts.

The week after my story appeared in the *Washington Post*, two rafters were shot at though not hit by an irate property owner who was in his view, most certainly, only upholding his God-given rights on Maryland's last frontier.

Even as the Youghiogheny River controversy continued to simmer, promising years of spirited arguments, lawsuits, and violence, yet another battle against government erupted.

It was over government "aid" in Oakland. The county's only subsidized low-cost housing project, one hundred prefabricated townhouses, sat at the edge of town, on the Sang Run Road. Bradley Manor, built by a Baltimore developer, had fallen into disrepair almost immediately upon its completion a decade before. The problems should have come as no surprise: Working in the winter, construction workers had to use torches to melt the ground so that foundation blocks could be laid. Buildings leaked, and there were obvious structural flaws. But instead of going after the developer right away, federal officials waited until the housing had badly deteriorated and then sought to lavish $5.8 million on the county to fix up the homes. The gift required local consent.

The rugged individualists of Oakland said no.

The action came as no surprise to Duane Yoder, Gary's first cousin and director of the county's community action agency. An advocate of the state project, Duane Yoder had returned to Garrett after working for several years in Southern Maryland and on the Eastern Shore and had come to the conclusion that the land of his birth was "isolated from the mainstream "

"There is a difference in perception up here," he said from his Oakland office. In his view, the position that "we don't need anyone" taken by many in Garrett was only a "security blanket" people grabbed on to so as to avoid unfavorable comparisons between this seemingly incongruous wedge of Maryland and the rest of the state.

In education and income, Garrett always turned up near the bottom among Maryland's twenty-three counties and Baltimore City. But in any measurement of per capita pride (some would say stubbornness), Garrett certainly ranked near the top.

"The time has come to say no," proclaimed Oakland Mayor Harvey D. (Hub) Swartzentruber. "I'm willing to shut the door and lock it." The stand Swartzentruber took was perfectly in tune with the prevailing ethic of Garrett County.

An old order Amish turned Lutheran, Swartzentruber owned Hub's Harness Shop in Oakland for thirty-six years. Before that, he had driven a milk truck— in fact, had the first milk route in the county, back in 1918. Hub's shop was across from the ornate old B&O train station and the city truck scales, which he attended for nothing, collecting $1.50 each from occasional users. "Twelve years ago," he told me, "I was gonna retire. Everybody said, 'You can't, you can't.'" Hub, who became mayor in 1968, finally closed his shop in 1981. However, he continued to serve as Oakland's chief executive and won re-election to an eighth term in 1982 by a two-to-one margin. He was eighty-two.

Hub Swartzentruber seemed to symbolize the personal tenacity of many in a land where longevity appears to be less an accident of fate than the reward for a good and righteous life of hard work and self-reliance. In this rugged land of harsh winters and hard times, it does not have to end the way it did for Austin Tasker. The land and the times have been good to at least some diligent and God-fearing folk who more than eked out a living on Maryland's last frontier.

In a town called Accident, seven miles north of Deep Creek Lake, they buried Walter H. Fratz one early autumn day. He was laid to rest in a shiny bronze casket behind the Zion Lutheran Church and right next to his first wife, Anna V. Fratz, who had died eleven years before at the age of seventy-two. The gravesite overlooked a corn field. Across the field, behind a row of pine trees, was his first store, which was now a warehouse for feed, seed, and farm supplies.

The eighty-year-old patriarch left a widow, five sons and four daughters, twenty-seven grandchildren, nine great-grandchildren, and a multimillion dollar business selling fuel, food, farm supplies, and trailers to the people of Garrett County. Until his last year, he could still be found sorting eggs in the chicken house in Accident. One of his sons recalled that, despite his wealth, Walter Fratz "always stayed here and worked. He took no vacation and he never traveled much. He never went in for fancy cars." At various times, there were two Plymouths, a Buick, and a Dodge.

As a teenager, Fratz had gone to Akron, Ohio, like a lot of people in Garrett, in search of work. He got jobs as a night desk clerk at a hotel and at the Goodyear rubber plant, where his sister already worked. All his siblings had gone to Ohio and all of them had stayed. But after a year or so, Walter Fratz returned home, to the place where his ancestor Leonhard Fratz had come in the 1850s, to the tabletop plateau of Maryland.

Fratz's minister recalled at Fratz's grave that in his later years the old man had reflected on his Ohio stay and on his return to Maryland, to Garrett County. "I could've stayed there and made it with the rest of those guys," the minister remembered Walter Fratz had said, "but I didn't do so bad, did I?"

About the Author

Eugene L. Meyer is a journalist and author with a special interest in history as it affects the present. A *Washington Post* staff writer, Meyer also worked for the late lamented *New York Herald Tribune* and the *Philadelphia Bulletin*.

His career might have peaked in 1966 when he interviewed the Beatles in their dressing room before a concert in Philadelphia, but he went on to achieve other heights. He investigated local officials, covered government and politics, mined Maryland for its mother lode of human interest stories, and whenever possible found excuses to write about life on and around the Chesapeake Bay and environs.

The Washington-Baltimore Newspaper Guild awarded him its top prizes for 1999 and 1995 in local news reporting, and for commentary and criticism published in 1996. His work has twice been nominated for the Pulitzer Prize, and has been cited for excellence by the American Bar Association, Sigma Delta Chi, the National Association of Home Builders, and the Maryland-Delaware-DC Press Association.

The Maryland Professional Chapter of the Society of Professional Journalists awarded him three citations for articles appearing in 1997 in *Chesapeake Bay Magazine*. In 1999, he received a St. George's Day Award from the Prince George's Historical Society for "meritorious effort in the preservation of the [county's] heritage."

His critically acclaimed first book, *Maryland Lost and Found: People and Places from Chesapeake to Appalachia*, was first published in 1986 by the Johns Hopkins University Press. His second book, *Chesapeake Country*, was published in 1990 by Abbeville Press. His work has appeared in a number of national magazines, including *Audubon, Family Circle, National Geographic Traveler*, and *Smithsonian*.

Meyer was a Washington Post Duke University Fellow in 1985 and the 1991 James Thurber Journalist-in-Residence at the Ohio State University. A graduate of Columbia College in the City of New York, Meyer lives in Silver Spring, Maryland, with his wife, Sandra, and sons David and Aaron.